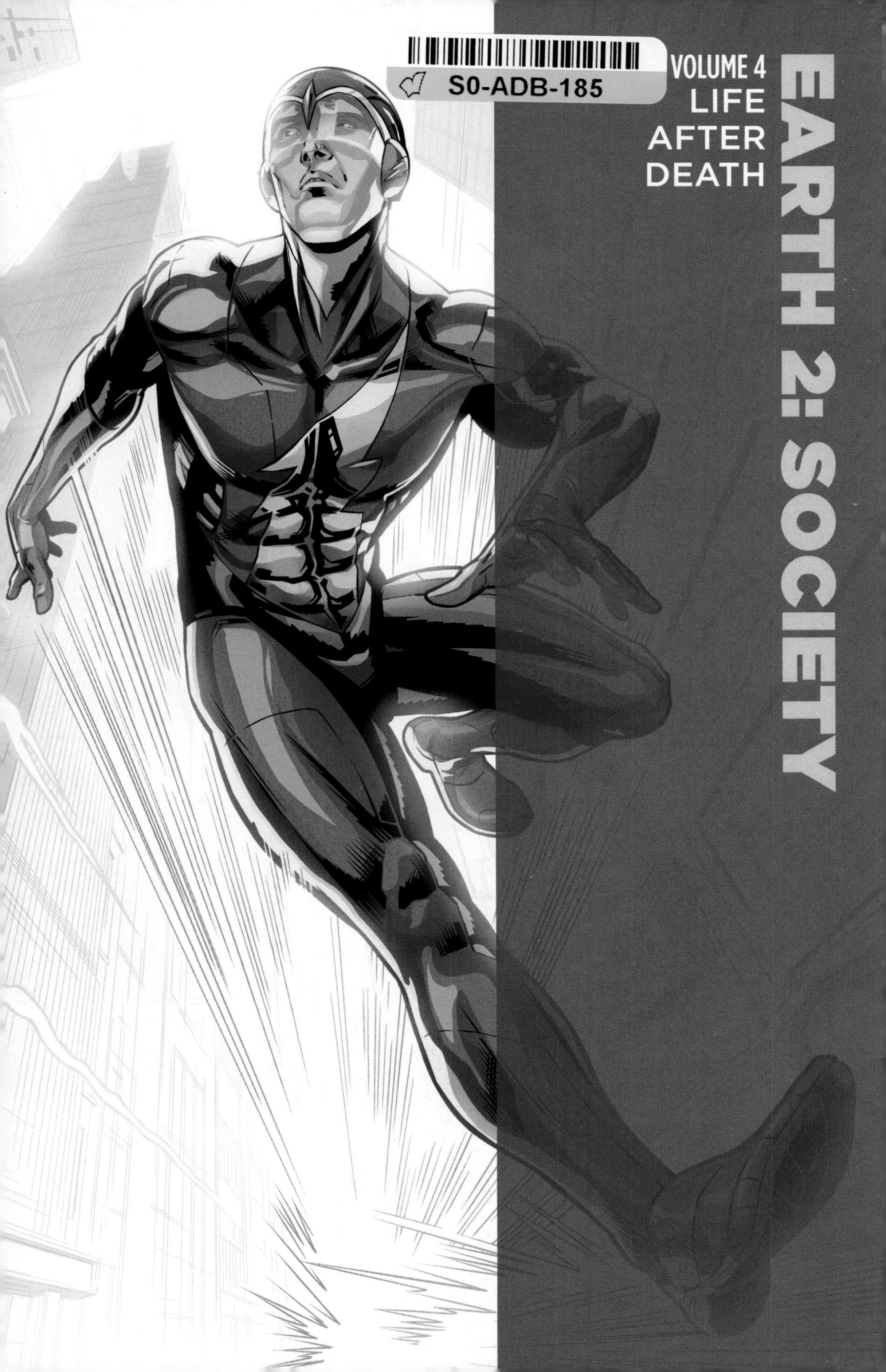
VOLUME 4
LIFE
AFTER
DEATH
EARTH 2: SOCIETY

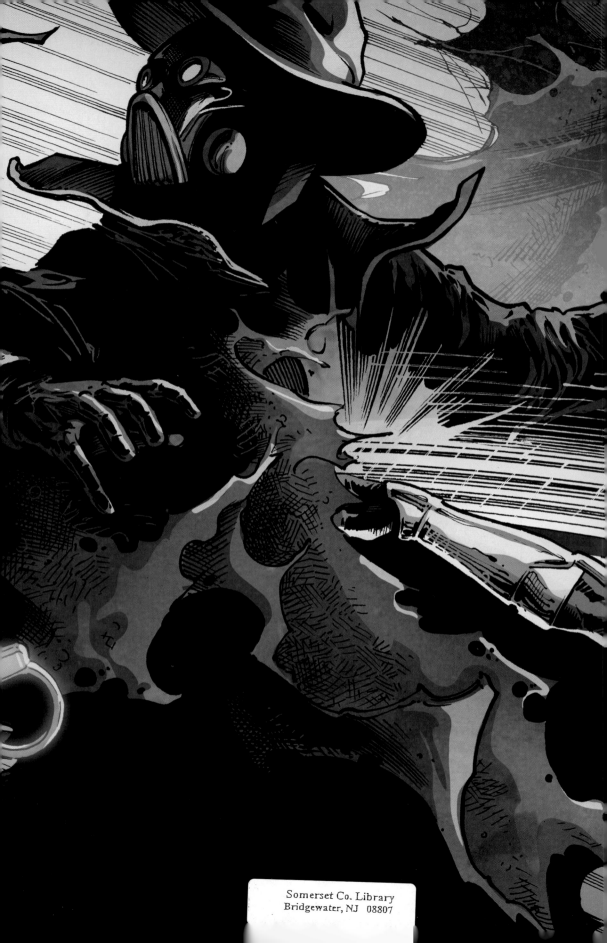

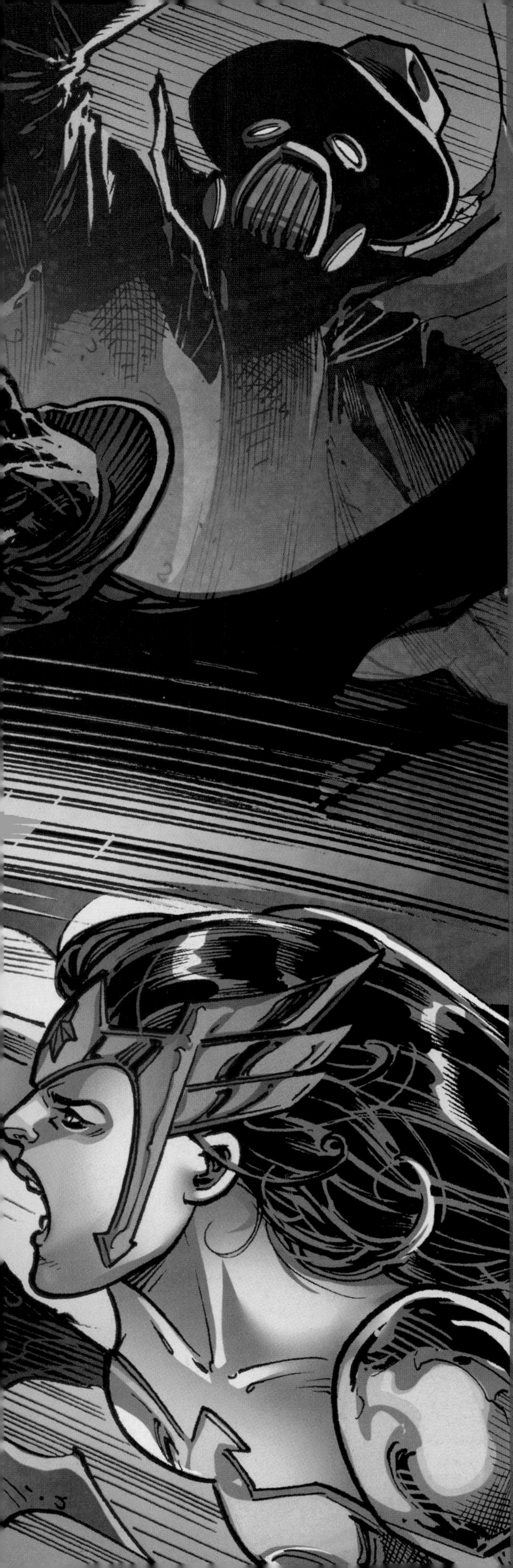

EARTH 2: SOCIETY

VOLUME 4
LIFE AFTER DEATH

WRITTEN BY
DAN ABNETT

ART BY
BRUNO REDONDO
VICENTE CIFUENTES
JUAN ALBARRAN

COLOR BY
REX LOKUS

LETTERS BY
TRAVIS LANHAM

COLLECTION COVER ART BY
BRUNO REDONDO &
ALEJANDRO SANCHEZ

SUPERMAN CREATED BY
JERRY SIEGEL &
JOE SHUSTER
BY SPECIAL ARRANGEMENT
WITH THE JERRY SIEGEL FAMILY

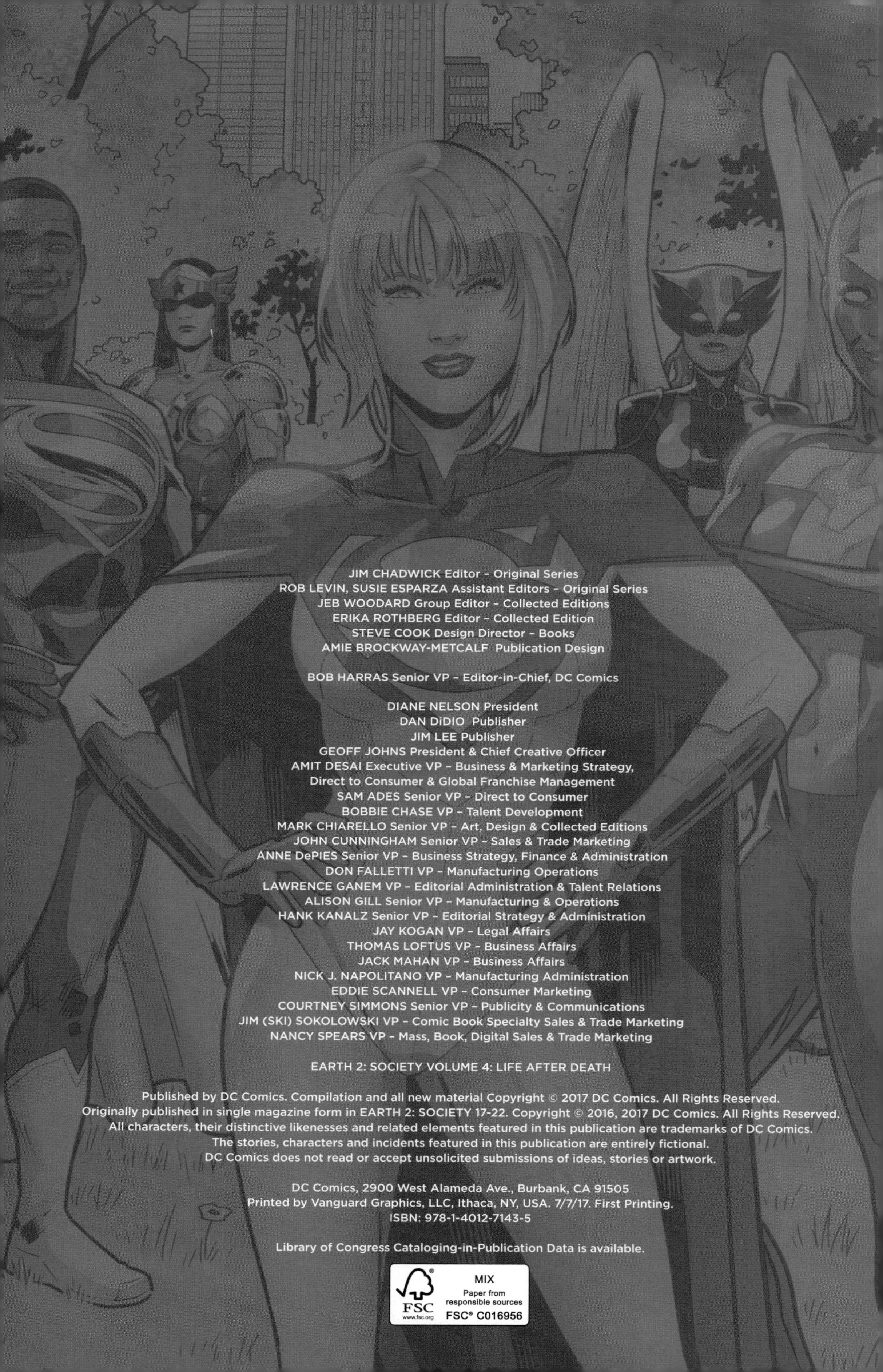

JIM CHADWICK Editor - Original Series
ROB LEVIN, SUSIE ESPARZA Assistant Editors - Original Series
JEB WOODARD Group Editor - Collected Editions
ERIKA ROTHBERG Editor - Collected Edition
STEVE COOK Design Director - Books
AMIE BROCKWAY-METCALF Publication Design

BOB HARRAS Senior VP - Editor-in-Chief, DC Comics

DIANE NELSON President
DAN DiDIO Publisher
JIM LEE Publisher
GEOFF JOHNS President & Chief Creative Officer
AMIT DESAI Executive VP - Business & Marketing Strategy, Direct to Consumer & Global Franchise Management
SAM ADES Senior VP - Direct to Consumer
BOBBIE CHASE VP - Talent Development
MARK CHIARELLO Senior VP - Art, Design & Collected Editions
JOHN CUNNINGHAM Senior VP - Sales & Trade Marketing
ANNE DePIES Senior VP - Business Strategy, Finance & Administration
DON FALLETTI VP - Manufacturing Operations
LAWRENCE GANEM VP - Editorial Administration & Talent Relations
ALISON GILL Senior VP - Manufacturing & Operations
HANK KANALZ Senior VP - Editorial Strategy & Administration
JAY KOGAN VP - Legal Affairs
THOMAS LOFTUS VP - Business Affairs
JACK MAHAN VP - Business Affairs
NICK J. NAPOLITANO VP - Manufacturing Administration
EDDIE SCANNELL VP - Consumer Marketing
COURTNEY SIMMONS Senior VP - Publicity & Communications
JIM (SKI) SOKOLOWSKI VP - Comic Book Specialty Sales & Trade Marketing
NANCY SPEARS VP - Mass, Book, Digital Sales & Trade Marketing

EARTH 2: SOCIETY VOLUME 4: LIFE AFTER DEATH

DC Comics, 2900 West Alameda Ave., Burbank, CA 91505
Printed by Vanguard Graphics, LLC, Ithaca, NY, USA. 7/7/17. First Printing.
ISBN: 978-1-4012-7143-5

Library of Congress Cataloging-in-Publication Data is available.

MIX
Paper from responsible sources
FSC® C016956

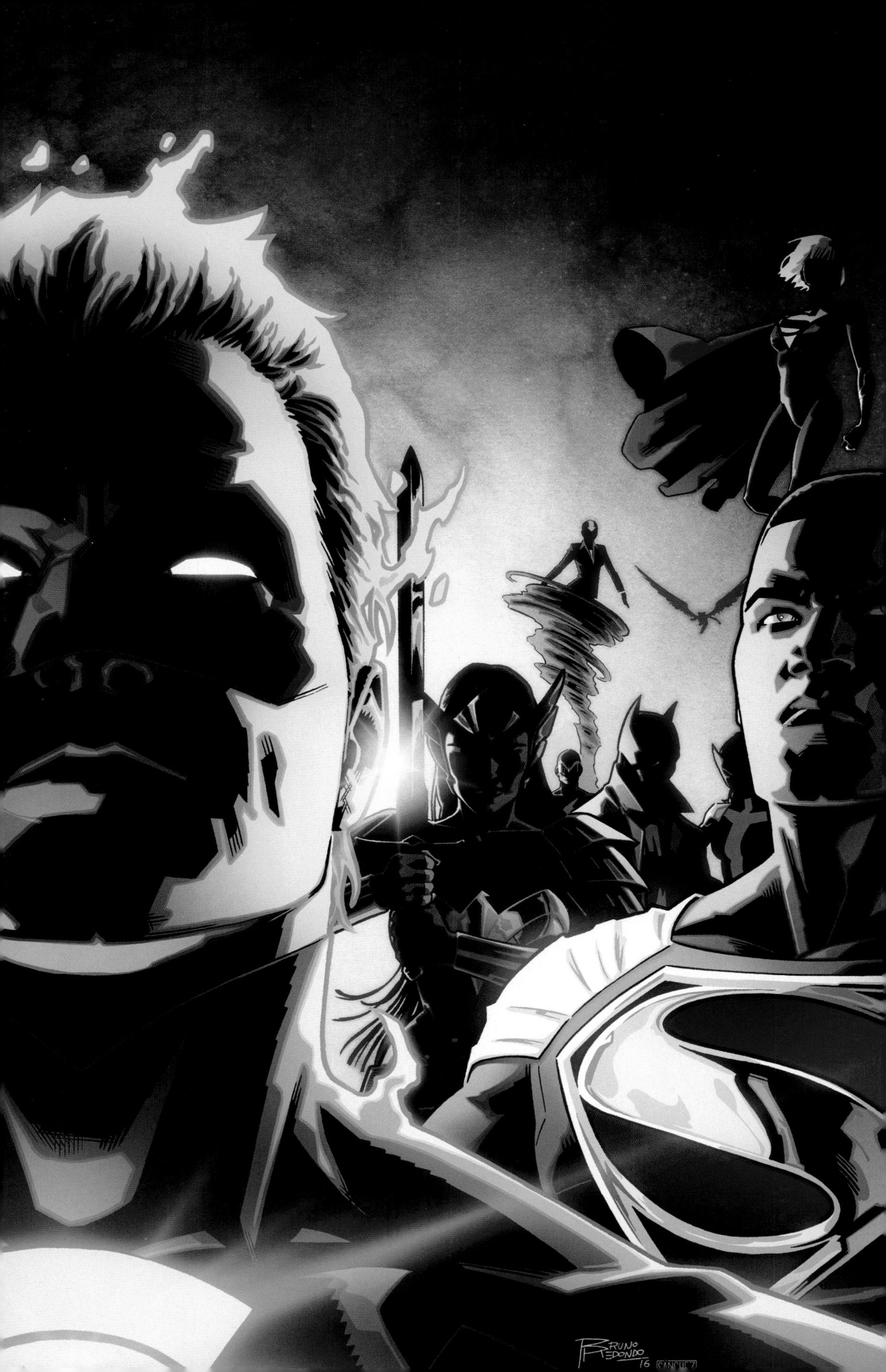
BRUNO REDONDO '16
SANCHEZ

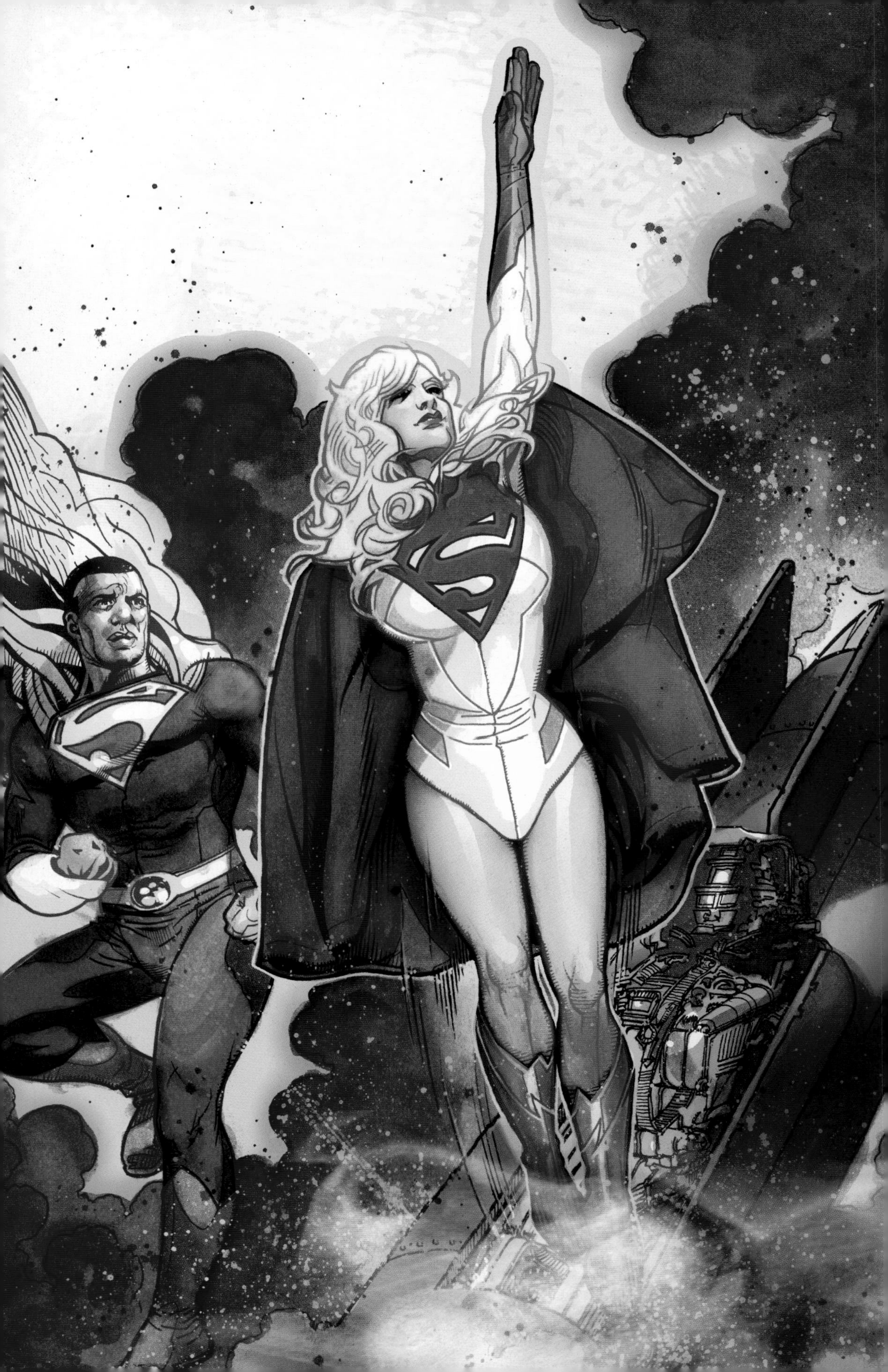

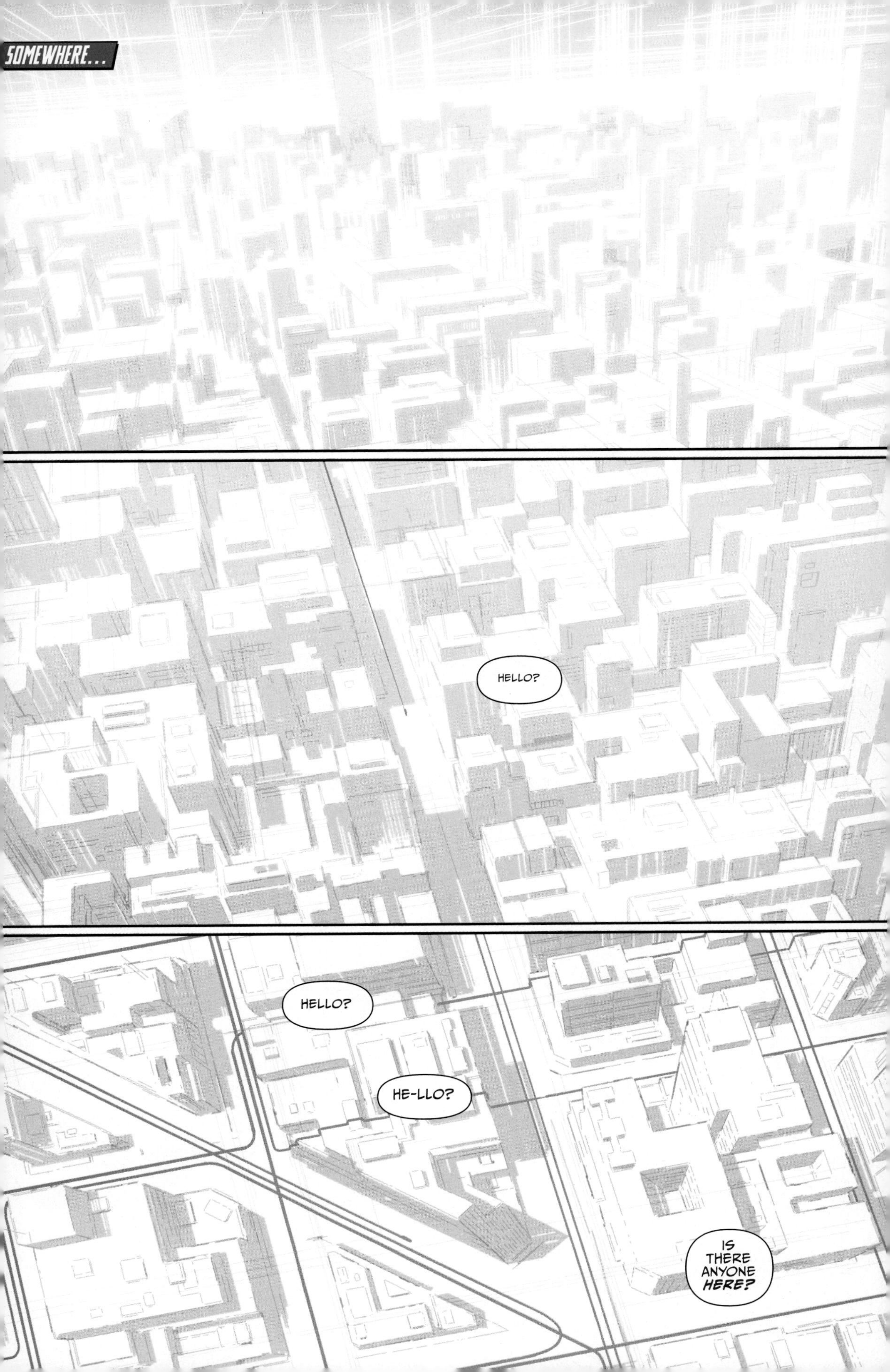
SOMEWHERE...
HELLO?
HELLO?
HE-LLO?
IS THERE ANYONE HERE?

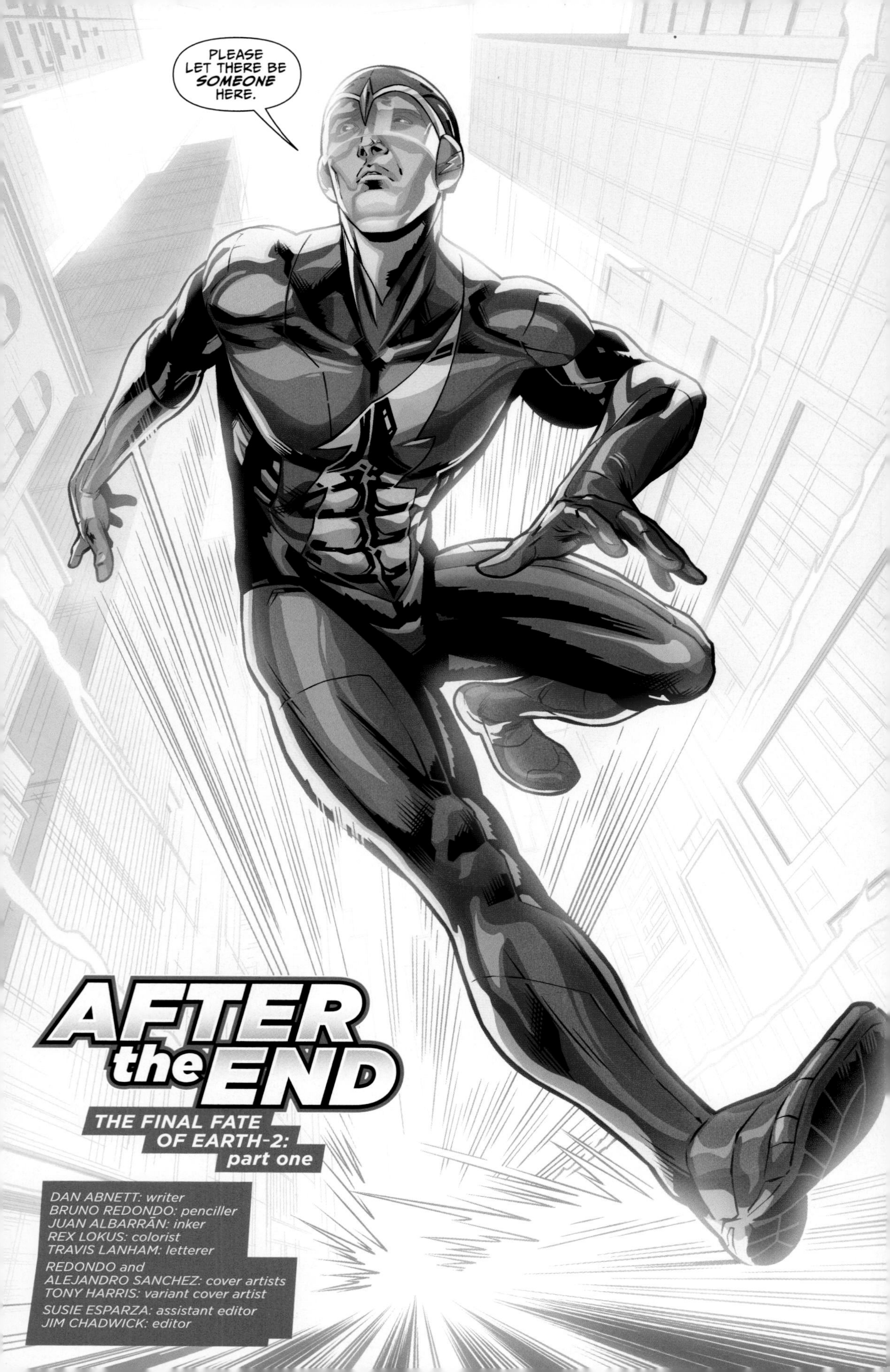

PLEASE LET THERE BE *SOMEONE* HERE.
AFTER the END
THE FINAL FATE OF EARTH-2: part one
DAN ABNETT: writer
BRUNO REDONDO: penciller
JUAN ALBARRÁN: inker
REX LOKUS: colorist
TRAVIS LANHAM: letterer
REDONDO and ALEJANDRO SANCHEZ: cover artists
TONY HARRIS: variant cover artist
SUSIE ESPARZA: assistant editor
JIM CHADWICK: editor

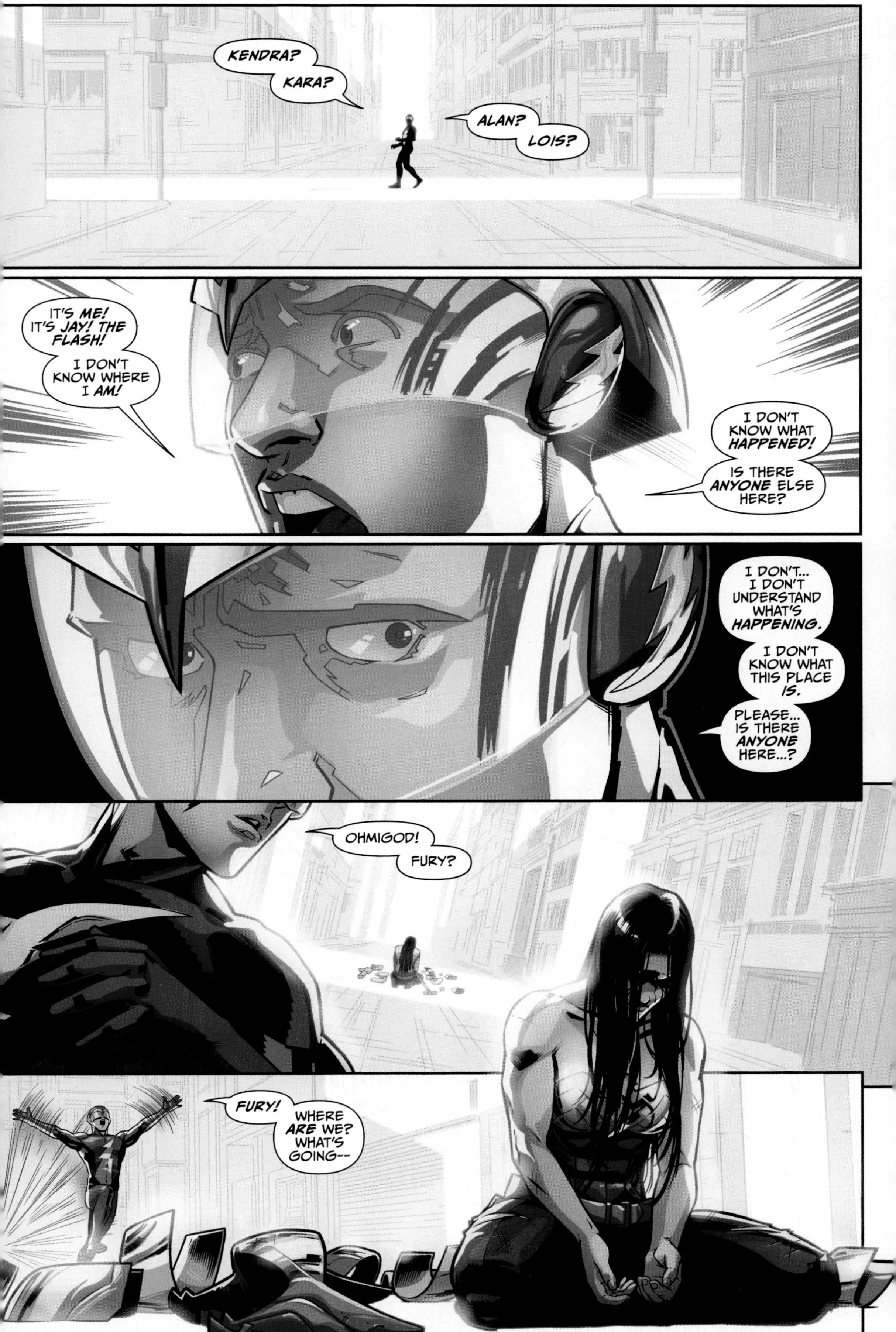
KENDRA?
KARA?
ALAN?
LOIS?
IT'S ME! IT'S JAY! THE FLASH!
I DON'T KNOW WHERE I AM!
I DON'T KNOW WHAT HAPPENED!
IS THERE ANYONE ELSE HERE?
I DON'T... I DON'T UNDERSTAND WHAT'S HAPPENING.
I DON'T KNOW WHAT THIS PLACE IS.
PLEASE... IS THERE ANYONE HERE...?
OHMIGOD!
FURY?
FURY!
WHERE ARE WE? WHAT'S GOING--

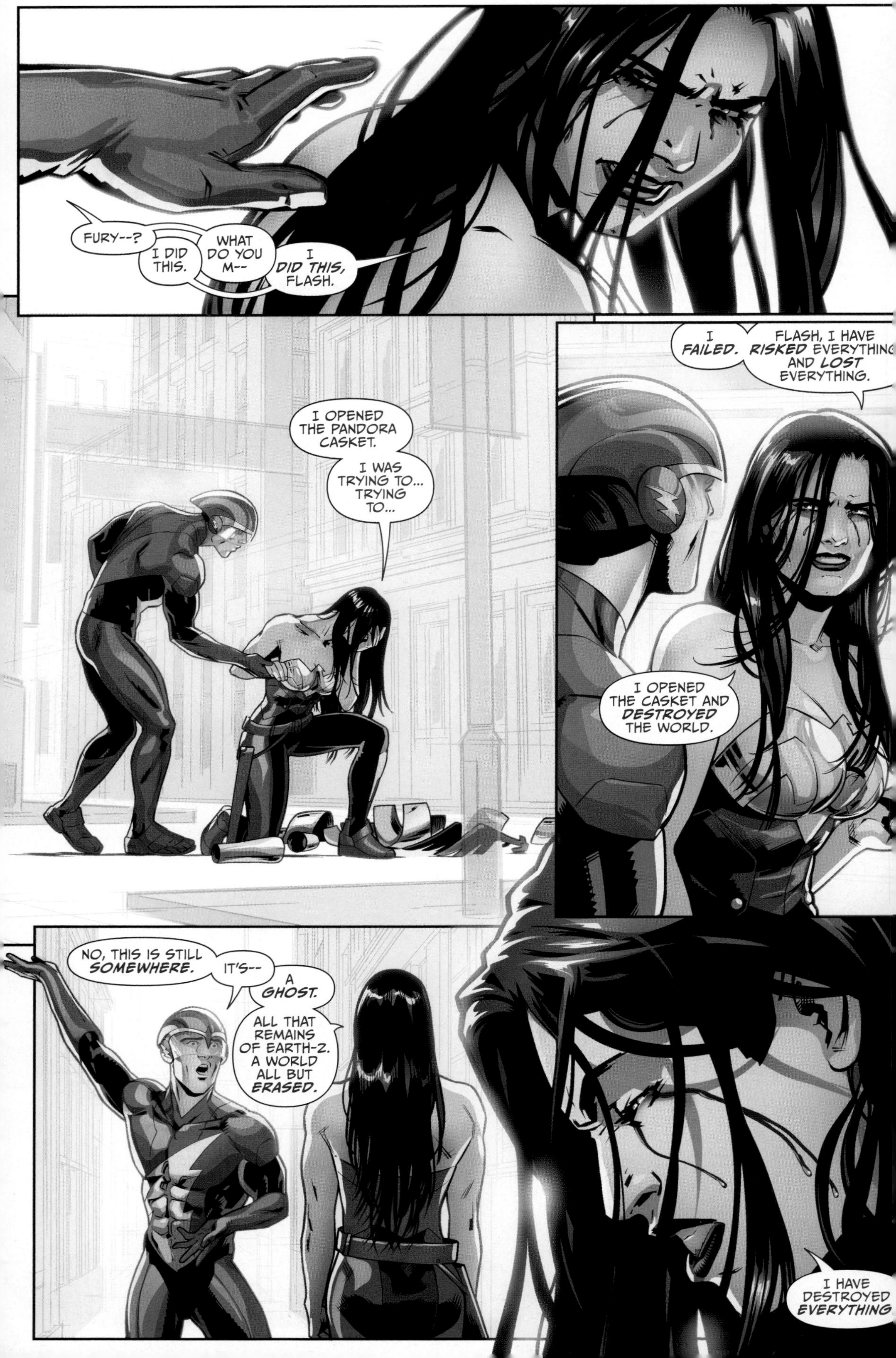

FURY--?
I DID THIS.
WHAT DO YOU M--
I DID THIS, FLASH.
I OPENED THE PANDORA CASKET.
I WAS TRYING TO... TRYING TO...
I FAILED.
FLASH, I HAVE RISKED EVERYTHING AND LOST EVERYTHING.
I OPENED THE CASKET AND DESTROYED THE WORLD.
NO, THIS IS STILL SOMEWHERE.
IT'S--
A GHOST.
ALL THAT REMAINS OF EARTH-2. A WORLD ALL BUT ERASED.
I HAVE DESTROYED EVERYTHING

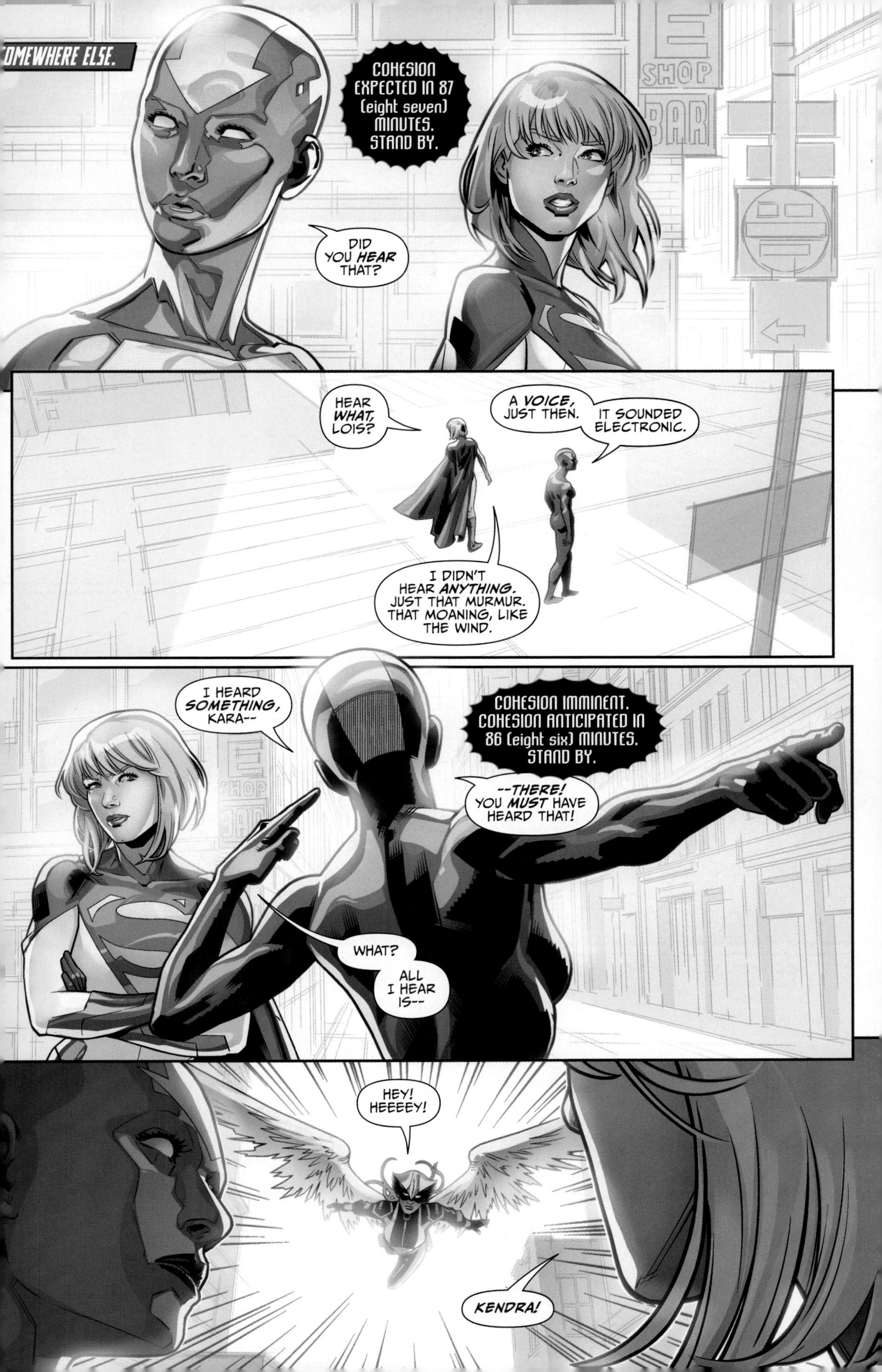
SOMEWHERE ELSE.
COHESION EXPECTED IN 87 (eight seven) MINUTES. STAND BY.
DID YOU HEAR THAT?
SHOP
BAR
HEAR WHAT, LOIS?
A VOICE, JUST THEN.
IT SOUNDED ELECTRONIC.
I DIDN'T HEAR ANYTHING. JUST THAT MURMUR. THAT MOANING, LIKE THE WIND.
I HEARD SOMETHING, KARA--
COHESION IMMINENT. COHESION ANTICIPATED IN 86 (eight six) MINUTES. STAND BY.
--THERE! YOU MUST HAVE HEARD THAT!
WHAT?
ALL I HEAR IS--
HEY! HEEEEY!
KENDRA!

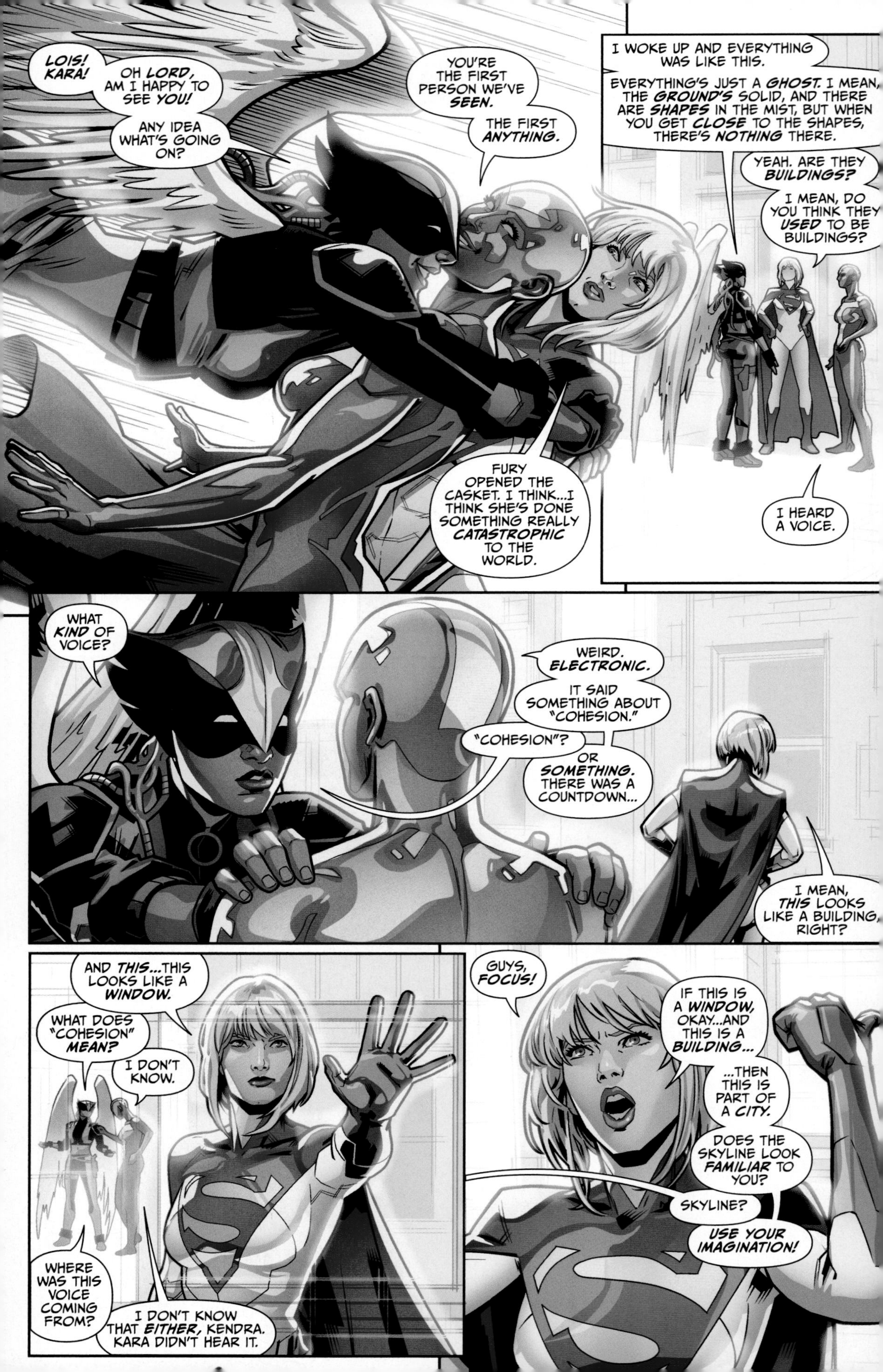
LOIS! KARA!
OH LORD, AM I HAPPY TO SEE YOU!
ANY IDEA WHAT'S GOING ON?
YOU'RE THE FIRST PERSON WE'VE SEEN.
THE FIRST ANYTHING.
FURY OPENED THE CASKET. I THINK...I THINK SHE'S DONE SOMETHING REALLY CATASTROPHIC TO THE WORLD.
I WOKE UP AND EVERYTHING WAS LIKE THIS.
EVERYTHING'S JUST A GHOST. I MEAN, THE GROUND'S SOLID, AND THERE ARE SHAPES IN THE MIST, BUT WHEN YOU GET CLOSE TO THE SHAPES, THERE'S NOTHING THERE.
YEAH. ARE THEY BUILDINGS?
I MEAN, DO YOU THINK THEY USED TO BE BUILDINGS?
I HEARD A VOICE.
WHAT KIND OF VOICE?
WEIRD. ELECTRONIC.
IT SAID SOMETHING ABOUT "COHESION."
"COHESION"?
OR SOMETHING. THERE WAS A COUNTDOWN...
I MEAN, THIS LOOKS LIKE A BUILDING, RIGHT?
AND THIS...THIS LOOKS LIKE A WINDOW.
WHAT DOES "COHESION" MEAN?
I DON'T KNOW.
WHERE WAS THIS VOICE COMING FROM?
I DON'T KNOW THAT EITHER, KENDRA. KARA DIDN'T HEAR IT.
GUYS, FOCUS!
IF THIS IS A WINDOW, OKAY...AND THIS IS A BUILDING...
...THEN THIS IS PART OF A CITY.
DOES THE SKYLINE LOOK FAMILIAR TO YOU?
SKYLINE?
USE YOUR IMAGINATION!

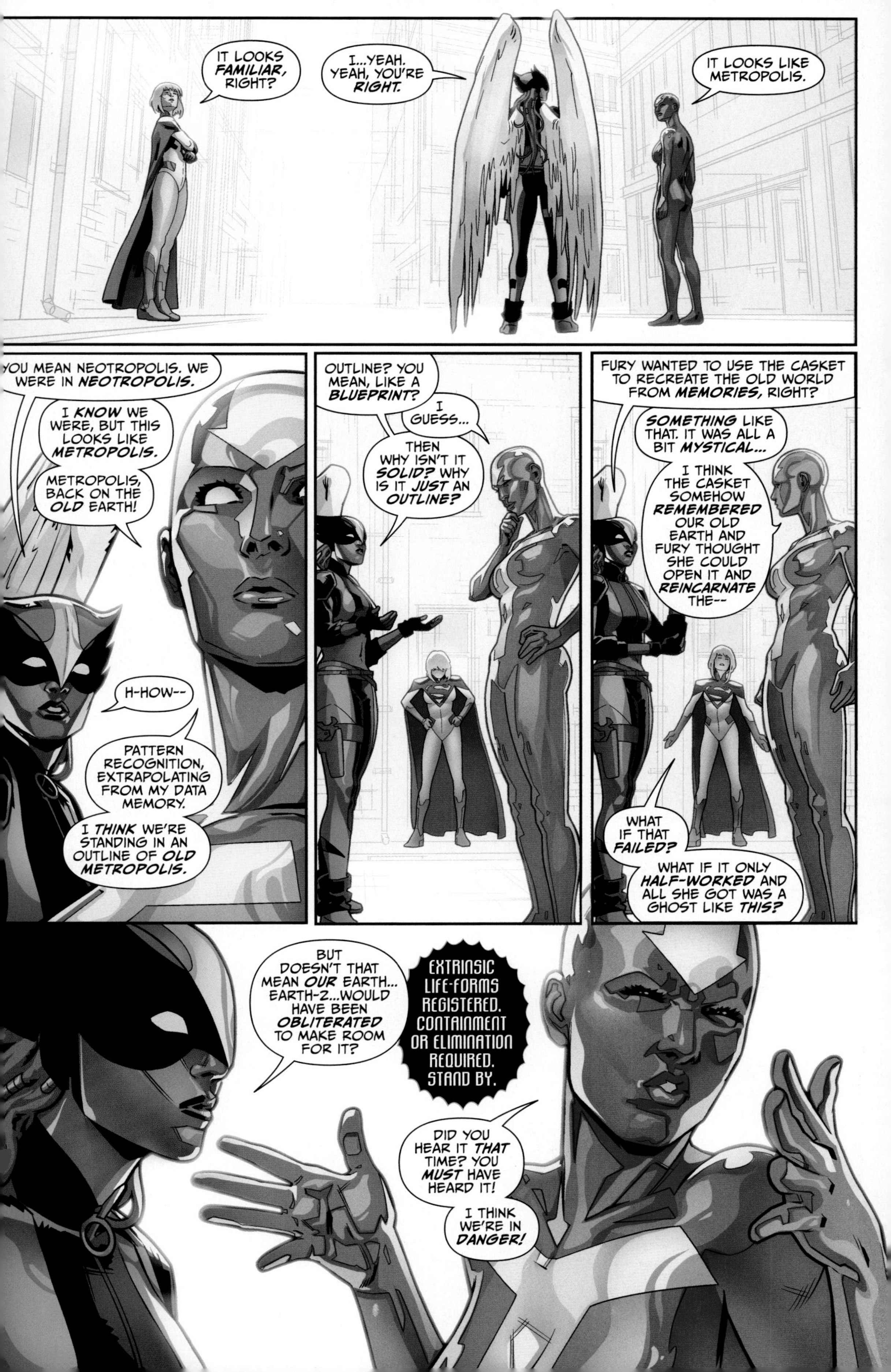
IT LOOKS FAMILIAR, RIGHT?
I...YEAH. YEAH, YOU'RE RIGHT.
IT LOOKS LIKE METROPOLIS.
YOU MEAN NEOTROPOLIS. WE WERE IN NEOTROPOLIS.
I KNOW WE WERE, BUT THIS LOOKS LIKE METROPOLIS.
METROPOLIS, BACK ON THE OLD EARTH!
H-HOW--
PATTERN RECOGNITION, EXTRAPOLATING FROM MY DATA MEMORY.
I THINK WE'RE STANDING IN AN OUTLINE OF OLD METROPOLIS.
OUTLINE? YOU MEAN, LIKE A BLUEPRINT?
I GUESS...
THEN WHY ISN'T IT SOLID? WHY IS IT JUST AN OUTLINE?
FURY WANTED TO USE THE CASKET TO RECREATE THE OLD WORLD FROM MEMORIES, RIGHT?
SOMETHING LIKE THAT. IT WAS ALL A BIT MYSTICAL...
I THINK THE CASKET SOMEHOW REMEMBERED OUR OLD EARTH AND FURY THOUGHT SHE COULD OPEN IT AND REINCARNATE THE--
WHAT IF THAT FAILED?
WHAT IF IT ONLY HALF-WORKED AND ALL SHE GOT WAS A GHOST LIKE THIS?
BUT DOESN'T THAT MEAN OUR EARTH... EARTH-2...WOULD HAVE BEEN OBLITERATED TO MAKE ROOM FOR IT?
EXTRINSIC LIFE-FORMS REGISTERED. CONTAINMENT OR ELIMINATION REQUIRED. STAND BY.
DID YOU HEAR IT THAT TIME? YOU MUST HAVE HEARD IT!
I THINK WE'RE IN DANGER!

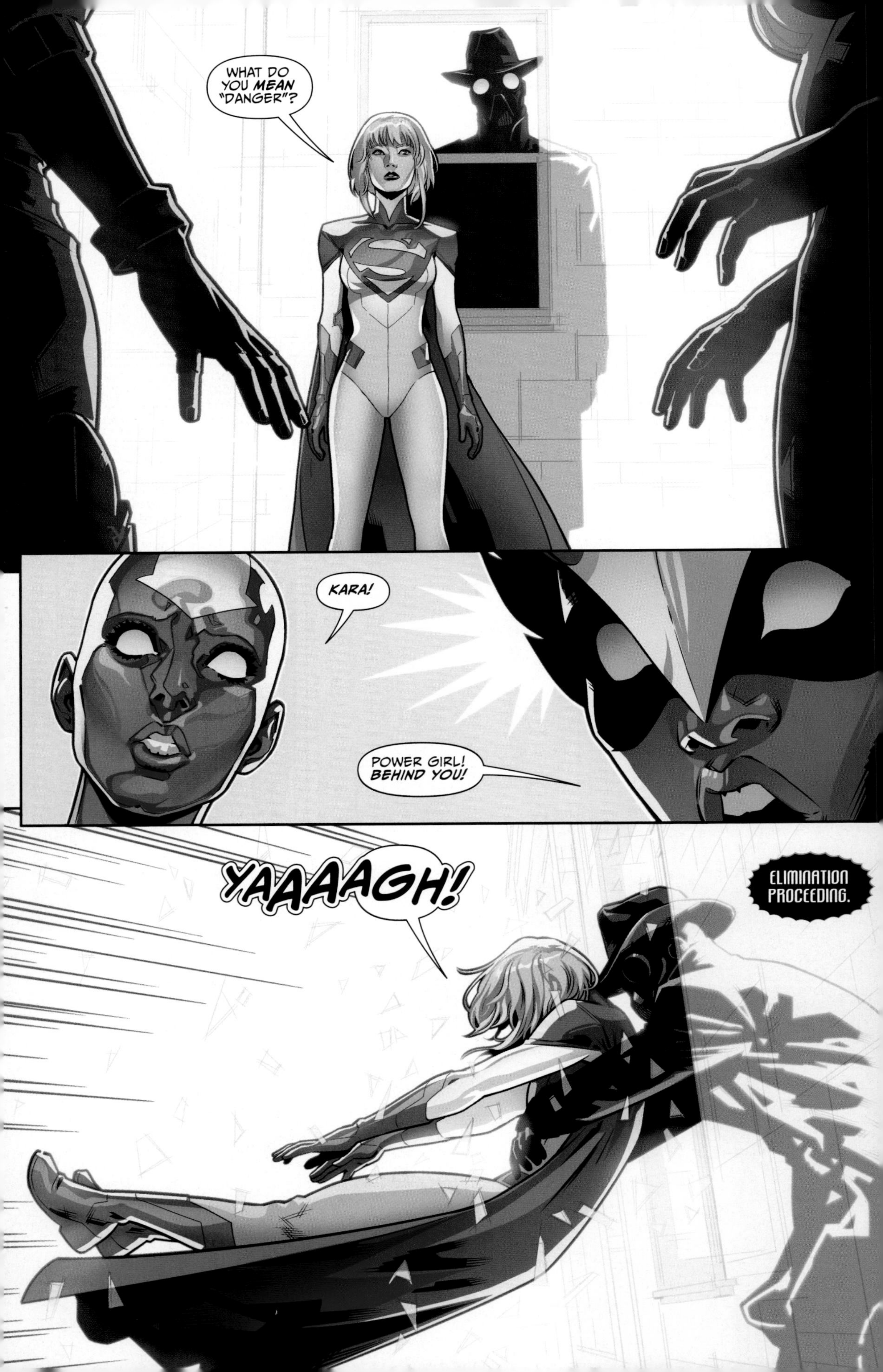
WHAT DO YOU MEAN "DANGER"?
KARA!
POWER GIRL! BEHIND YOU!
YAAAAGH!
ELIMINATION PROCEEDING.

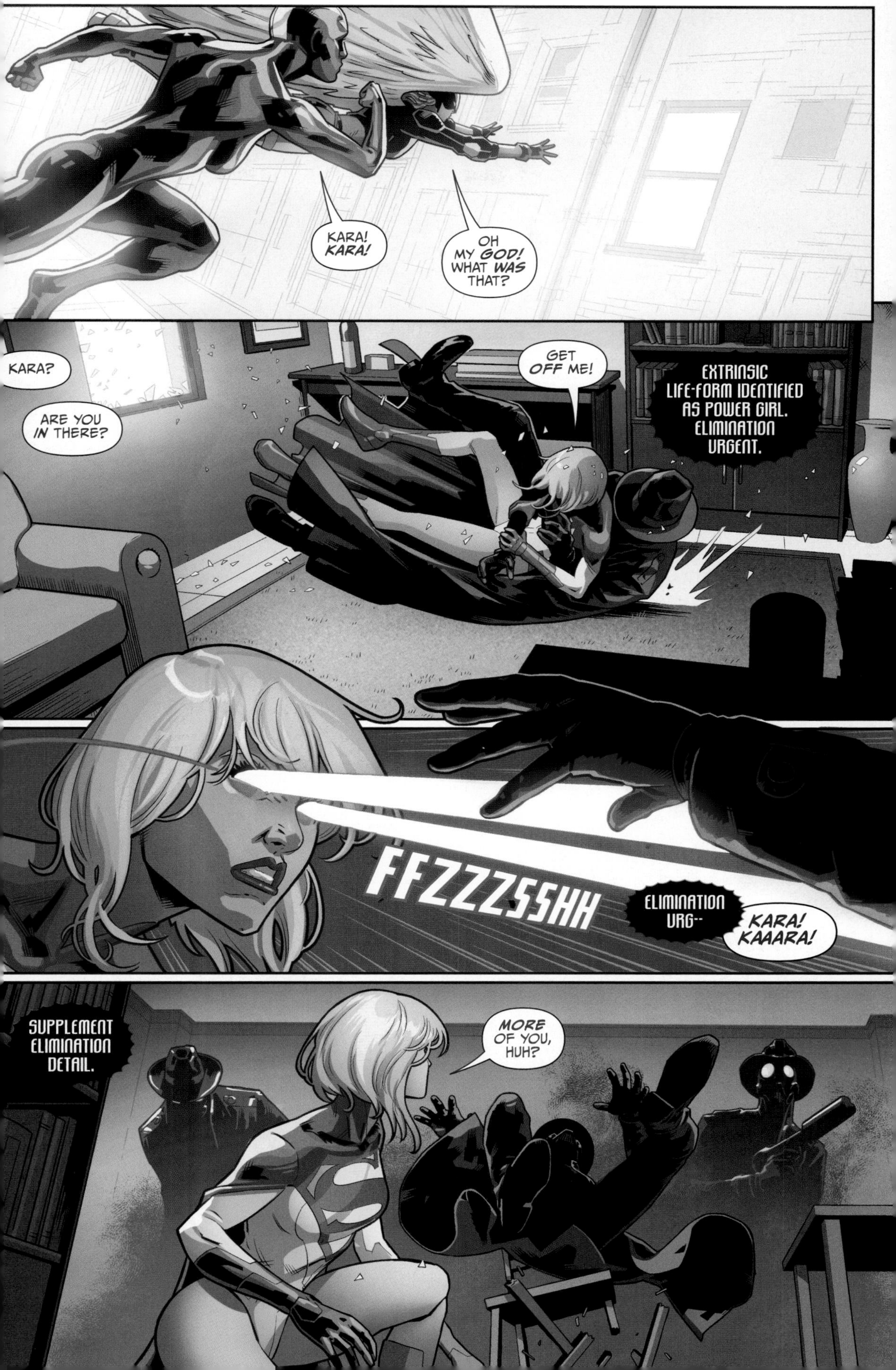
KARA! KARA!
OH MY GOD! WHAT WAS THAT?
KARA?
ARE YOU IN THERE?
GET OFF ME!
EXTRINSIC LIFE-FORM IDENTIFIED AS POWER GIRL. ELIMINATION URGENT.
FFZZZSSHH
ELIMINATION URG--
KARA! KAAARA!
SUPPLEMENT ELIMINATION DETAIL.
MORE OF YOU, HUH?

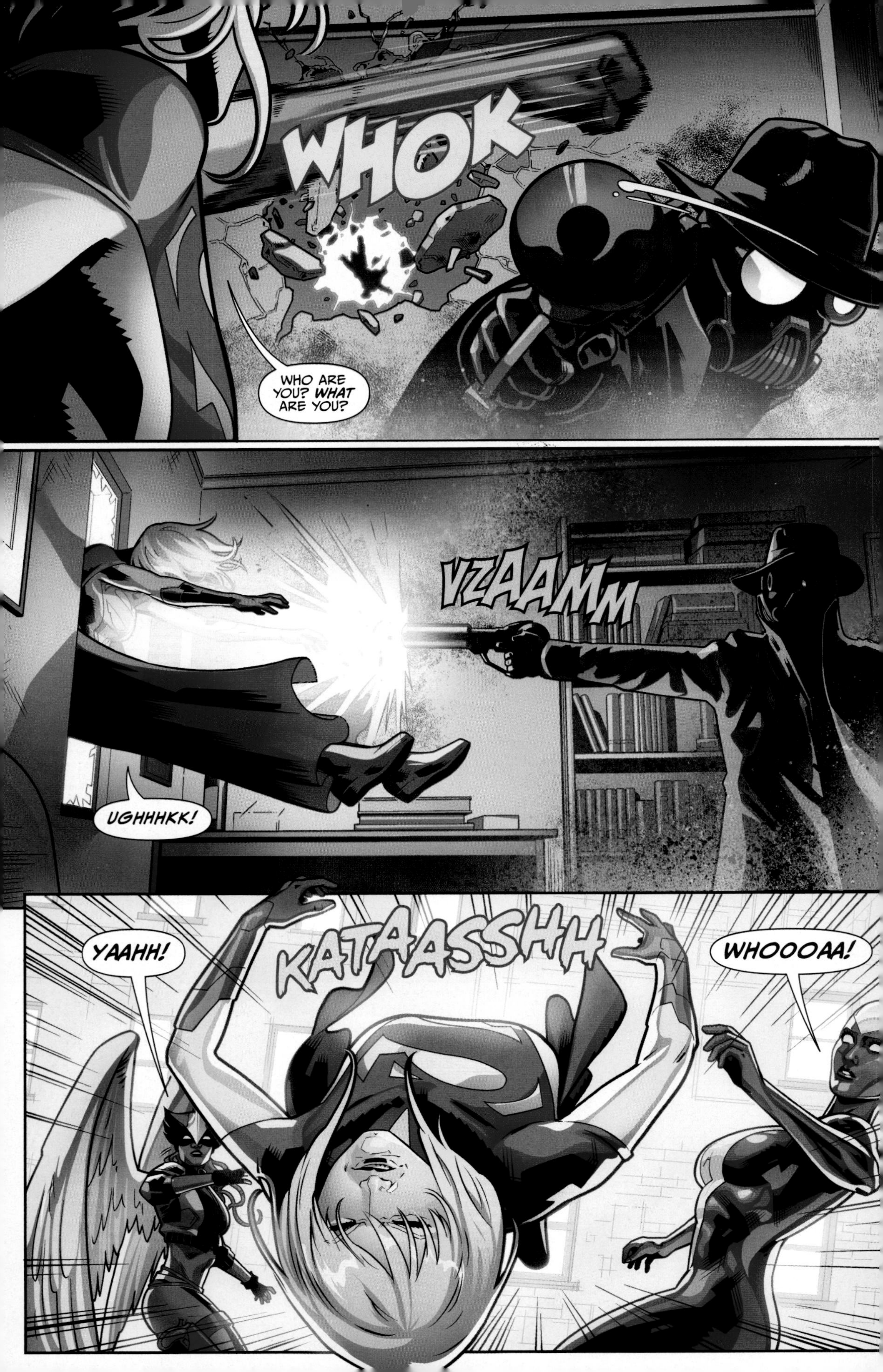
WHOK
WHO ARE YOU? WHAT ARE YOU?
VZAAMM
UGHHHKK!
YAAHH!
KATAASSHH
WHOOOAA!

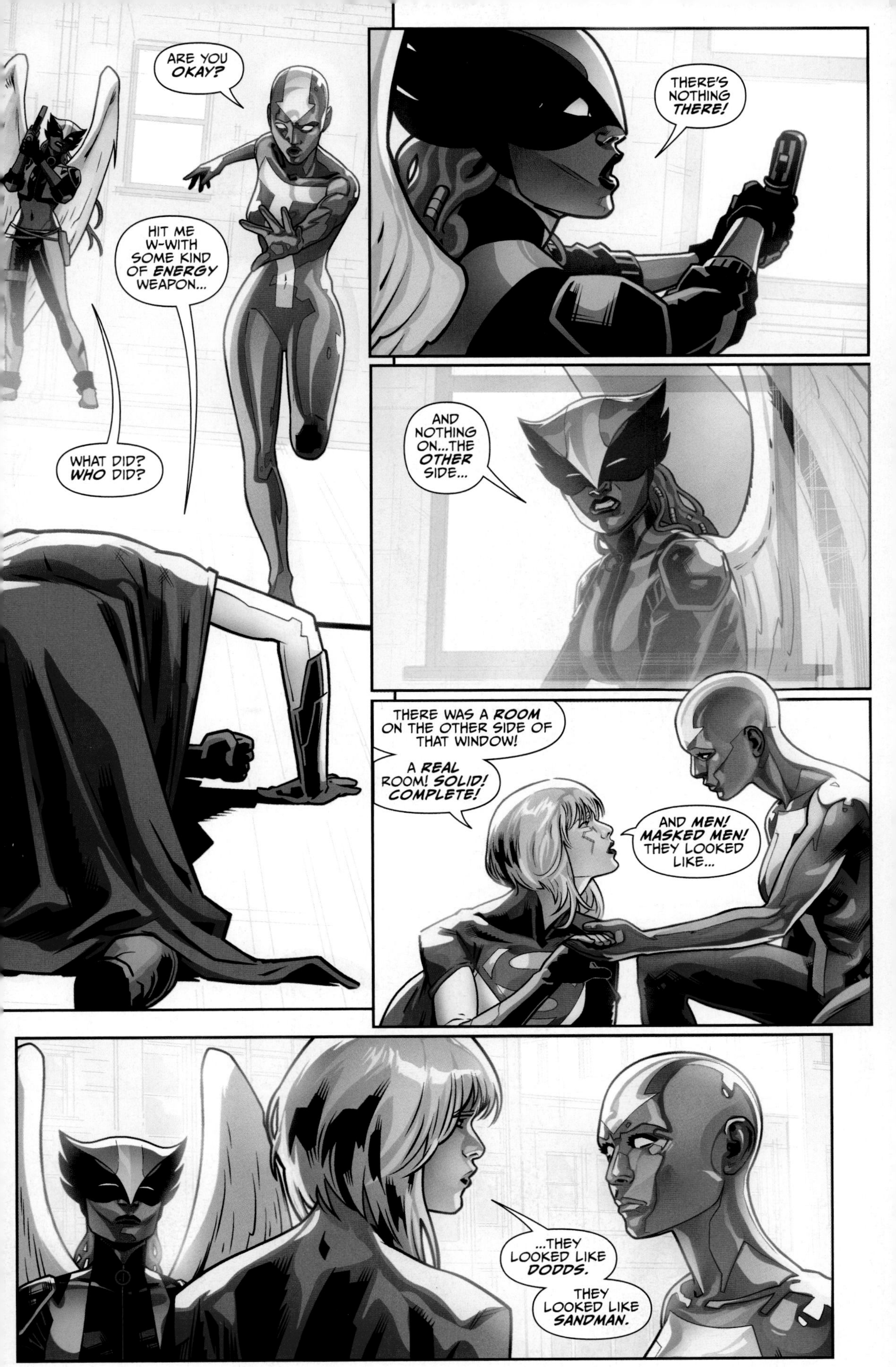
ARE YOU OKAY?
HIT ME W-WITH SOME KIND OF ENERGY WEAPON...
WHAT DID? WHO DID?
THERE'S NOTHING THERE!
AND NOTHING ON...THE OTHER SIDE...
THERE WAS A ROOM ON THE OTHER SIDE OF THAT WINDOW!
A REAL ROOM! SOLID! COMPLETE!
AND MEN! MASKED MEN! THEY LOOKED LIKE...
...THEY LOOKED LIKE DODDS.
THEY LOOKED LIKE SANDMAN.

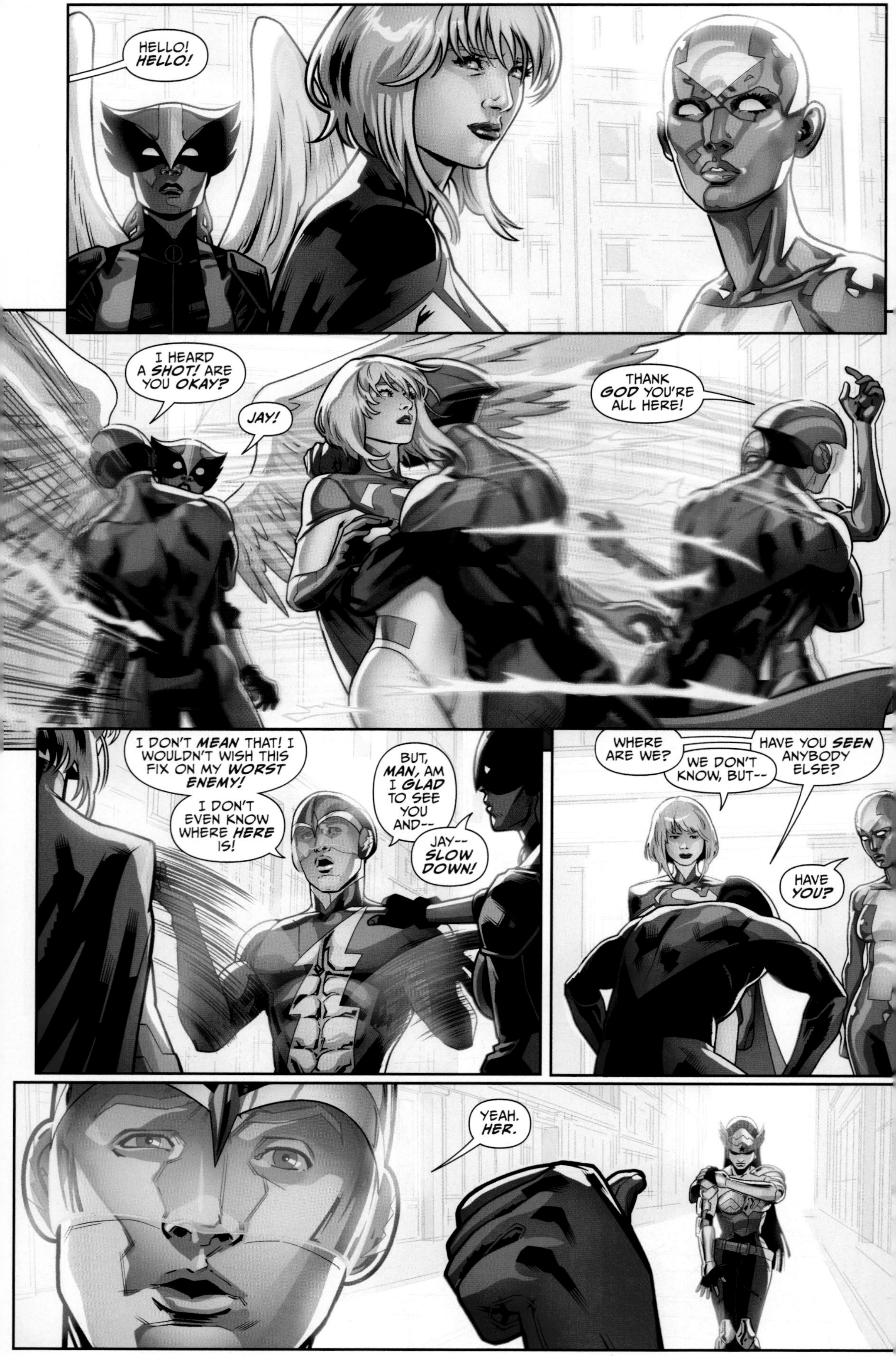
HELLO! HELLO!
I HEARD A SHOT! ARE YOU OKAY?
JAY!
THANK GOD YOU'RE ALL HERE!
I DON'T MEAN THAT! I WOULDN'T WISH THIS FIX ON MY WORST ENEMY!
I DON'T EVEN KNOW WHERE HERE IS!
BUT, MAN, AM I GLAD TO SEE YOU AND--
JAY-- SLOW DOWN!
WHERE ARE WE?
WE DON'T KNOW, BUT--
HAVE YOU SEEN ANYBODY ELSE?
HAVE YOU?
YEAH. HER.

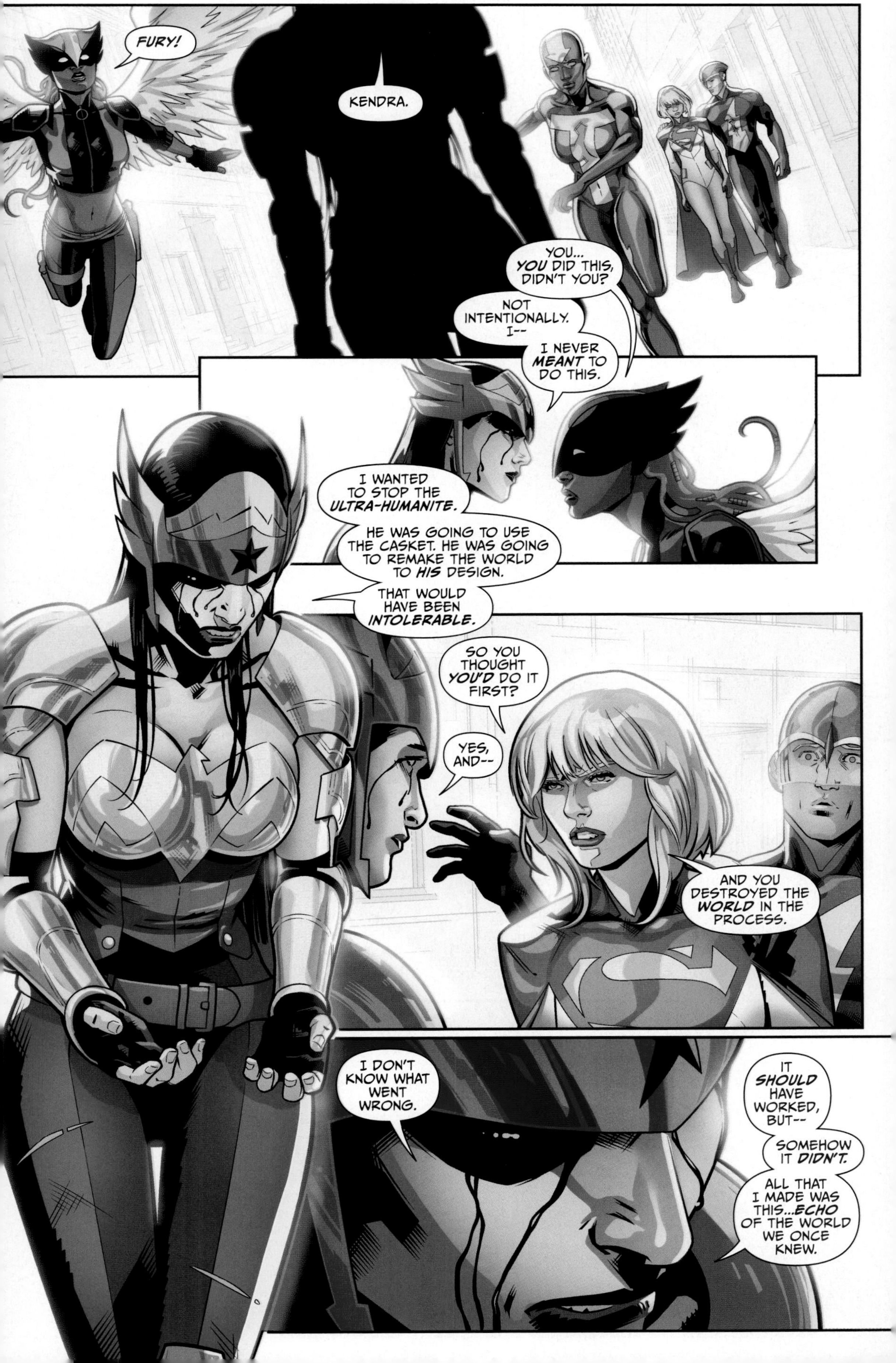
FURY!
KENDRA.
YOU... YOU DID THIS, DIDN'T YOU?
NOT INTENTIONALLY. I--
I NEVER MEANT TO DO THIS.
I WANTED TO STOP THE ULTRA-HUMANITE.
HE WAS GOING TO USE THE CASKET. HE WAS GOING TO REMAKE THE WORLD TO HIS DESIGN.
THAT WOULD HAVE BEEN INTOLERABLE.
SO YOU THOUGHT YOU'D DO IT FIRST?
YES, AND--
AND YOU DESTROYED THE WORLD IN THE PROCESS.
I DON'T KNOW WHAT WENT WRONG.
IT SHOULD HAVE WORKED, BUT--
SOMEHOW IT DIDN'T.
ALL THAT I MADE WAS THIS...ECHO OF THE WORLD WE ONCE KNEW.

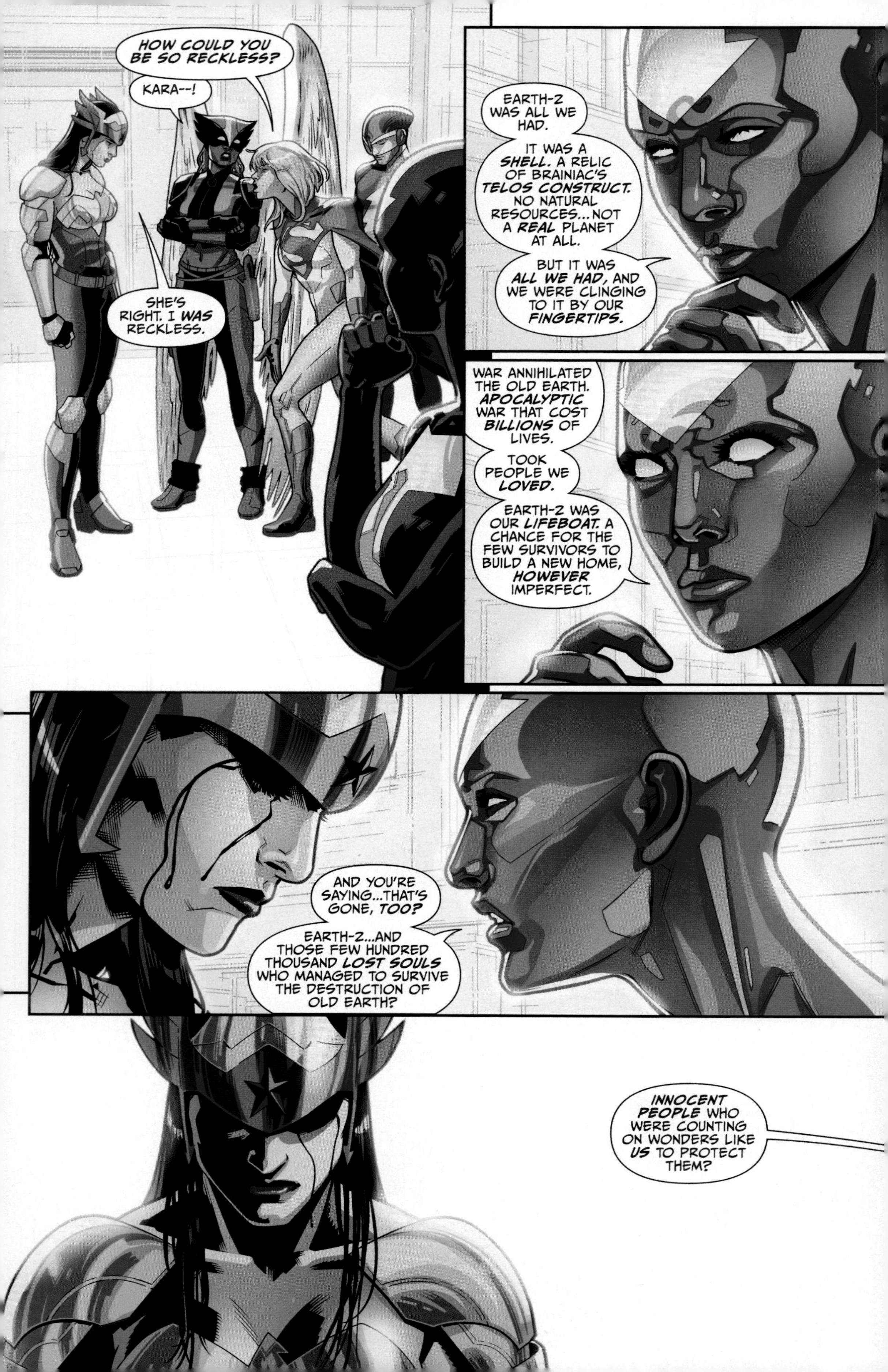
HOW COULD YOU BE SO RECKLESS?
KARA--!
SHE'S RIGHT. I WAS RECKLESS.
EARTH-2 WAS ALL WE HAD.
IT WAS A SHELL. A RELIC OF BRAINIAC'S TELOS CONSTRUCT. NO NATURAL RESOURCES...NOT A REAL PLANET AT ALL.
BUT IT WAS ALL WE HAD, AND WE WERE CLINGING TO IT BY OUR FINGERTIPS.
WAR ANNIHILATED THE OLD EARTH. APOCALYPTIC WAR THAT COST BILLIONS OF LIVES.
TOOK PEOPLE WE LOVED.
EARTH-2 WAS OUR LIFEBOAT. A CHANCE FOR THE FEW SURVIVORS TO BUILD A NEW HOME, HOWEVER IMPERFECT.
AND YOU'RE SAYING...THAT'S GONE, TOO?
EARTH-2...AND THOSE FEW HUNDRED THOUSAND LOST SOULS WHO MANAGED TO SURVIVE THE DESTRUCTION OF OLD EARTH?
INNOCENT PEOPLE WHO WERE COUNTING ON WONDERS LIKE US TO PROTECT THEM?

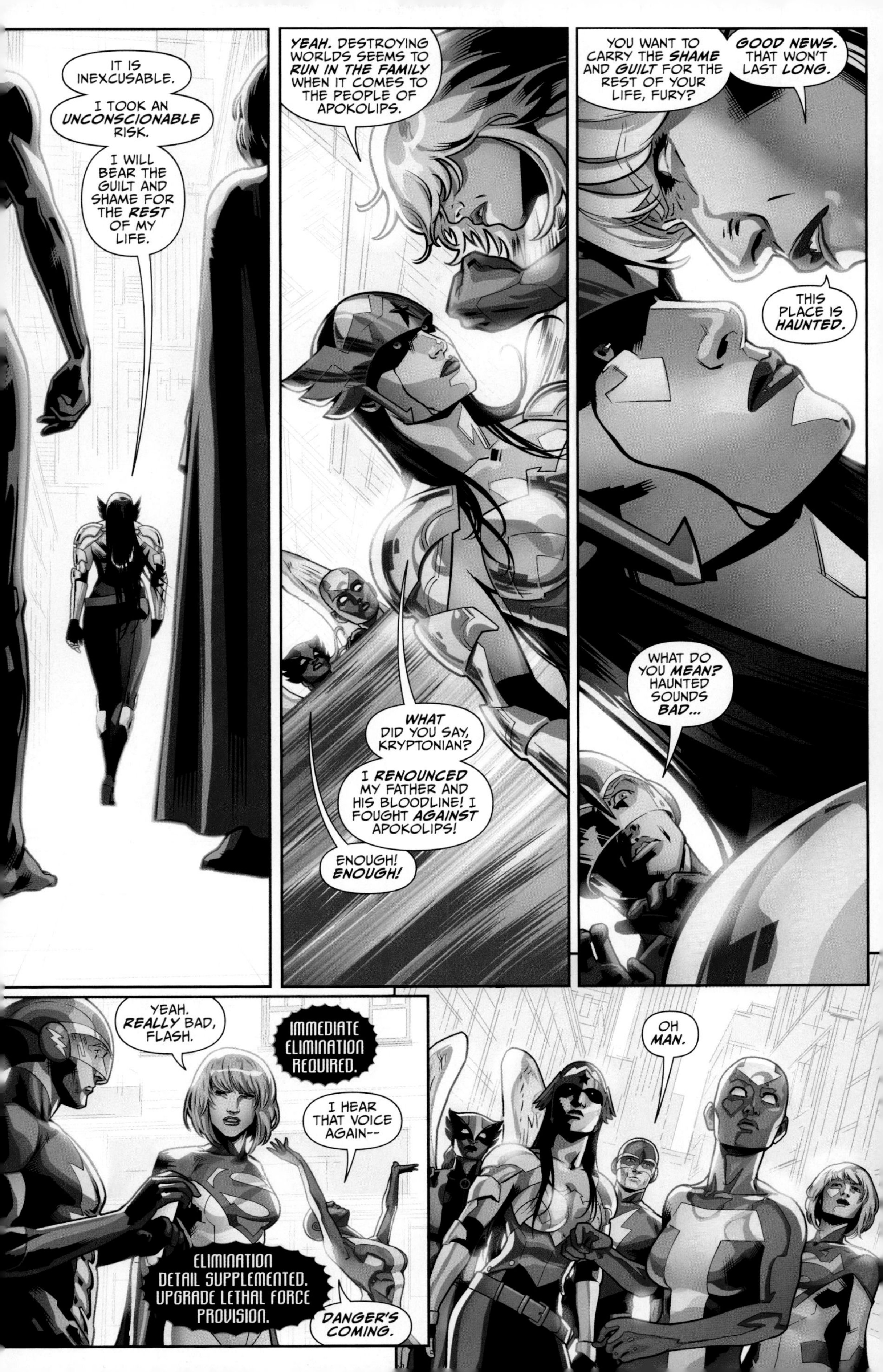
IT IS INEXCUSABLE.
I TOOK AN UNCONSCIONABLE RISK.
I WILL BEAR THE GUILT AND SHAME FOR THE REST OF MY LIFE.
YEAH. DESTROYING WORLDS SEEMS TO RUN IN THE FAMILY WHEN IT COMES TO THE PEOPLE OF APOKOLIPS.
WHAT DID YOU SAY, KRYPTONIAN?
I RENOUNCED MY FATHER AND HIS BLOODLINE! I FOUGHT AGAINST APOKOLIPS!
ENOUGH! ENOUGH!
YOU WANT TO CARRY THE SHAME AND GUILT FOR THE REST OF YOUR LIFE, FURY?
GOOD NEWS. THAT WON'T LAST LONG.
THIS PLACE IS HAUNTED.
WHAT DO YOU MEAN? HAUNTED SOUNDS BAD...
YEAH. REALLY BAD, FLASH.
IMMEDIATE ELIMINATION REQUIRED.
I HEAR THAT VOICE AGAIN--
ELIMINATION DETAIL SUPPLEMENTED. UPGRADE LETHAL FORCE PROVISION.
DANGER'S COMING.
OH MAN.

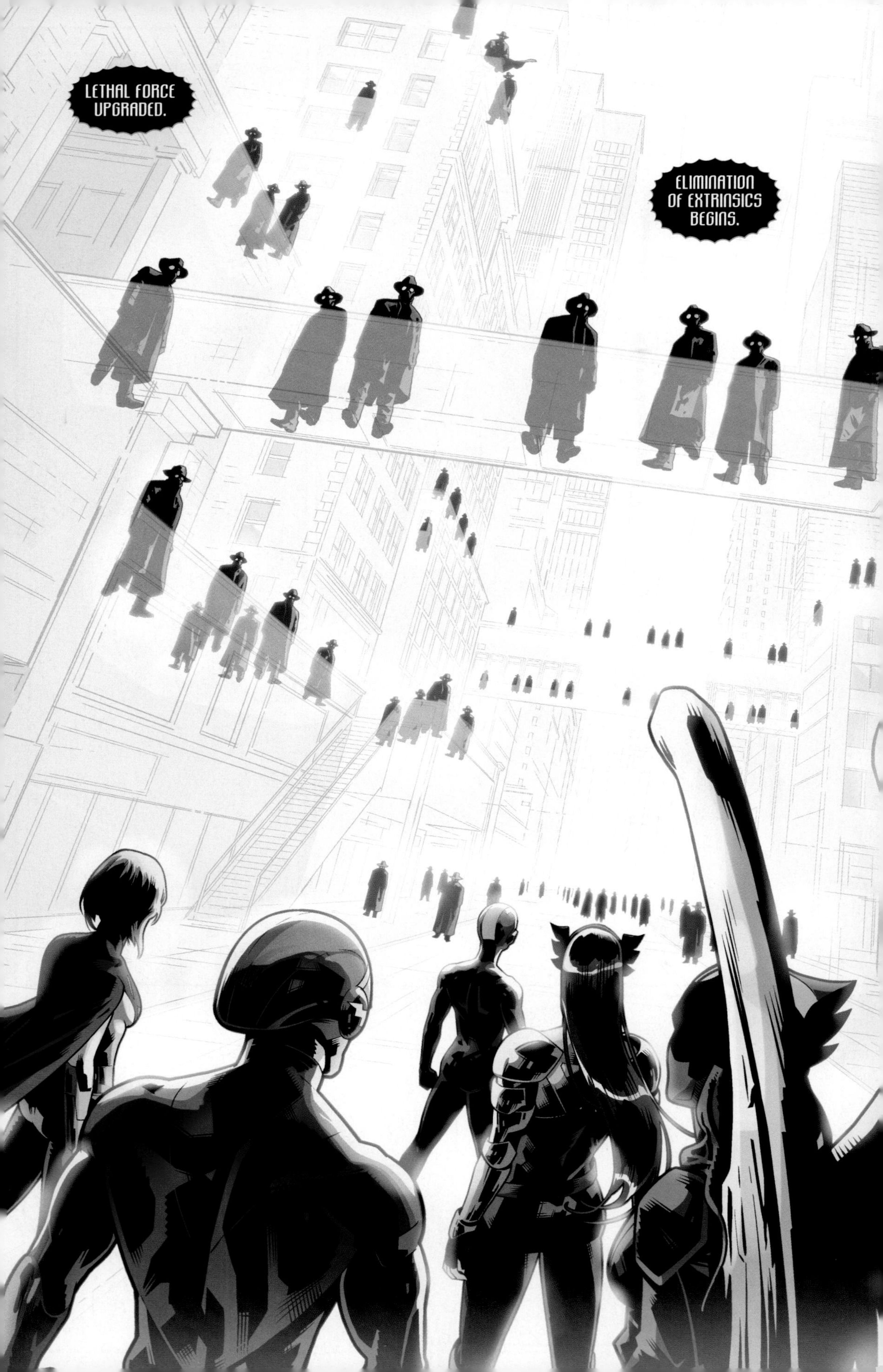
LETHAL FORCE UPGRADED.
ELIMINATION OF EXTRINSICS BEGINS.

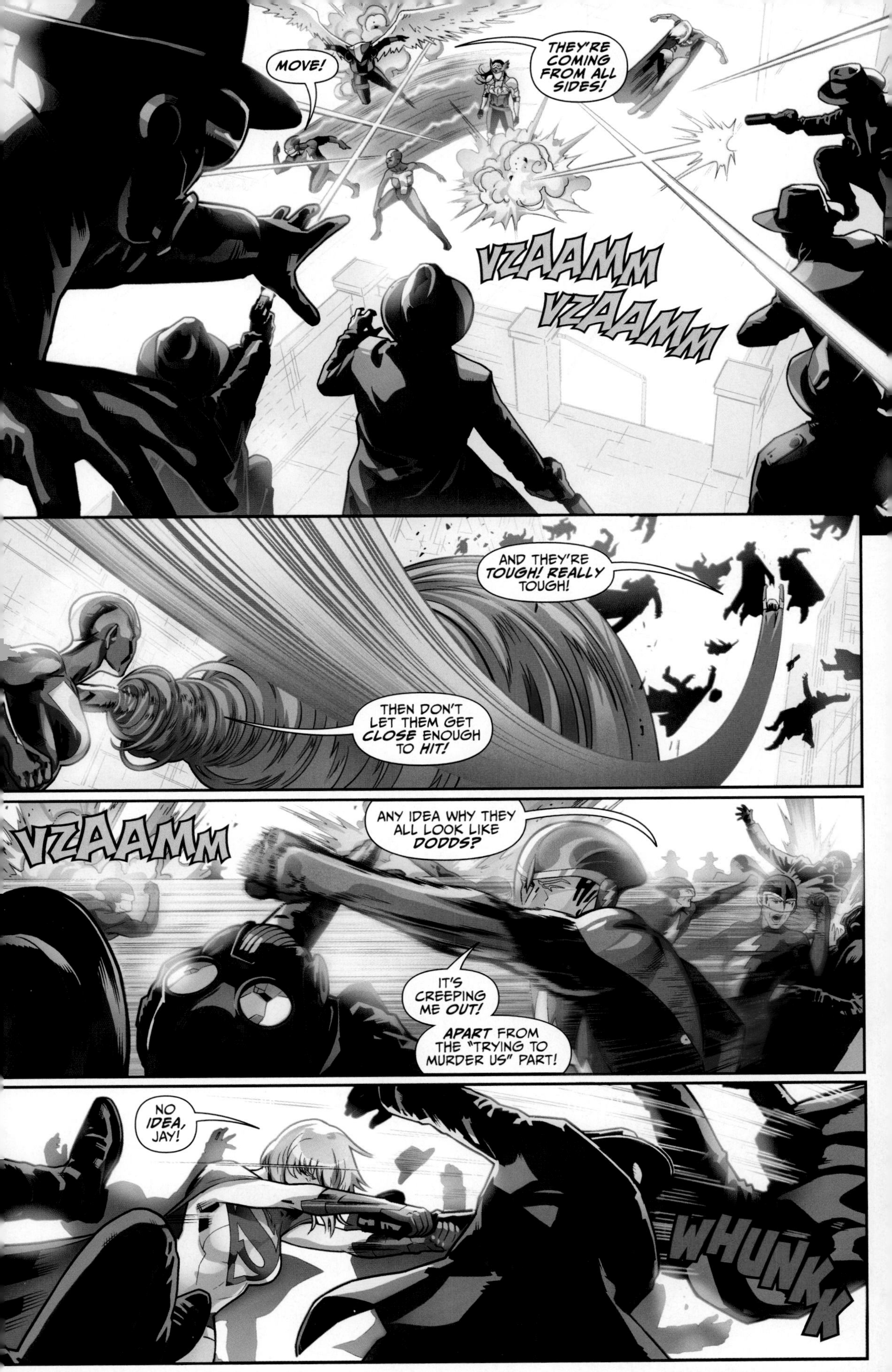
MOVE!
THEY'RE COMING FROM ALL SIDES!
VZAAMM
VZAAMM
AND THEY'RE TOUGH! REALLY TOUGH!
THEN DON'T LET THEM GET CLOSE ENOUGH TO HIT!
VZAAMM
ANY IDEA WHY THEY ALL LOOK LIKE DODDS?
IT'S CREEPING ME OUT!
APART FROM THE "TRYING TO MURDER US" PART!
NO IDEA, JAY!
WHUNKK

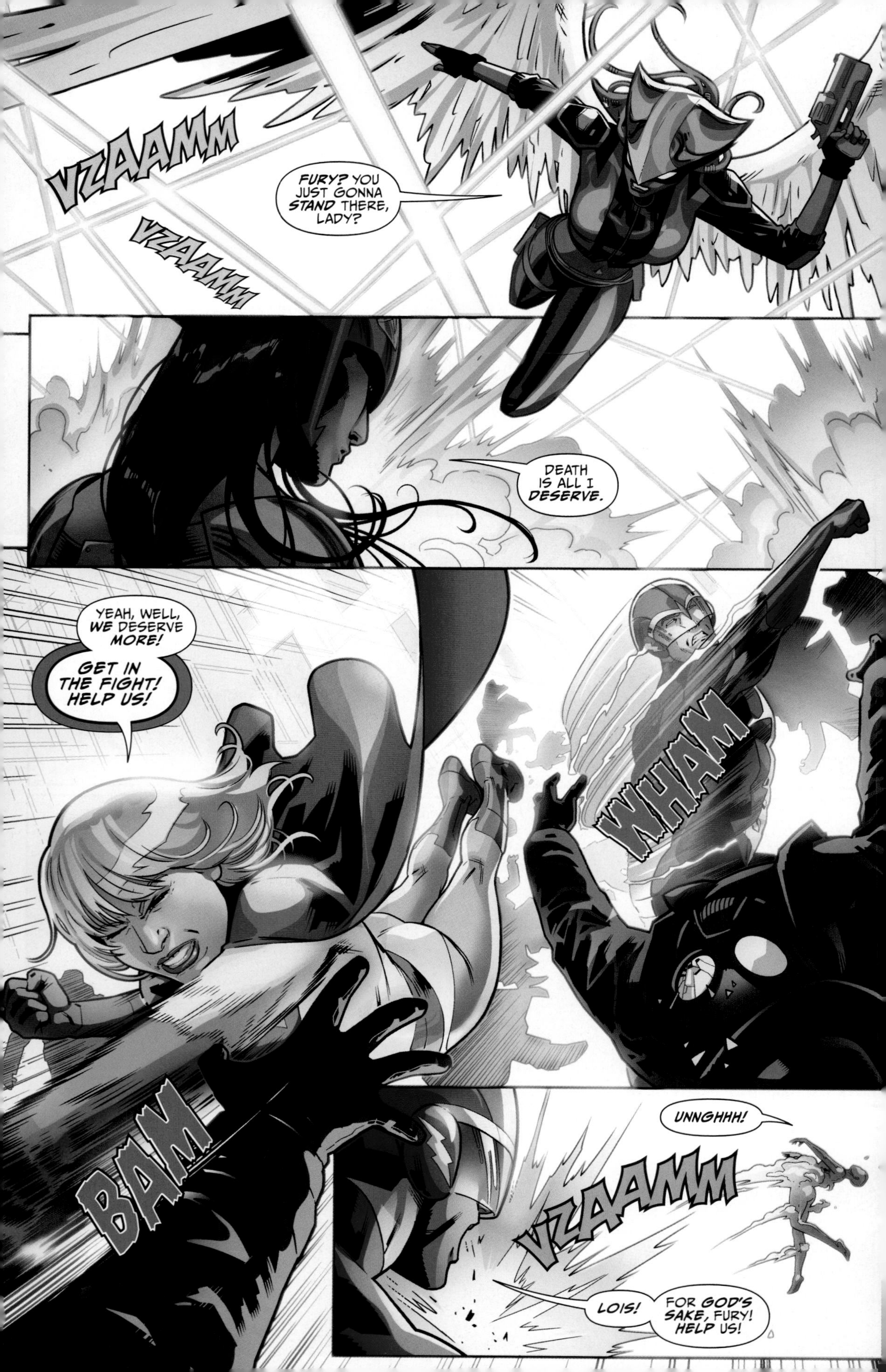
VZAAMM
VZAAMM
FURY? YOU JUST GONNA STAND THERE, LADY?
DEATH IS ALL I DESERVE.
YEAH, WELL, WE DESERVE MORE!
GET IN THE FIGHT! HELP US!
WHAM
BAM
UNNGHHH!
VZAAMM
LOIS!
FOR GOD'S SAKE, FURY! HELP US!

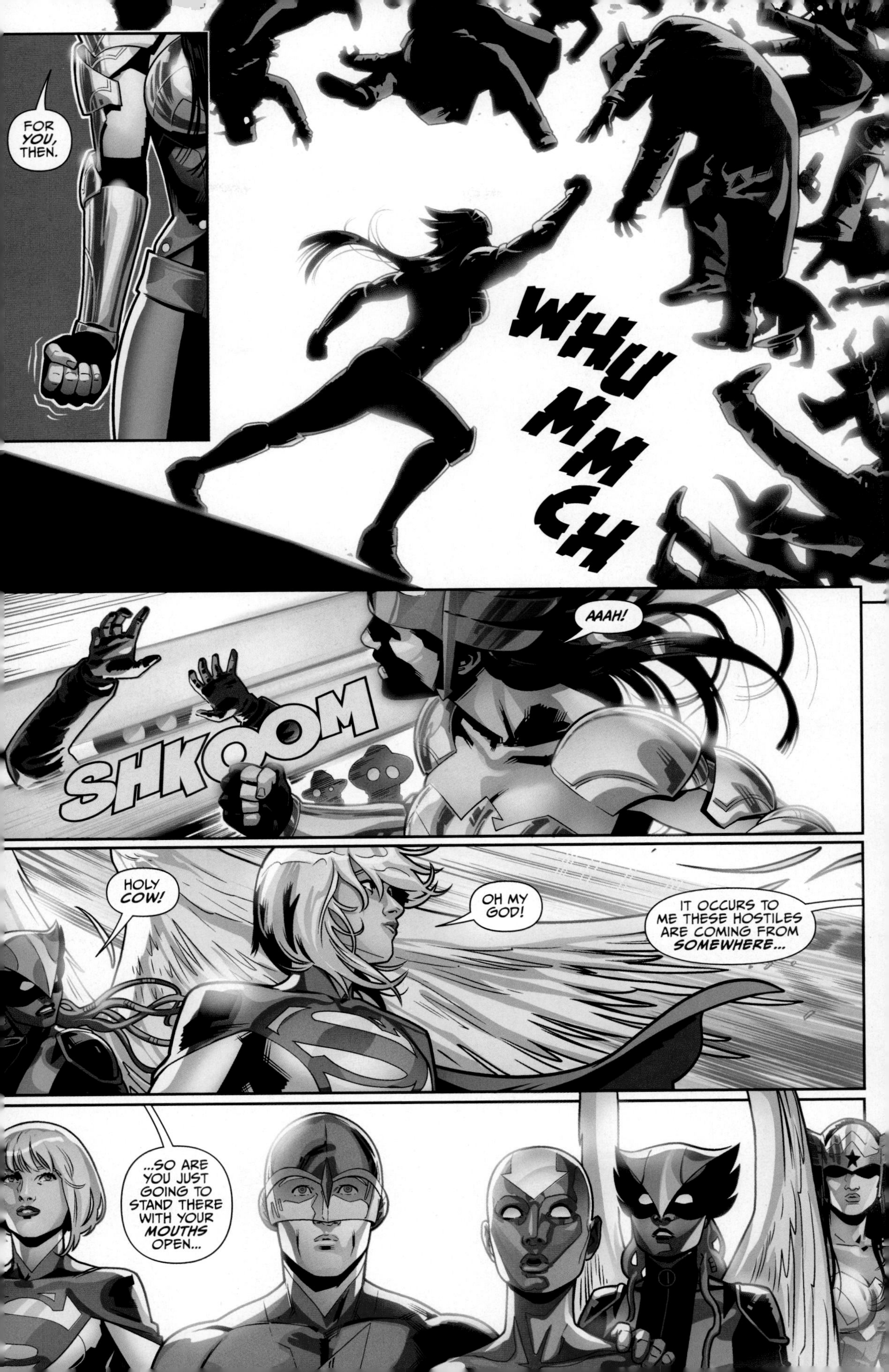
FOR YOU, THEN.
WHUMMMCH
AAAH!
SHKOOM
HOLY COW!
OH MY GOD!
IT OCCURS TO ME THESE HOSTILES ARE COMING FROM SOMEWHERE...
...SO ARE YOU JUST GOING TO STAND THERE WITH YOUR MOUTHS OPEN...

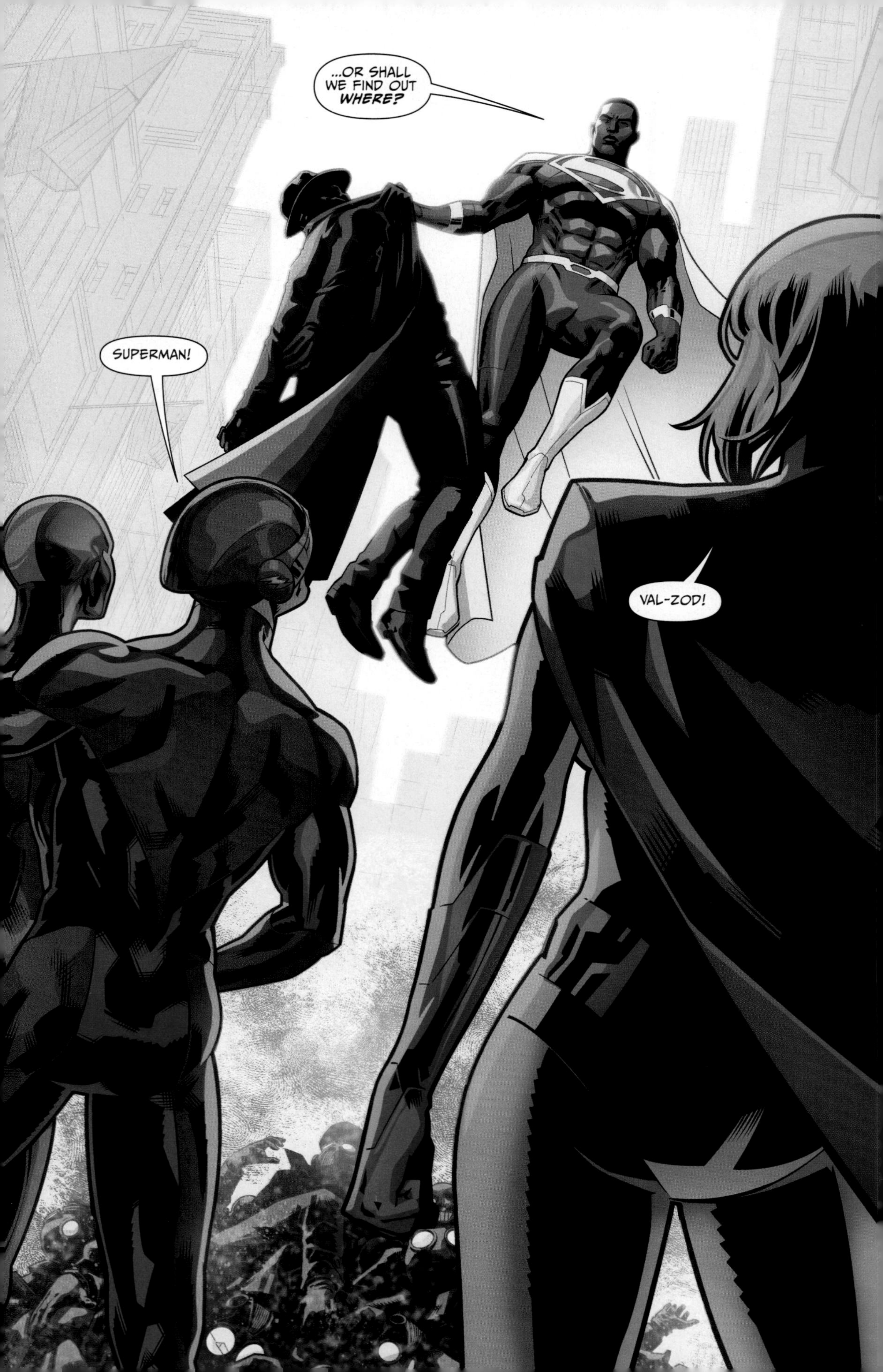
...OR SHALL WE FIND OUT WHERE?
SUPERMAN!
VAL-ZOD!

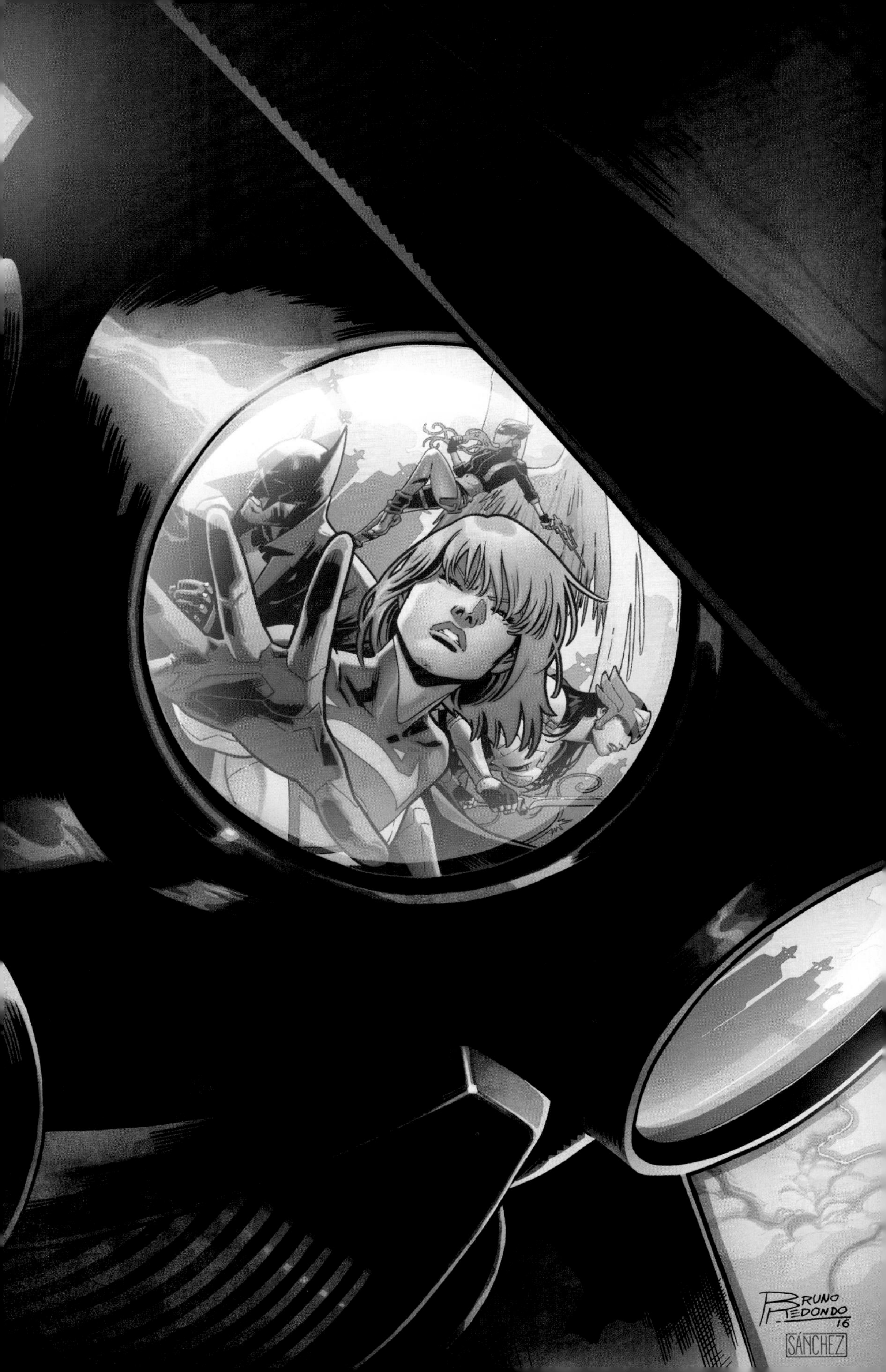
BRUNO REDONDO 16
SÁNCHEZ

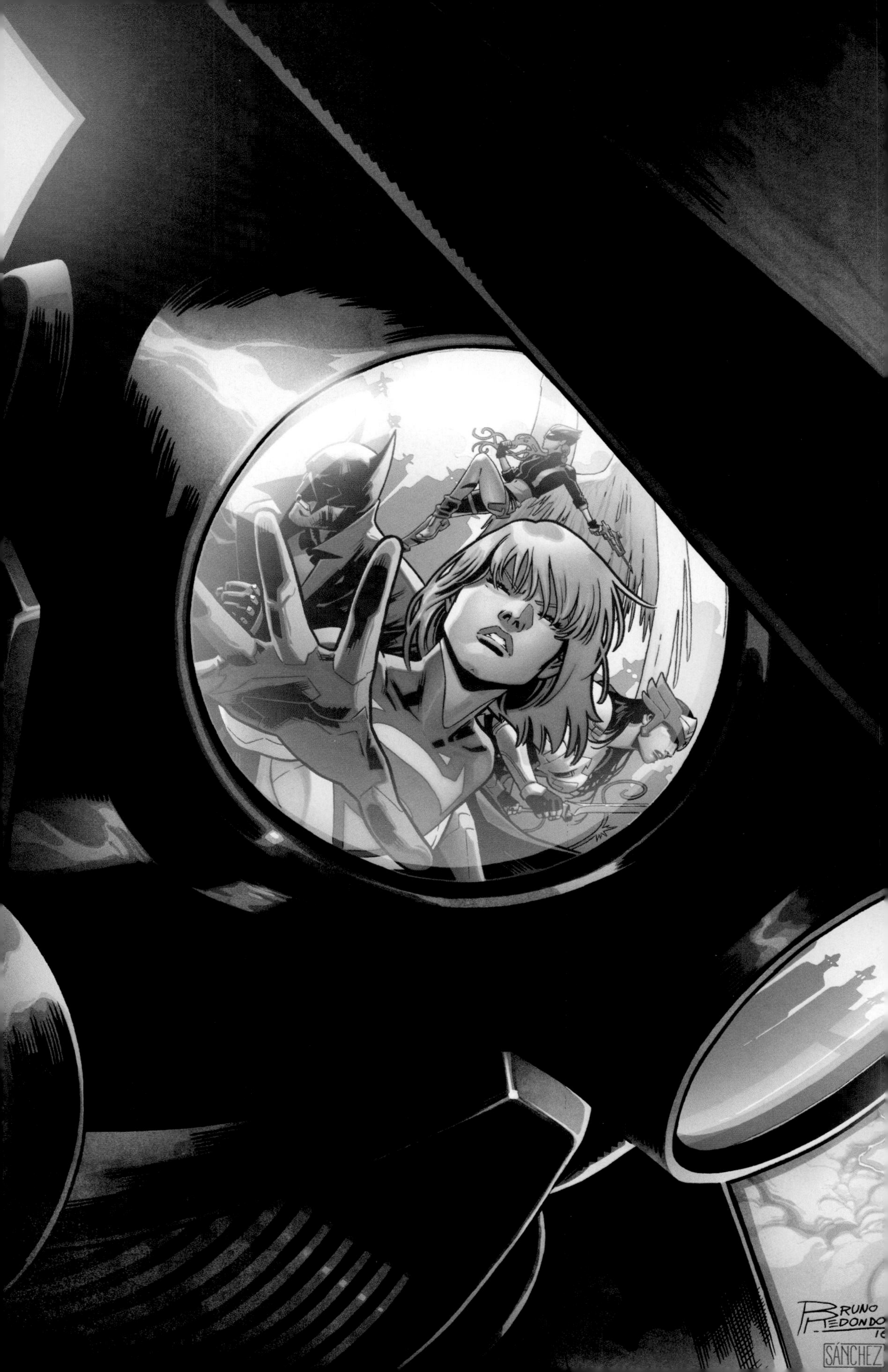
BRUNO REDONDO

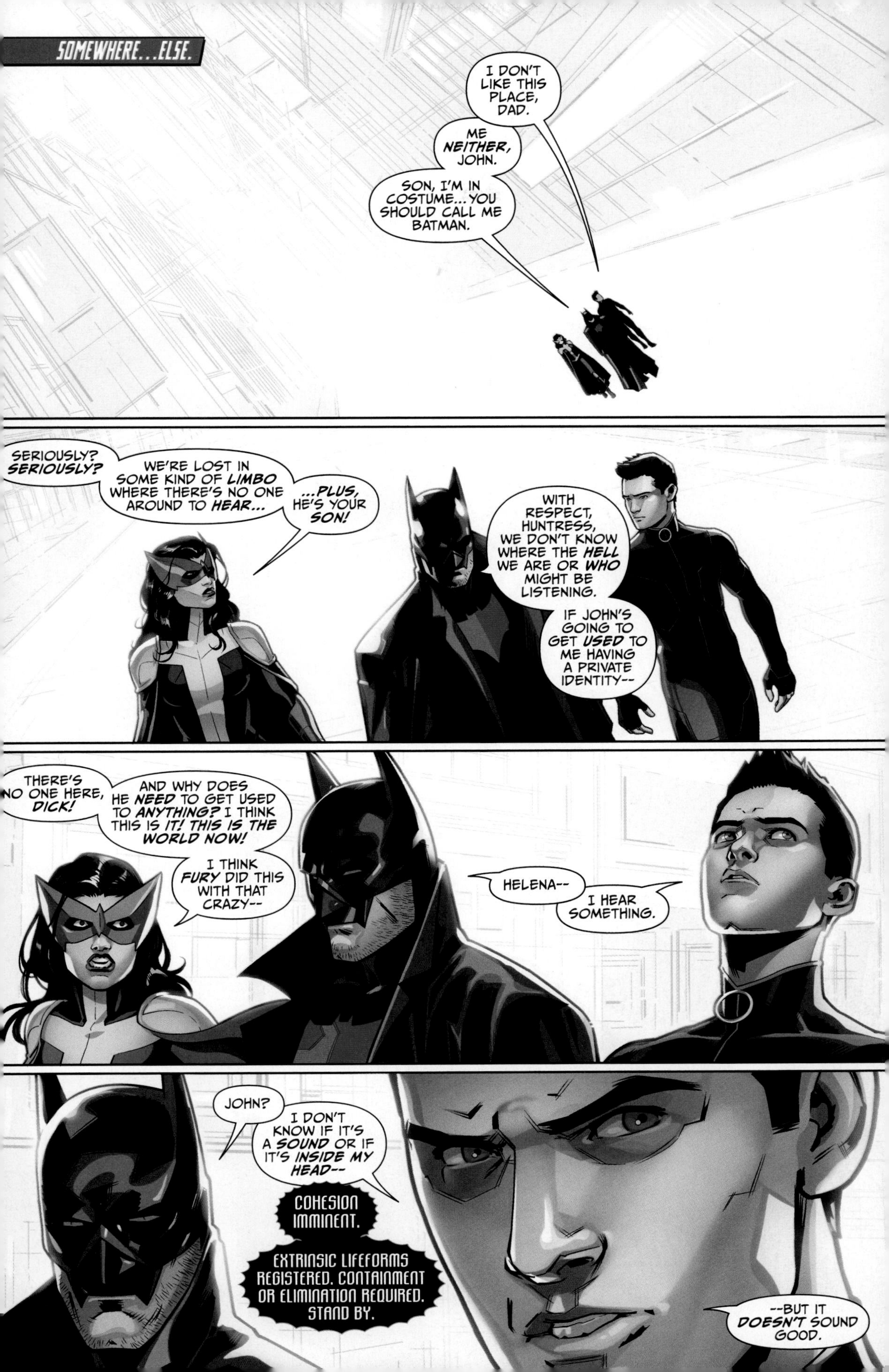
SOMEWHERE...ELSE.
I DON'T LIKE THIS PLACE, DAD.
ME NEITHER, JOHN.
SON, I'M IN COSTUME...YOU SHOULD CALL ME BATMAN.
SERIOUSLY? SERIOUSLY?
WE'RE LOST IN SOME KIND OF LIMBO WHERE THERE'S NO ONE AROUND TO HEAR...
...PLUS, HE'S YOUR SON!
WITH RESPECT, HUNTRESS, WE DON'T KNOW WHERE THE HELL WE ARE OR WHO MIGHT BE LISTENING.
IF JOHN'S GOING TO GET USED TO ME HAVING A PRIVATE IDENTITY--
THERE'S NO ONE HERE, DICK!
AND WHY DOES HE NEED TO GET USED TO ANYTHING? I THINK THIS IS IT! THIS IS THE WORLD NOW!
I THINK FURY DID THIS WITH THAT CRAZY--
HELENA--
I HEAR SOMETHING.
JOHN?
I DON'T KNOW IF IT'S A SOUND OR IF IT'S INSIDE MY HEAD--
COHESION IMMINENT.
EXTRINSIC LIFEFORMS REGISTERED. CONTAINMENT OR ELIMINATION REQUIRED. STAND BY.
--BUT IT DOESN'T SOUND GOOD.

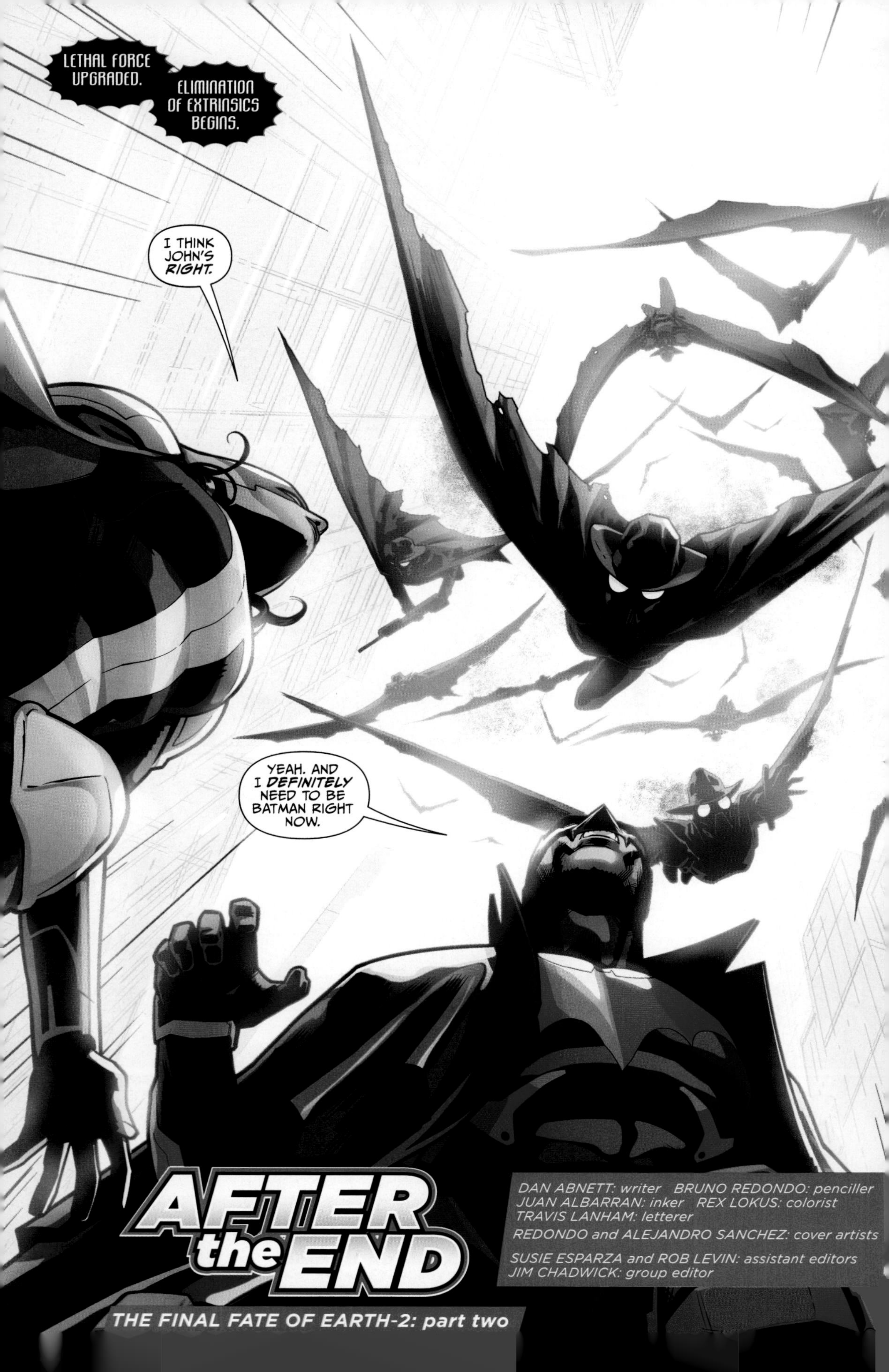
LETHAL FORCE UPGRADED.
ELIMINATION OF EXTRINSICS BEGINS.
I THINK JOHN'S RIGHT.
YEAH. AND I DEFINITELY NEED TO BE BATMAN RIGHT NOW.
AFTER the END
THE FINAL FATE OF EARTH-2: part two
DAN ABNETT: writer BRUNO REDONDO: penciller
JUAN ALBARRAN: inker REX LOKUS: colorist
TRAVIS LANHAM: letterer
REDONDO and ALEJANDRO SANCHEZ: cover artists
SUSIE ESPARZA and ROB LEVIN: assistant editors
JIM CHADWICK: group editor

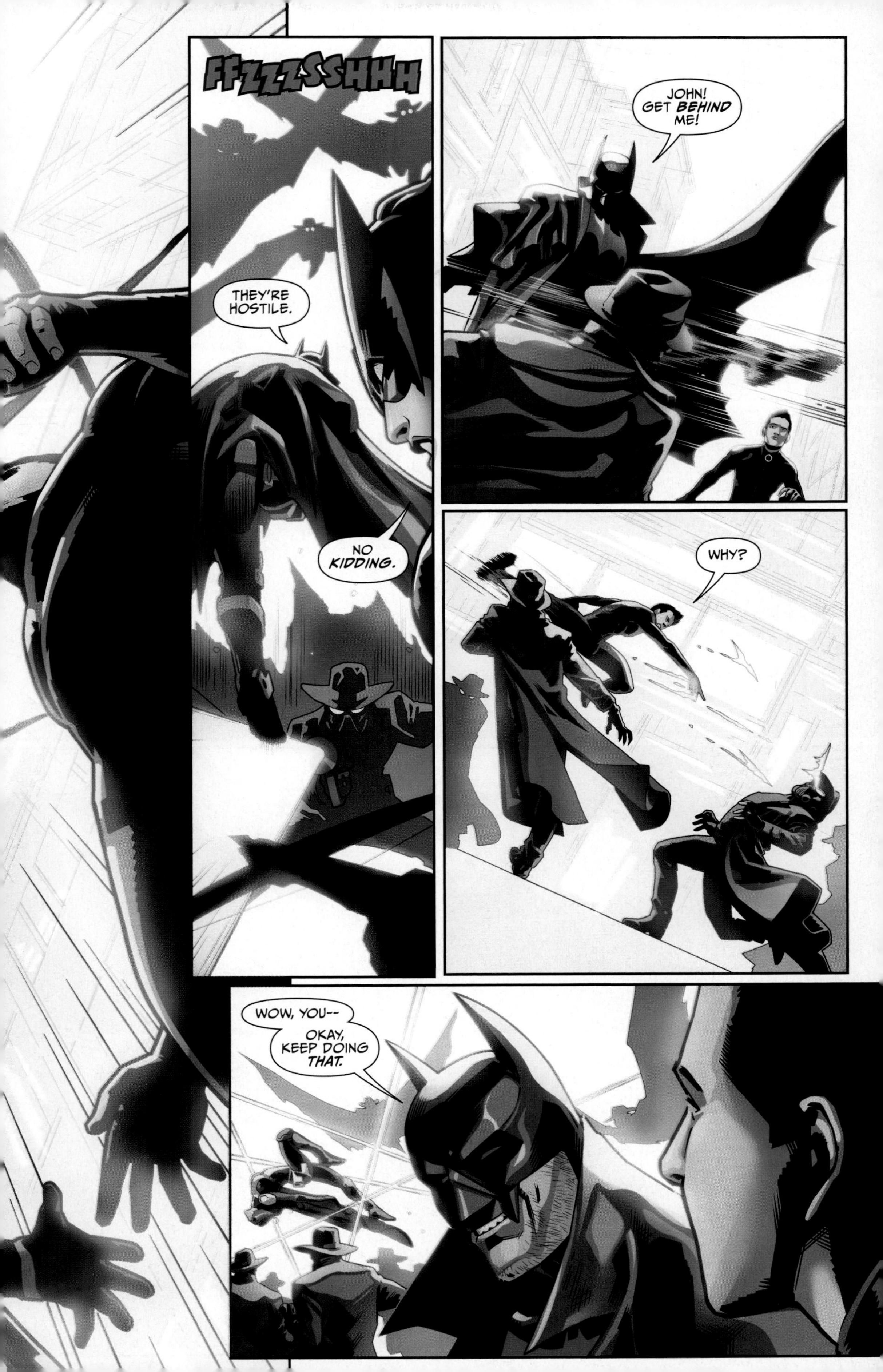
FFZZZSSHHH
THEY'RE HOSTILE.
NO KIDDING.
JOHN! GET BEHIND ME!
WHY?
WOW, YOU--
OKAY, KEEP DOING THAT.

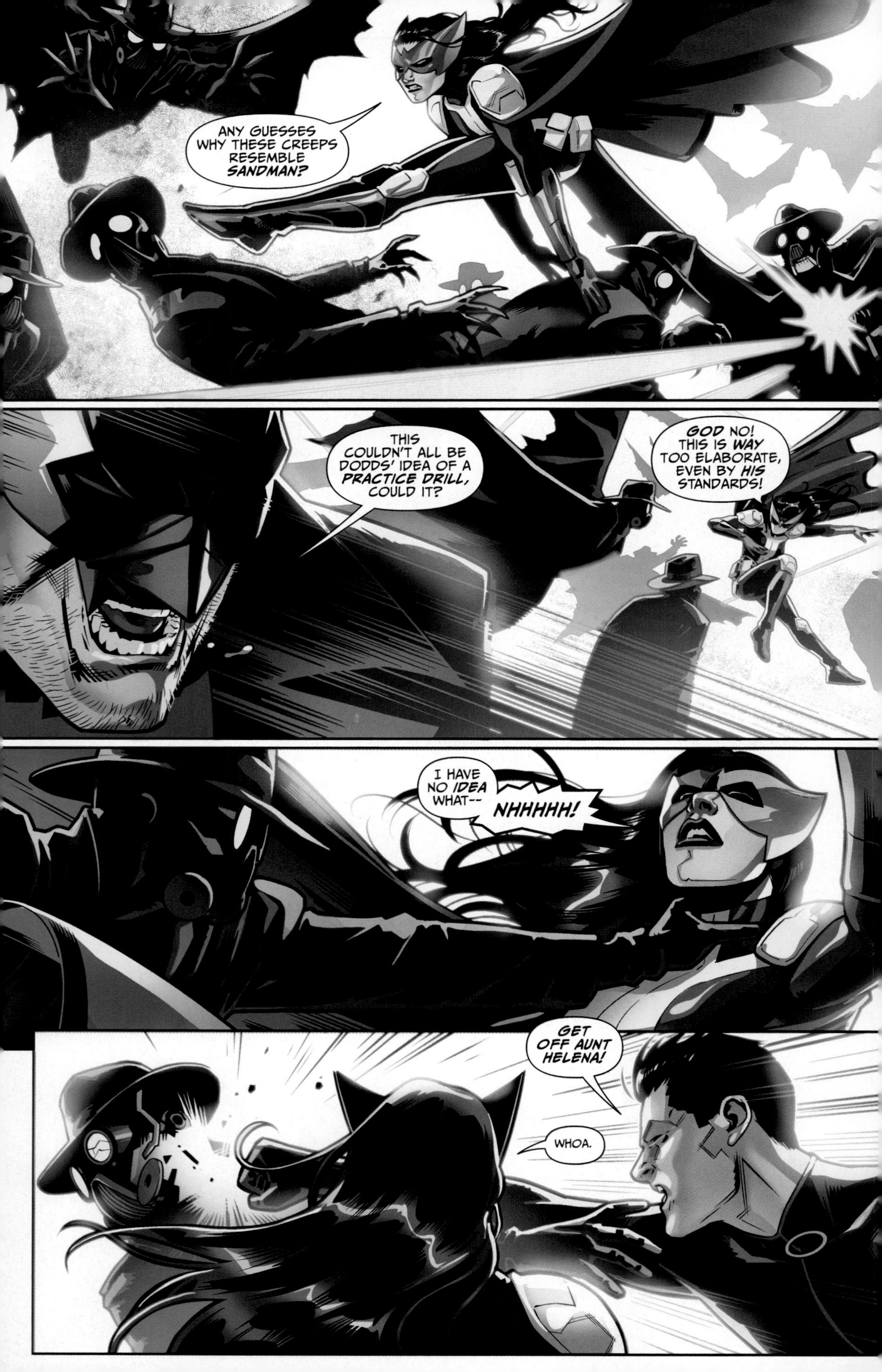
ANY GUESSES WHY THESE CREEPS RESEMBLE SANDMAN?
THIS COULDN'T ALL BE DODDS' IDEA OF A PRACTICE DRILL, COULD IT?
GOD NO! THIS IS WAY TOO ELABORATE, EVEN BY HIS STANDARDS!
I HAVE NO IDEA WHAT--
NHHHHH!
GET OFF AUNT HELENA!
WHOA.

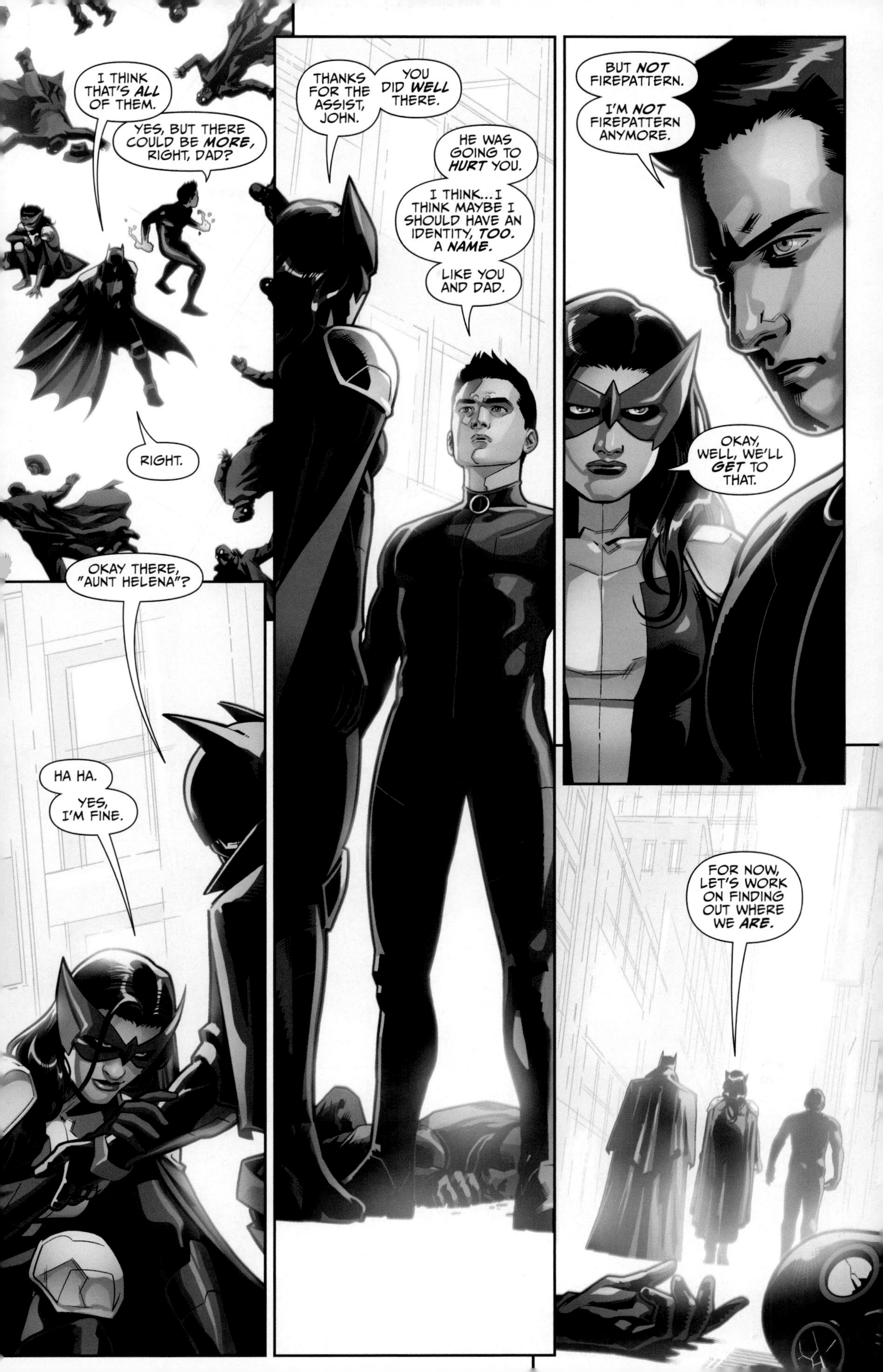
I THINK THAT'S ALL OF THEM.
YES, BUT THERE COULD BE MORE, RIGHT, DAD?
RIGHT.
OKAY THERE, "AUNT HELENA"?
HA HA.
YES, I'M FINE.
THANKS FOR THE ASSIST, JOHN.
YOU DID WELL THERE.
HE WAS GOING TO HURT YOU.
I THINK... I THINK MAYBE I SHOULD HAVE AN IDENTITY, TOO. A NAME.
LIKE YOU AND DAD.
BUT NOT FIREPATTERN.
I'M NOT FIREPATTERN ANYMORE.
OKAY, WELL, WE'LL GET TO THAT.
FOR NOW, LET'S WORK ON FINDING OUT WHERE WE ARE.

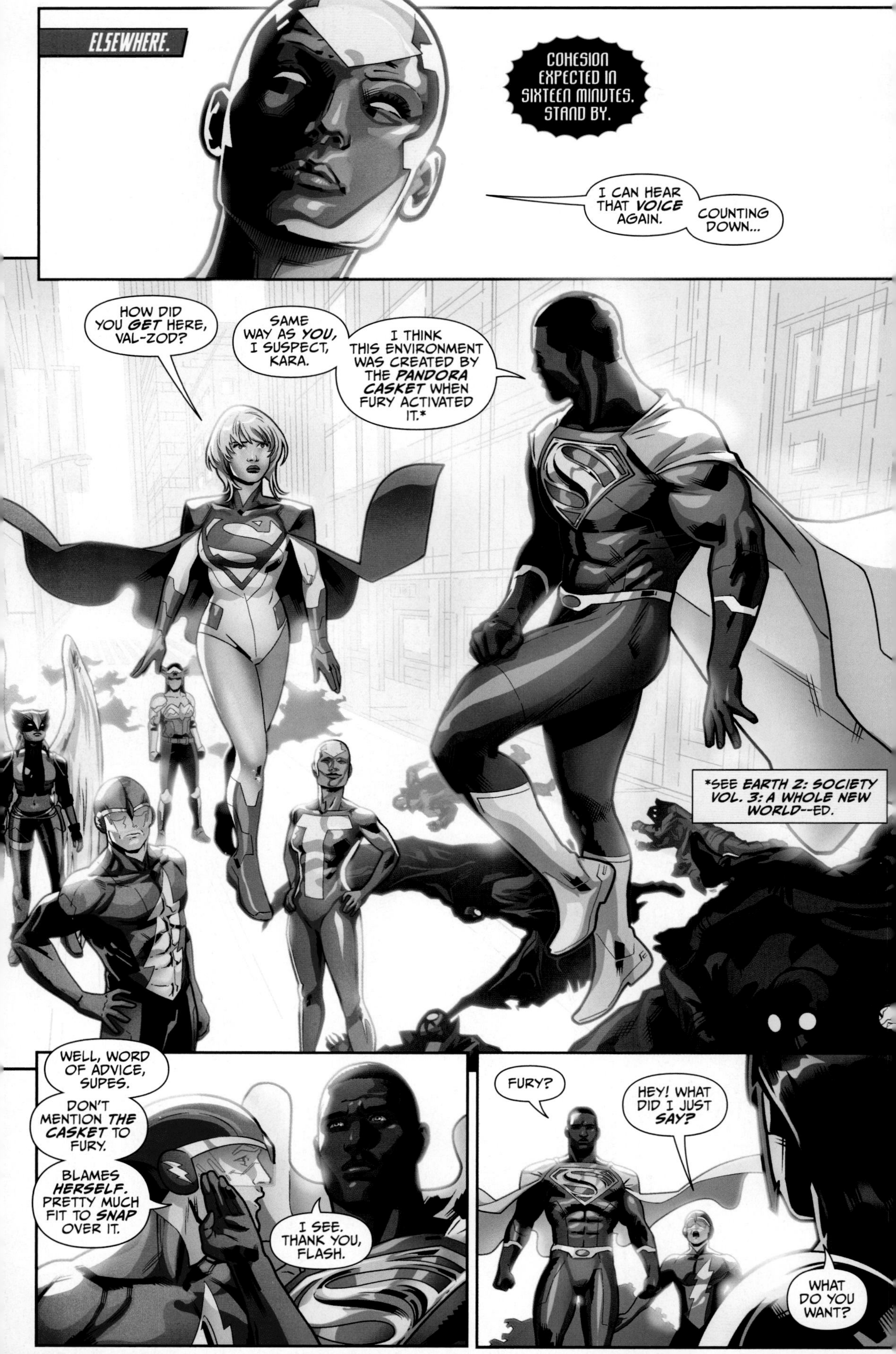
ELSEWHERE.
COHESION EXPECTED IN SIXTEEN MINUTES. STAND BY.
I CAN HEAR THAT VOICE AGAIN.
COUNTING DOWN...
HOW DID YOU GET HERE, VAL-ZOD?
SAME WAY AS YOU, I SUSPECT, KARA.
I THINK THIS ENVIRONMENT WAS CREATED BY THE PANDORA CASKET WHEN FURY ACTIVATED IT.*
*SEE EARTH 2: SOCIETY VOL. 3: A WHOLE NEW WORLD--ED.
WELL, WORD OF ADVICE, SUPES.
DON'T MENTION THE CASKET TO FURY.
BLAMES HERSELF. PRETTY MUCH FIT TO SNAP OVER IT.
I SEE. THANK YOU, FLASH.
FURY?
HEY! WHAT DID I JUST SAY?
WHAT DO YOU WANT?

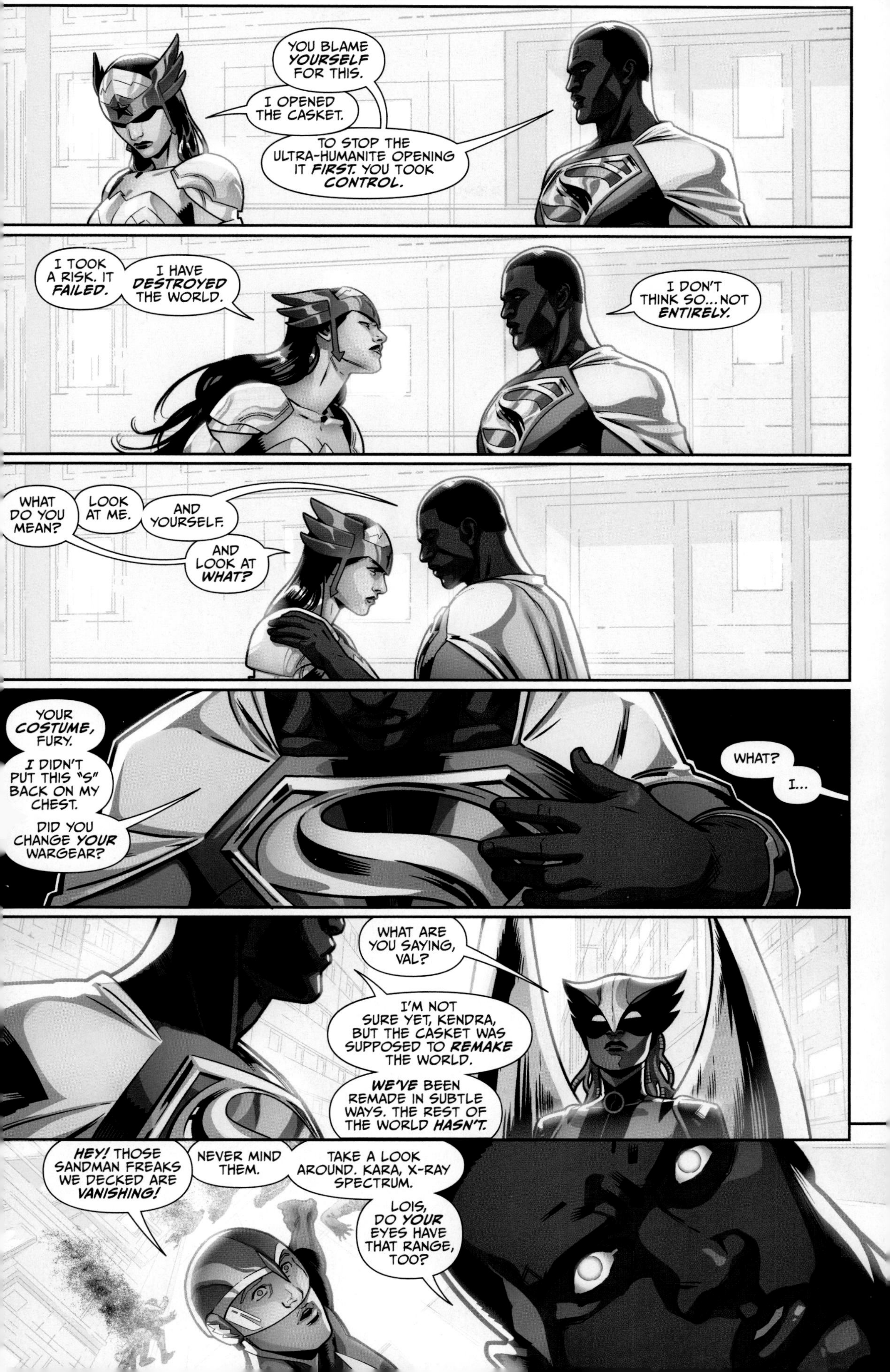
YOU BLAME YOURSELF FOR THIS.
I OPENED THE CASKET.
TO STOP THE ULTRA-HUMANITE OPENING IT FIRST. YOU TOOK CONTROL.
I TOOK A RISK. IT FAILED.
I HAVE DESTROYED THE WORLD.
I DON'T THINK SO...NOT ENTIRELY.
WHAT DO YOU MEAN?
LOOK AT ME.
AND YOURSELF.
AND LOOK AT WHAT?
YOUR COSTUME, FURY.
I DIDN'T PUT THIS "S" BACK ON MY CHEST.
DID YOU CHANGE YOUR WARGEAR?
WHAT?
I...
WHAT ARE YOU SAYING, VAL?
I'M NOT SURE YET, KENDRA, BUT THE CASKET WAS SUPPOSED TO REMAKE THE WORLD.
WE'VE BEEN REMADE IN SUBTLE WAYS. THE REST OF THE WORLD HASN'T.
HEY! THOSE SANDMAN FREAKS WE DECKED ARE VANISHING!
NEVER MIND THEM.
TAKE A LOOK AROUND. KARA, X-RAY SPECTRUM.
LOIS, DO YOUR EYES HAVE THAT RANGE, TOO?

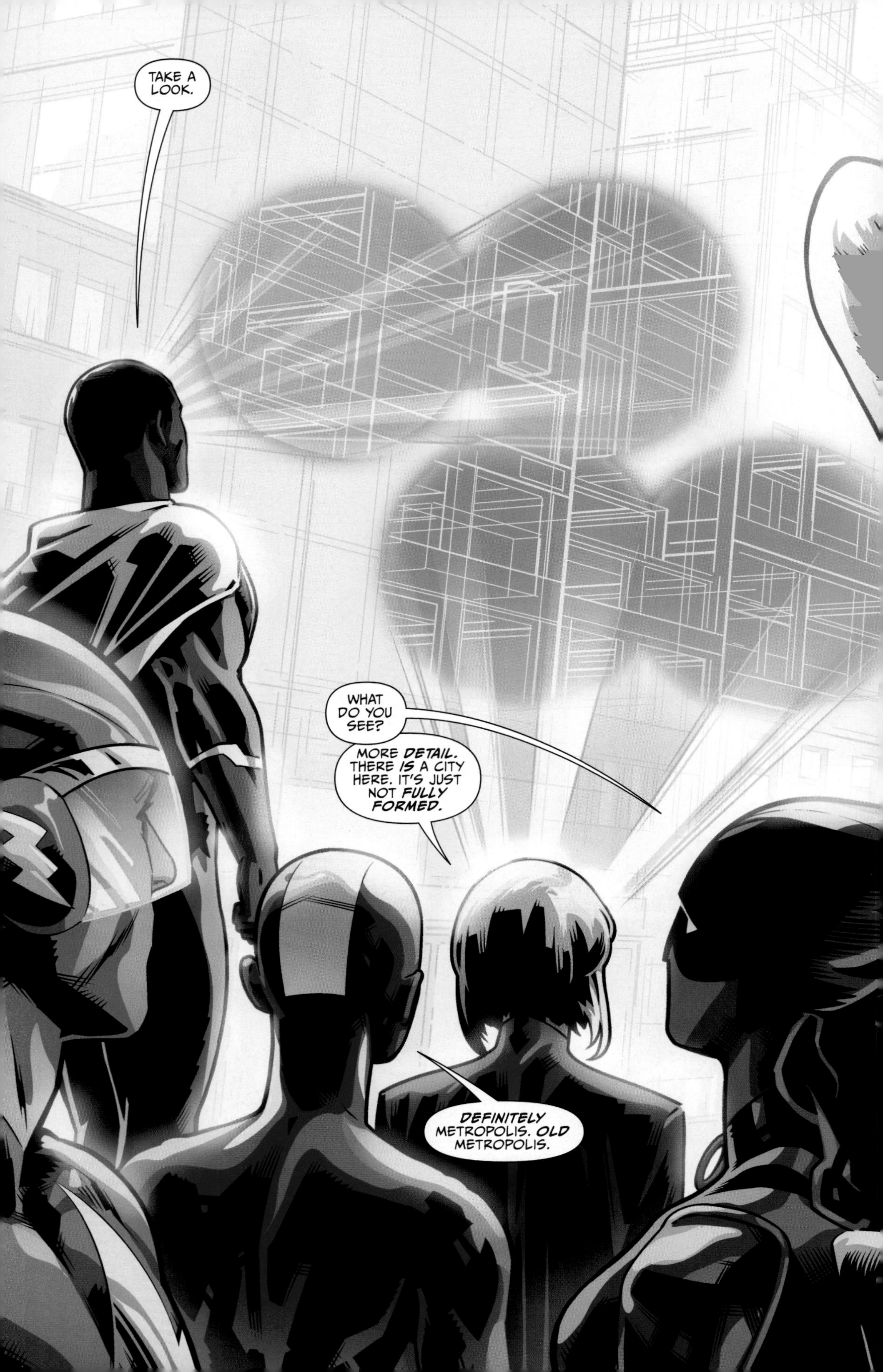
TAKE A LOOK.
WHAT DO YOU SEE?
MORE DETAIL. THERE IS A CITY HERE. IT'S JUST NOT FULLY FORMED.
DEFINITELY METROPOLIS. OLD METROPOLIS.

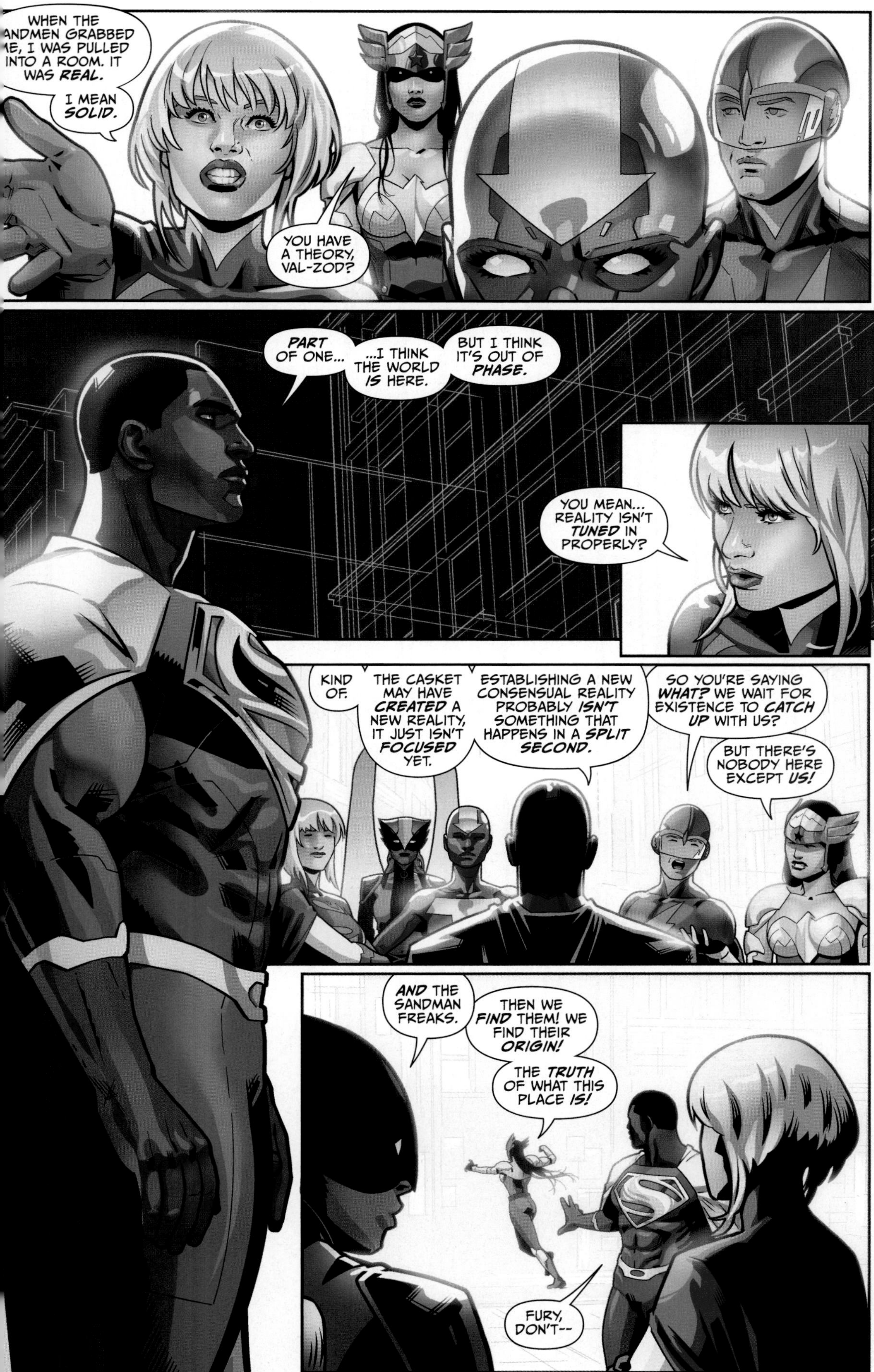
WHEN THE SANDMEN GRABBED ME, I WAS PULLED INTO A ROOM. IT WAS REAL.
I MEAN SOLID.
YOU HAVE A THEORY, VAL-ZOD?
PART OF ONE...
...I THINK THE WORLD IS HERE.
BUT I THINK IT'S OUT OF PHASE.
YOU MEAN... REALITY ISN'T TUNED IN PROPERLY?
KIND OF.
THE CASKET MAY HAVE CREATED A NEW REALITY, IT JUST ISN'T FOCUSED YET.
ESTABLISHING A NEW CONSENSUAL REALITY PROBABLY ISN'T SOMETHING THAT HAPPENS IN A SPLIT SECOND.
SO YOU'RE SAYING WHAT? WE WAIT FOR EXISTENCE TO CATCH UP WITH US?
BUT THERE'S NOBODY HERE EXCEPT US!
AND THE SANDMAN FREAKS.
THEN WE FIND THEM! WE FIND THEIR ORIGIN!
THE TRUTH OF WHAT THIS PLACE IS!
FURY, DON'T--

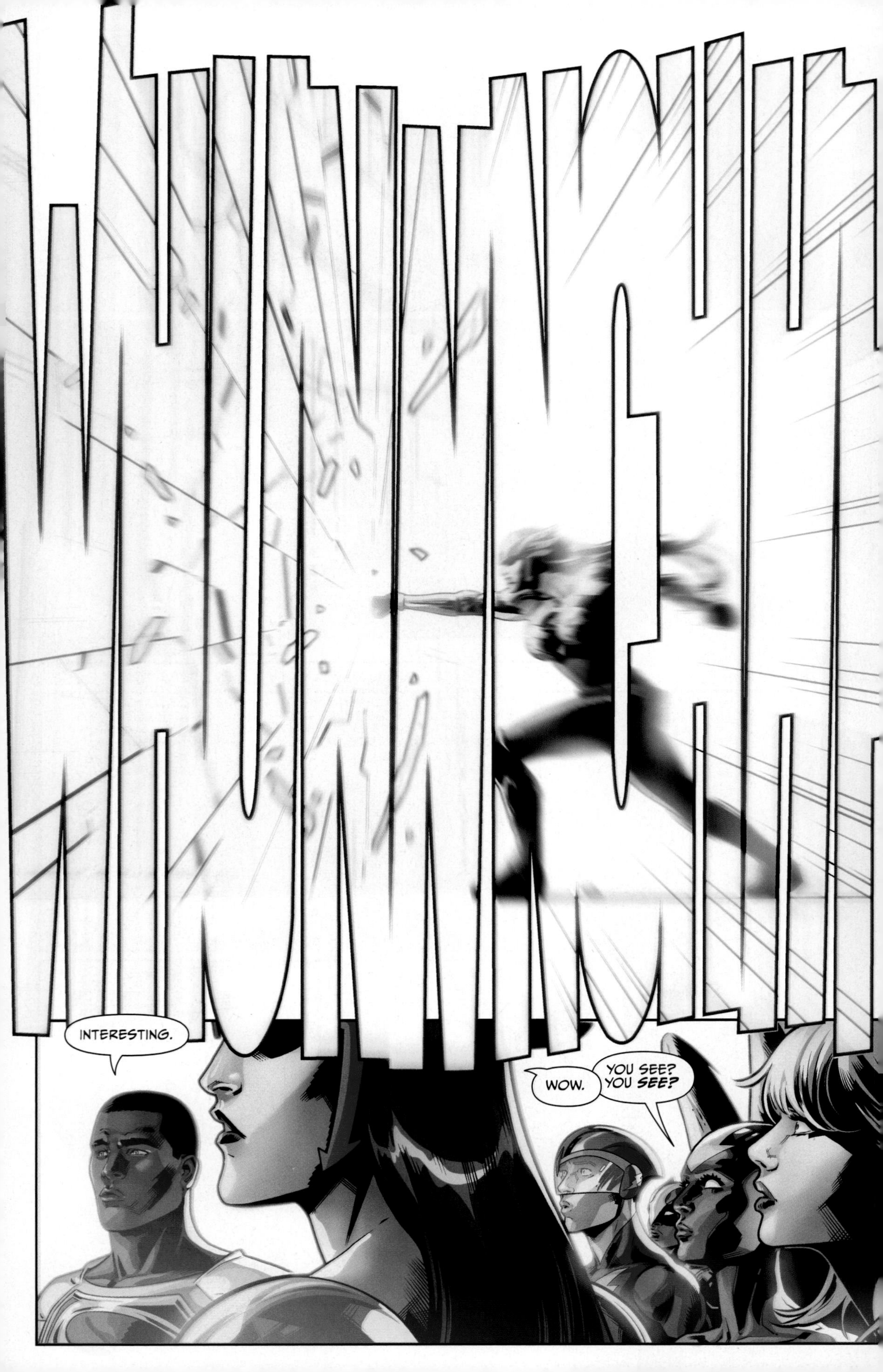
INTERESTING.
WOW.
YOU SEE? YOU *SEE?*

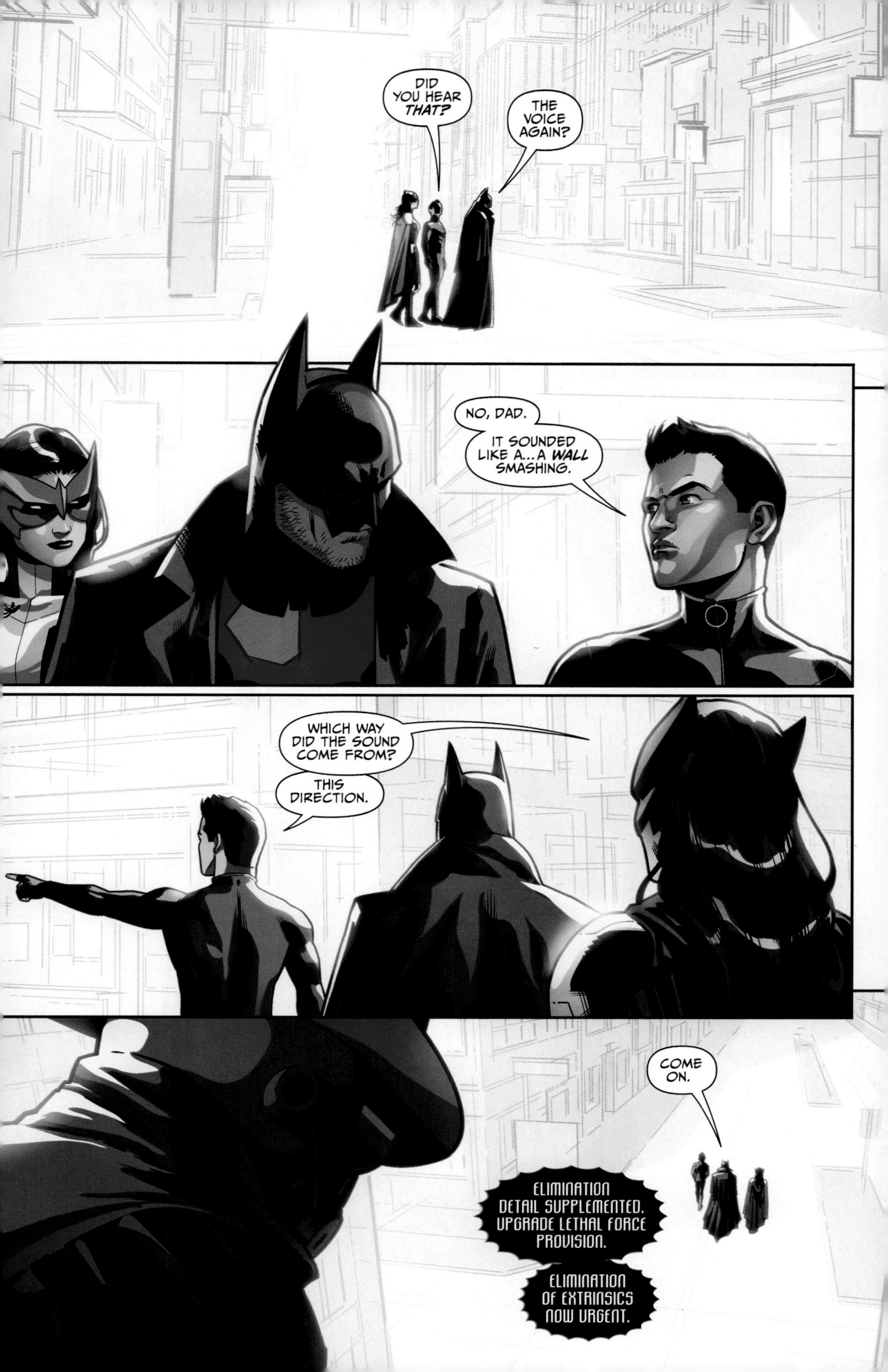
DID YOU HEAR *THAT?*
THE VOICE AGAIN?
NO, DAD.
IT SOUNDED LIKE A... A *WALL* SMASHING.
WHICH WAY DID THE SOUND COME FROM?
THIS DIRECTION.
COME ON.
ELIMINATION DETAIL SUPPLEMENTED. UPGRADE LETHAL FORCE PROVISION.
ELIMINATION OF EXTRINSICS NOW URGENT.

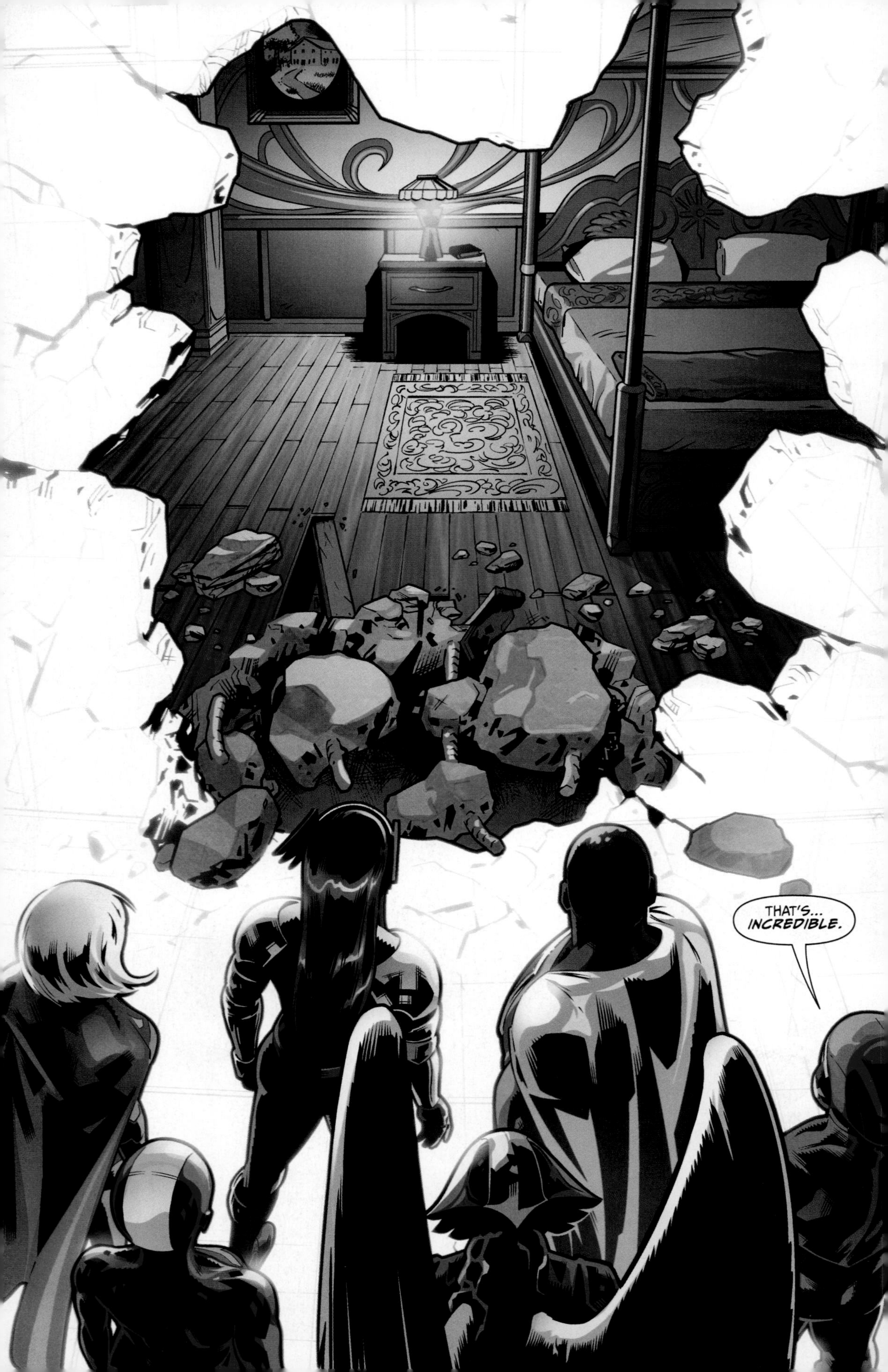
THAT'S... INCREDIBLE.

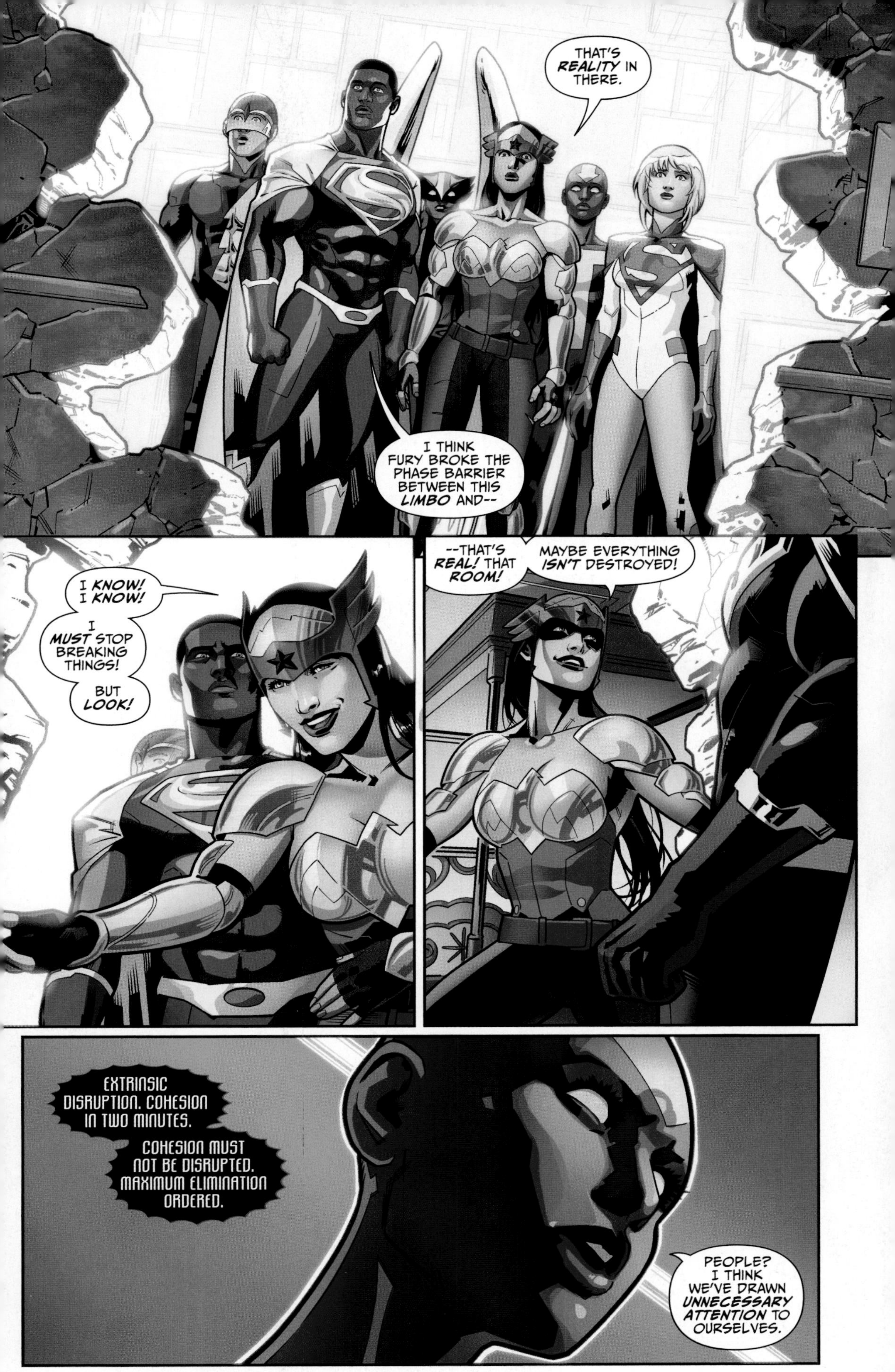
THAT'S REALITY IN THERE.
I THINK FURY BROKE THE PHASE BARRIER BETWEEN THIS LIMBO AND--
I KNOW! I KNOW!
I MUST STOP BREAKING THINGS!
BUT LOOK!
--THAT'S REAL! THAT ROOM!
MAYBE EVERYTHING ISN'T DESTROYED!
EXTRINSIC DISRUPTION. COHESION IN TWO MINUTES.
COHESION MUST NOT BE DISRUPTED. MAXIMUM ELIMINATION ORDERED.
PEOPLE? I THINK WE'VE DRAWN UNNECESSARY ATTENTION TO OURSELVES.

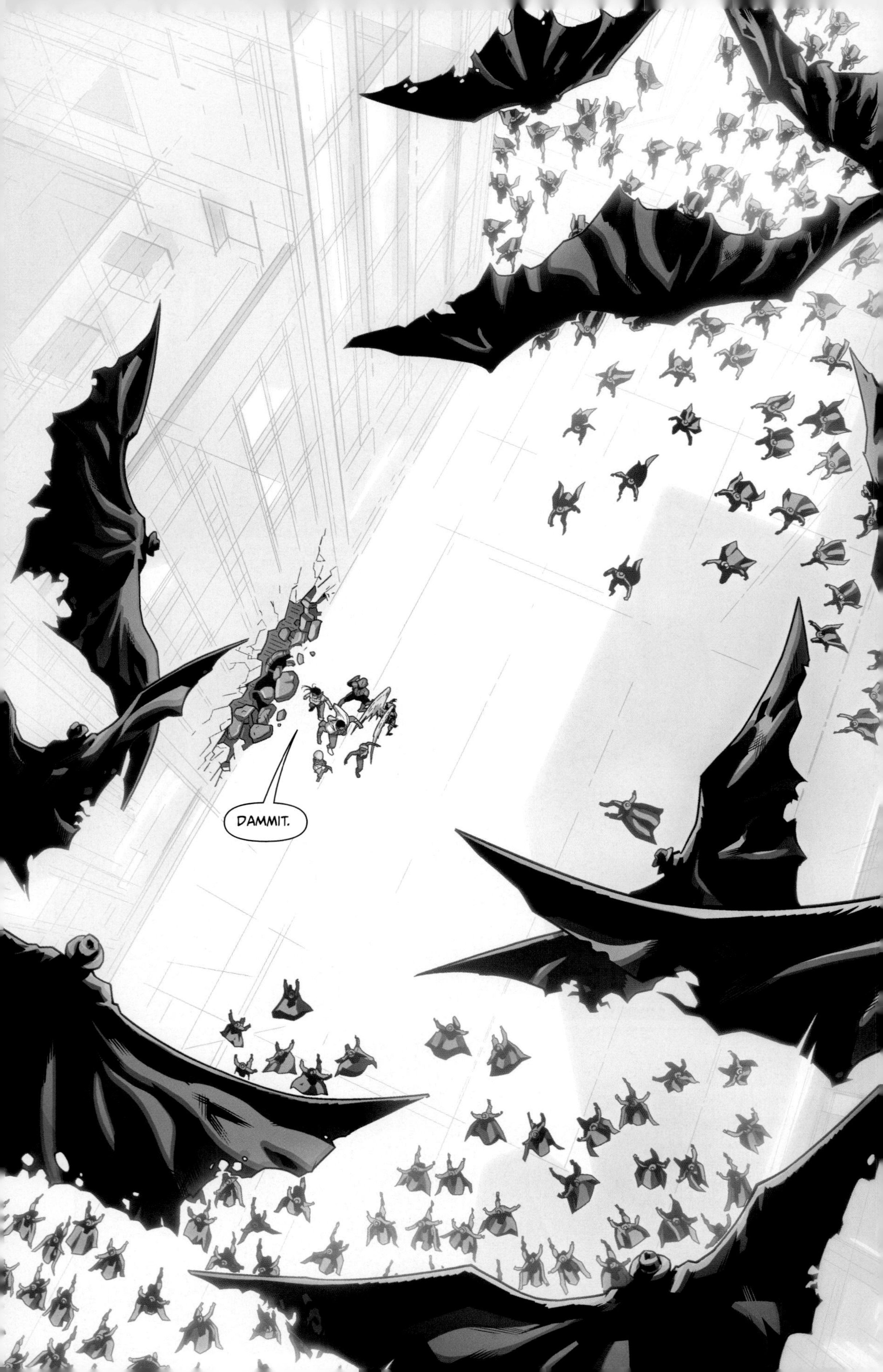
DAMMIT.

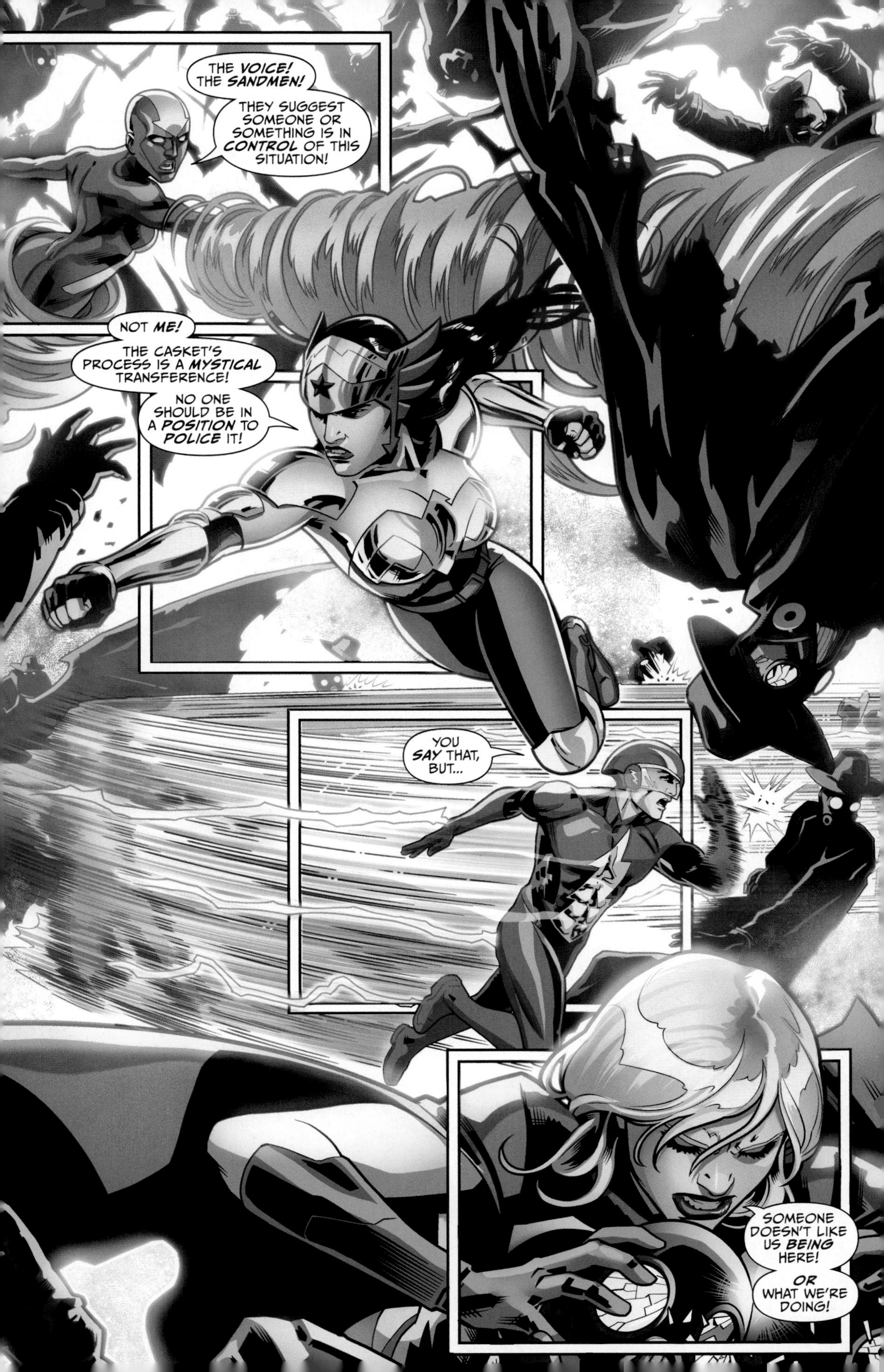
THE VOICE! THE SANDMEN!
THEY SUGGEST SOMEONE OR SOMETHING IS IN CONTROL OF THIS SITUATION!
NOT ME!
THE CASKET'S PROCESS IS A MYSTICAL TRANSFERENCE!
NO ONE SHOULD BE IN A POSITION TO POLICE IT!
YOU SAY THAT, BUT...
SOMEONE DOESN'T LIKE US BEING HERE!
OR WHAT WE'RE DOING!

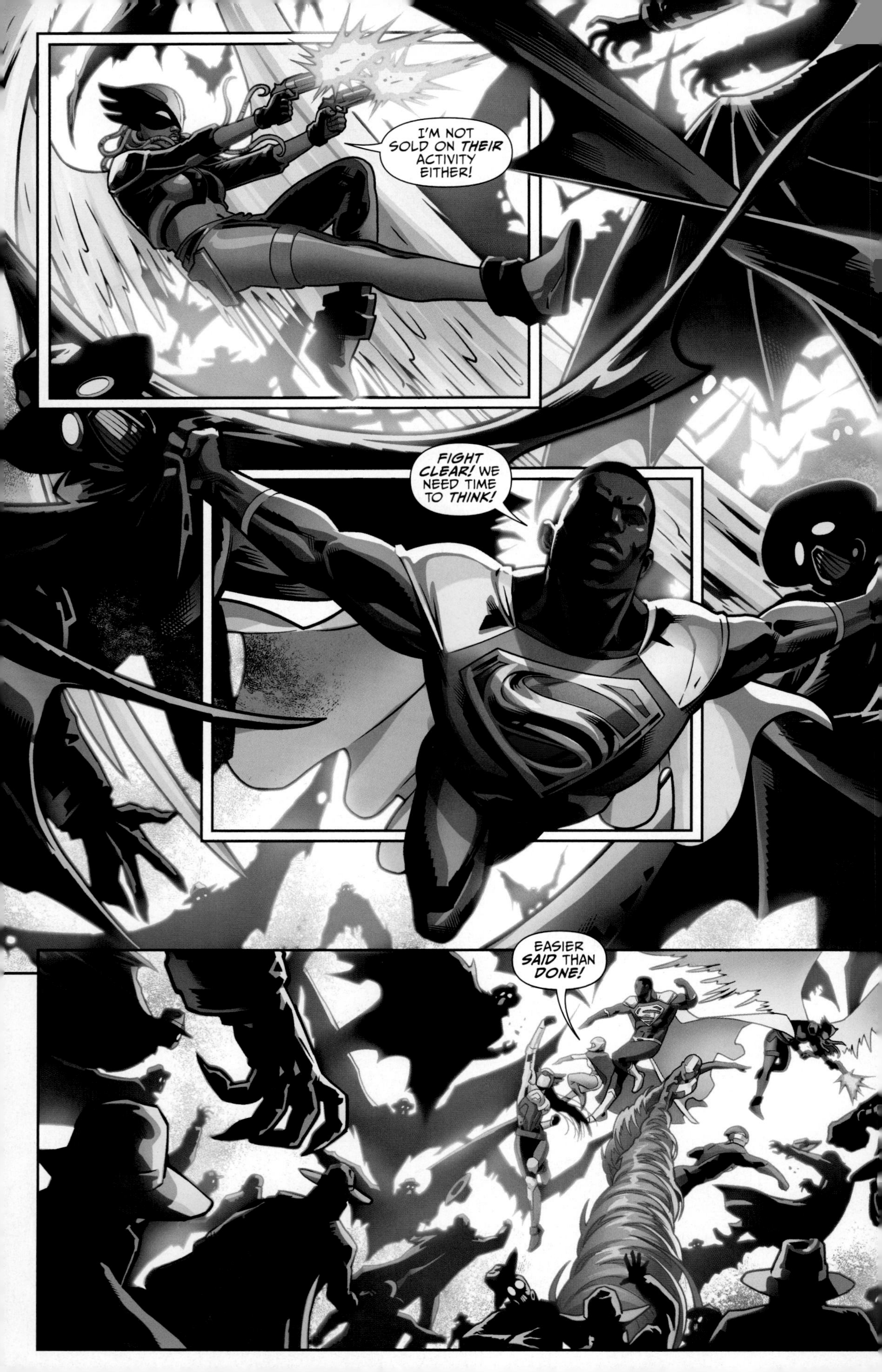
I'M NOT SOLD ON THEIR ACTIVITY EITHER!
FIGHT CLEAR! WE NEED TIME TO THINK!
EASIER SAID THAN DONE!

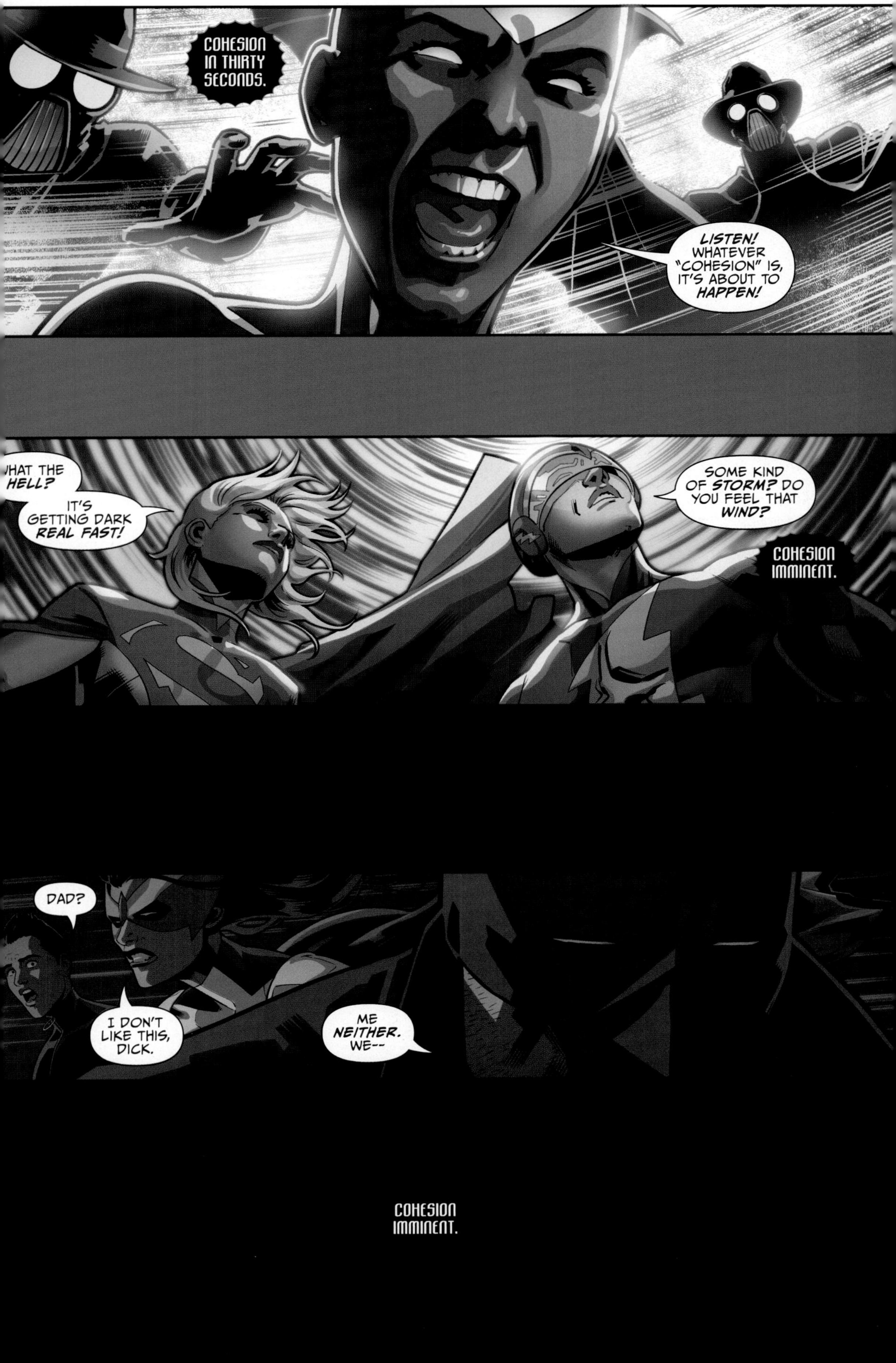
COHESION IN THIRTY SECONDS.
LISTEN! WHATEVER "COHESION" IS, IT'S ABOUT TO HAPPEN!
WHAT THE HELL?
IT'S GETTING DARK REAL FAST!
SOME KIND OF STORM? DO YOU FEEL THAT WIND?
COHESION IMMINENT.
DAD?
I DON'T LIKE THIS, DICK.
ME NEITHER. WE--
COHESION IMMINENT.

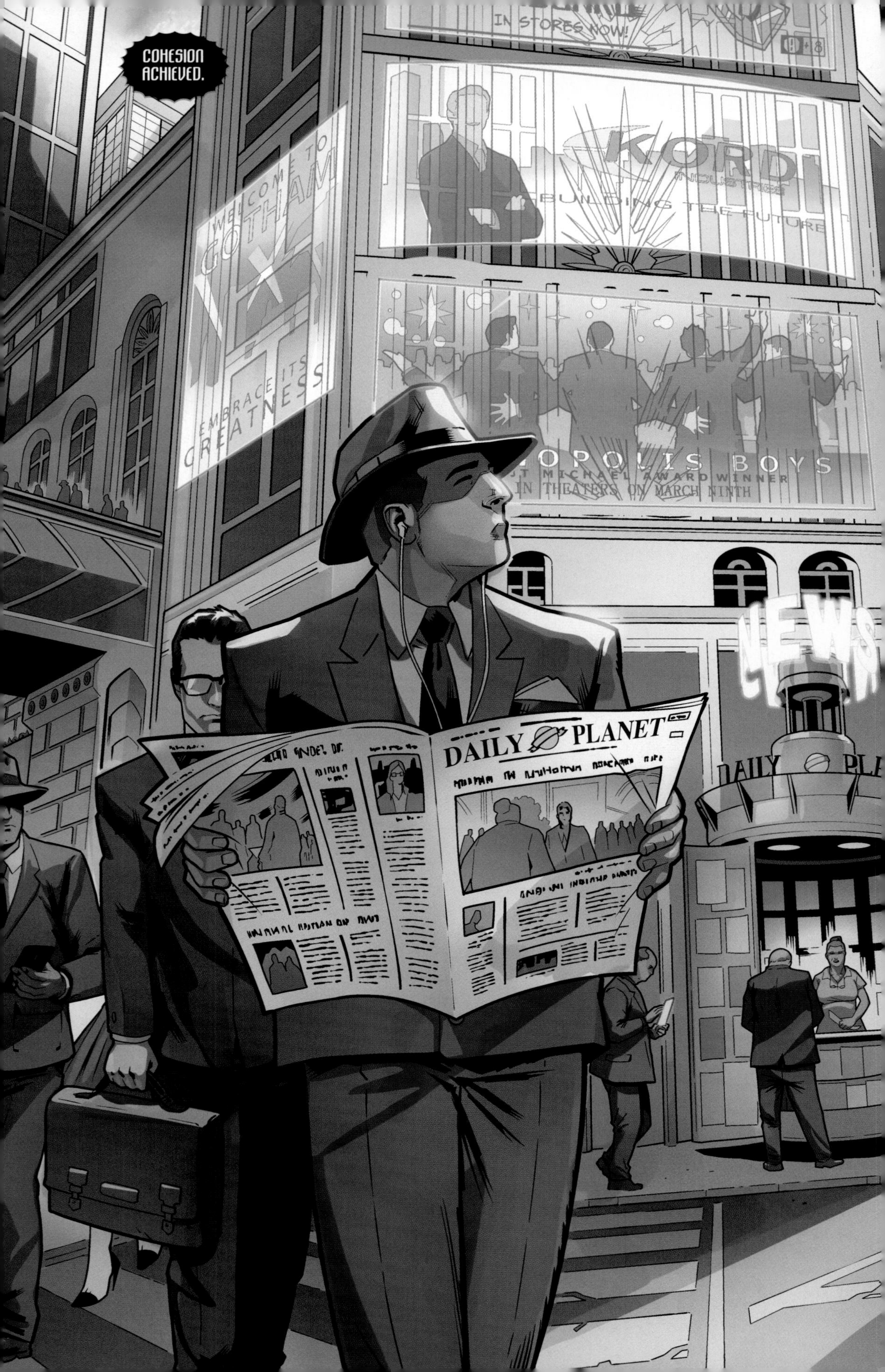
COHESION ACHIEVED.
IN STORES NOW!
WELCOME TO GOTHAM
EMBRACE ITS GREATNESS
KORD INDUSTRIES
BUILDING THE FUTURE
IN THEATERS ON MARCH NINTH
DAILY PLANET
NEWS

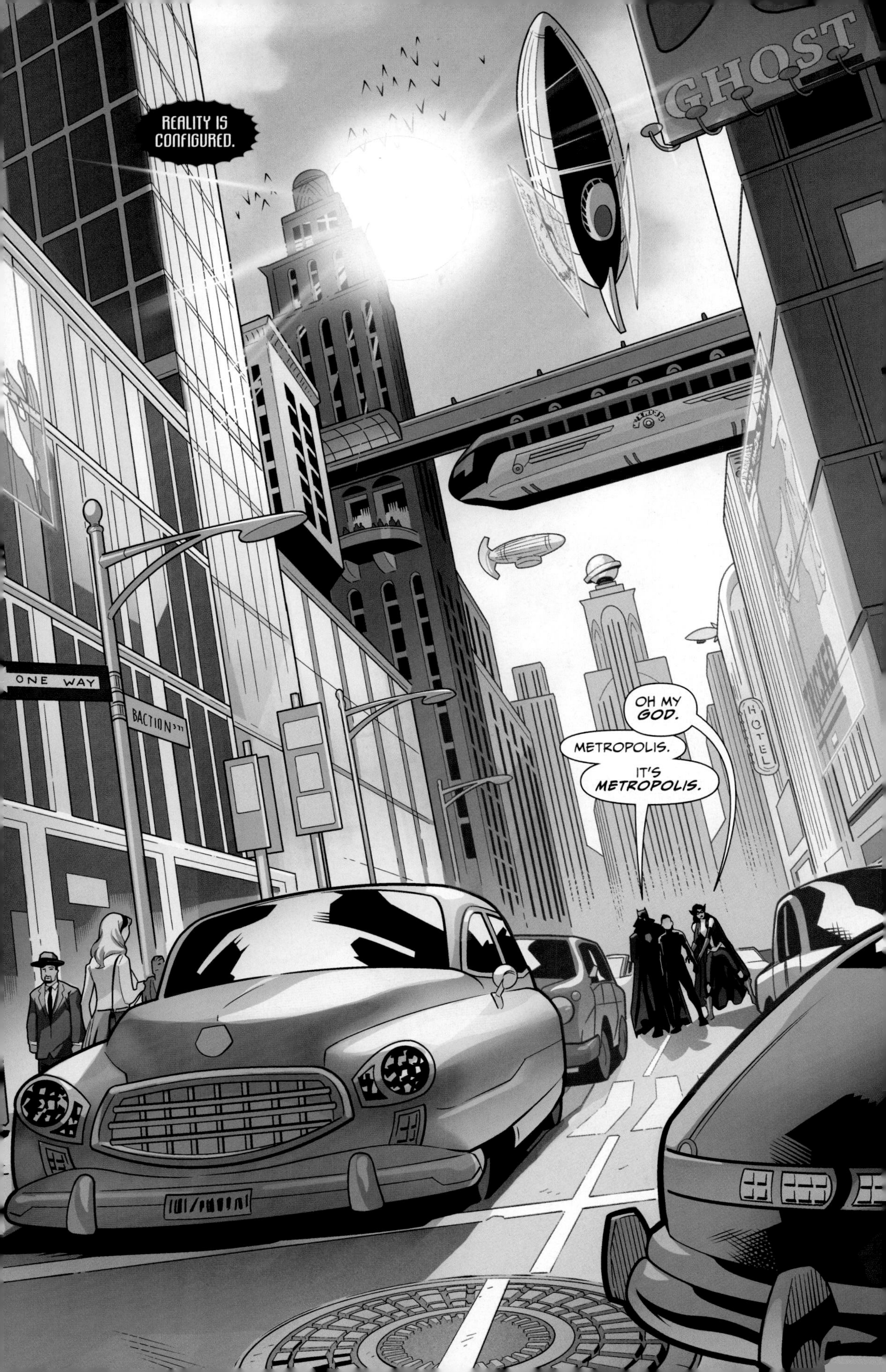
REALITY IS CONFIGURED.
GHOST
ONE WAY
OH MY GOD.
METROPOLIS.
IT'S METROPOLIS.
HOTEL

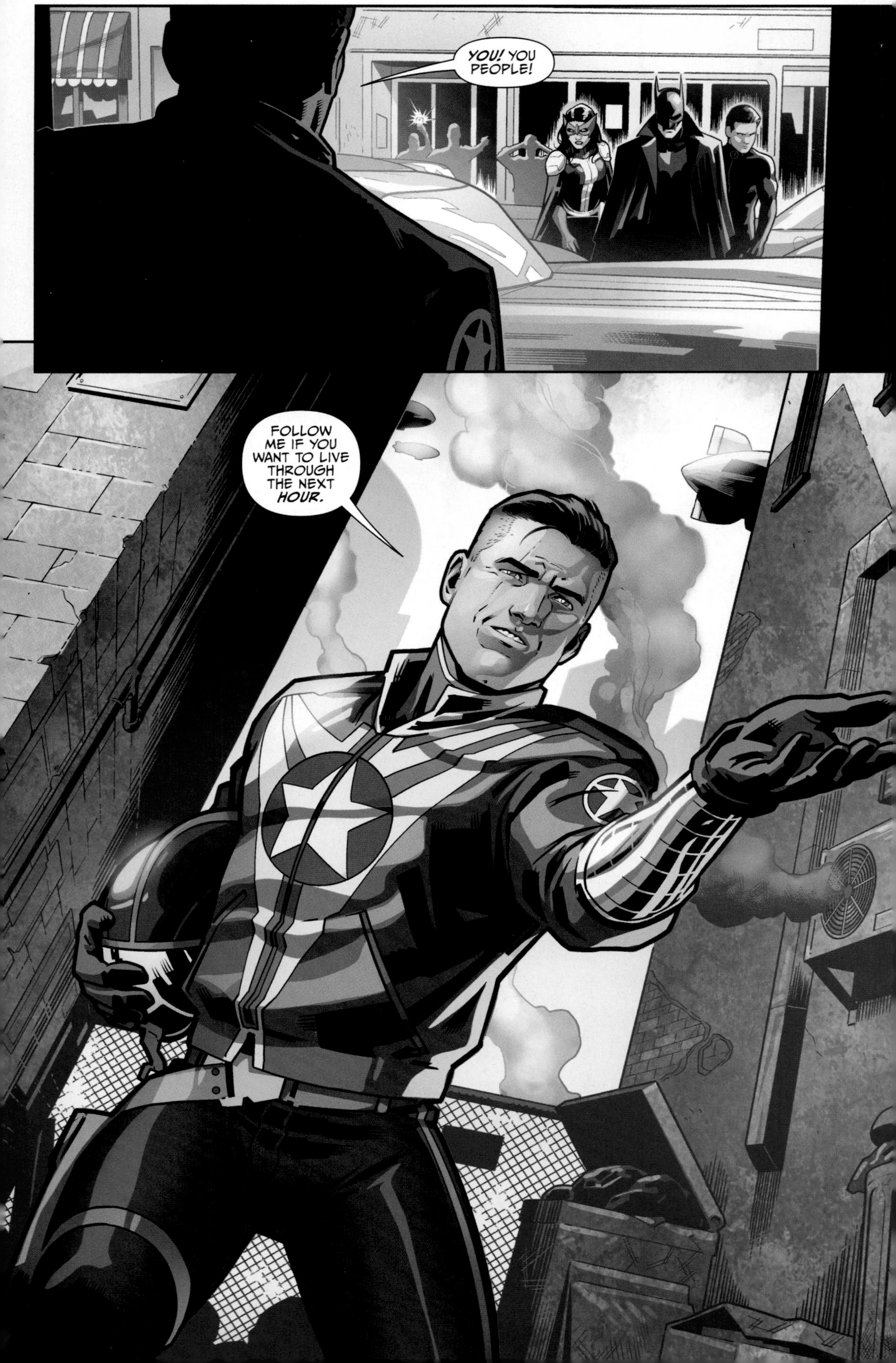
YOU! YOU PEOPLE!
FOLLOW ME IF YOU WANT TO LIVE THROUGH THE NEXT HOUR.

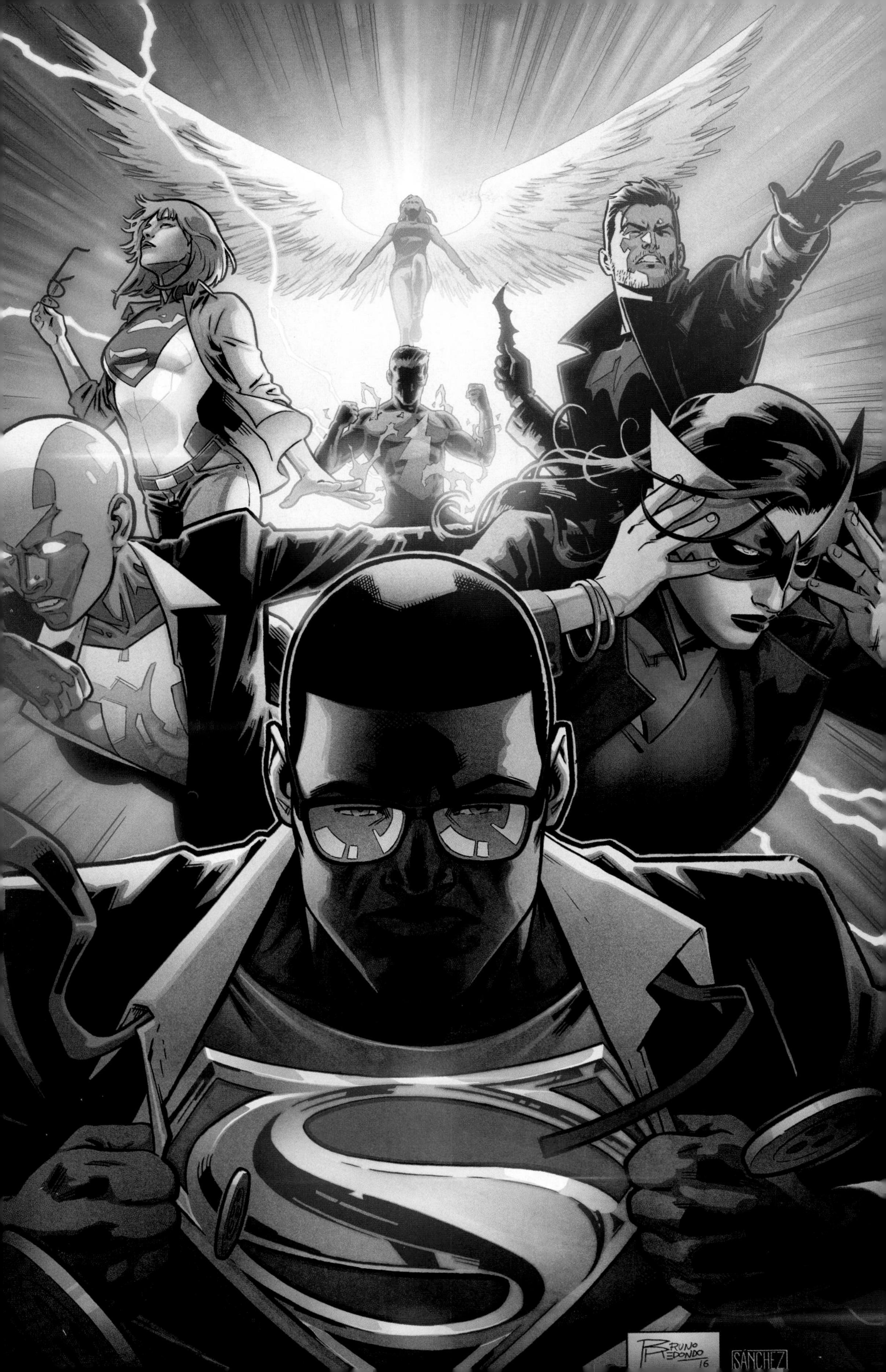
BRUNO REDONDO 16
SÁNCHEZ

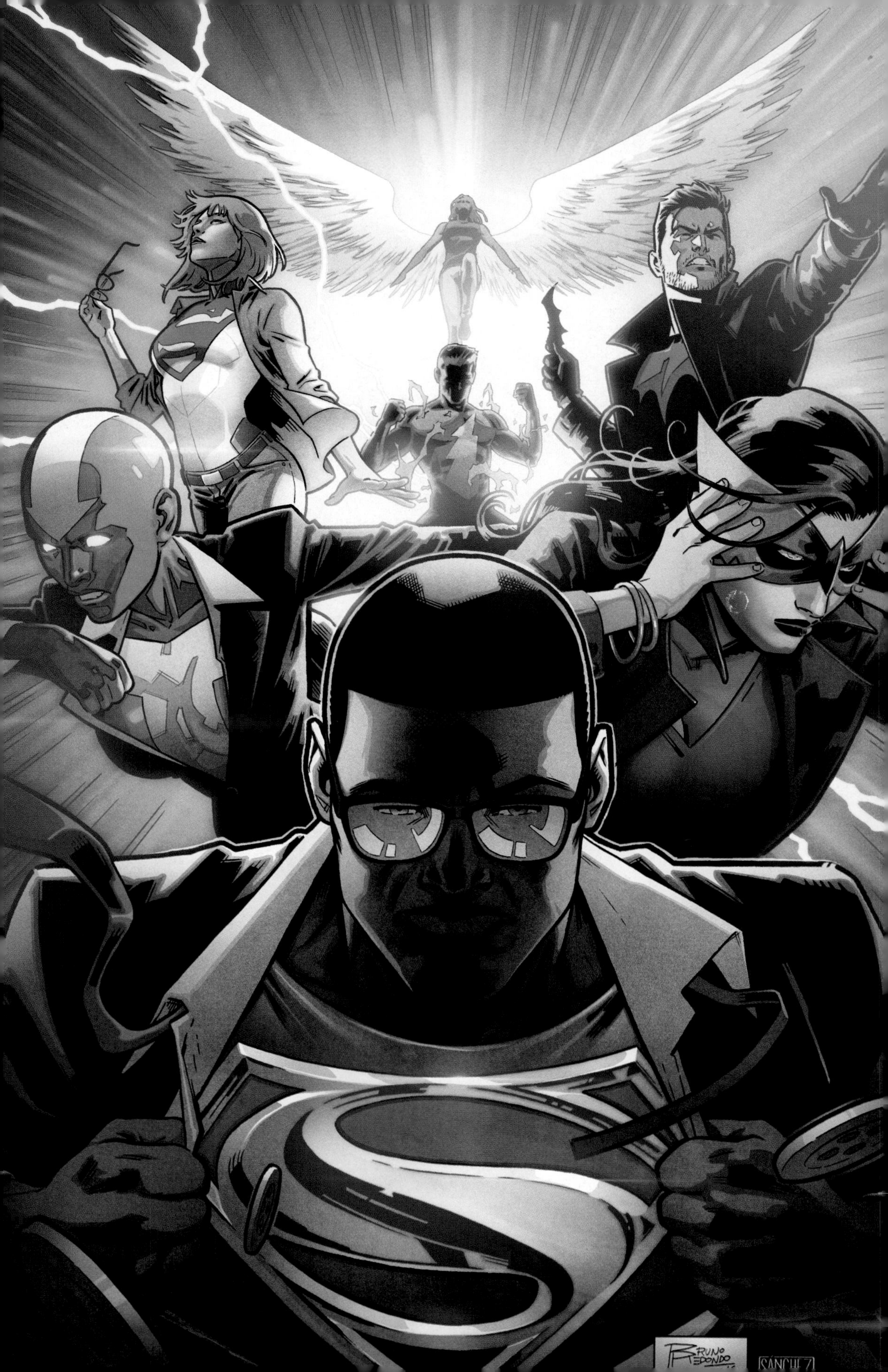
BRUNO REDONDO
SANCHEZ

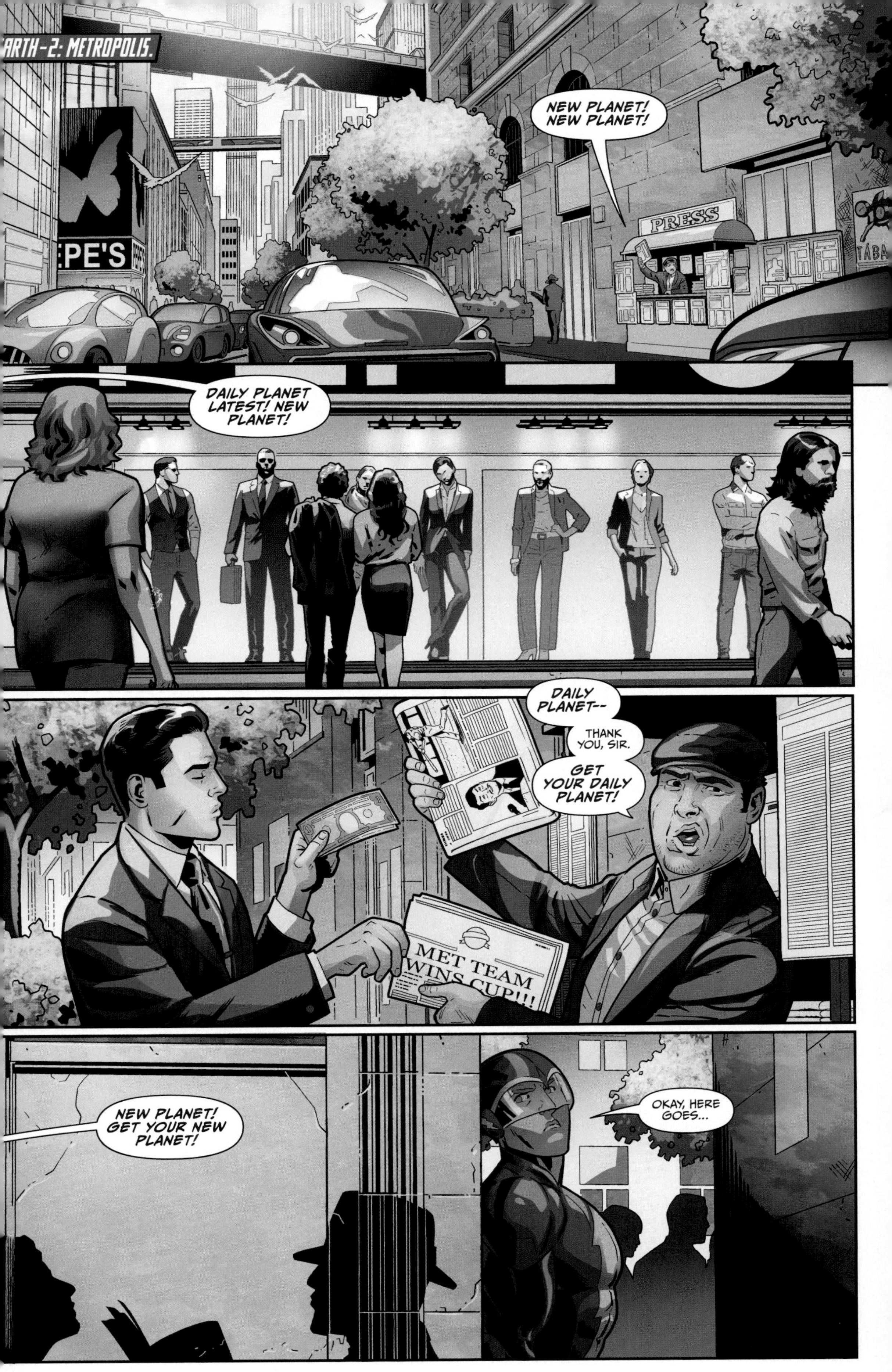
ARTH-2: METROPOLIS.
NEW PLANET! NEW PLANET!
PEPE'S
PRESS
TÁBA
DAILY PLANET LATEST! NEW PLANET!
DAILY PLANET--
THANK YOU, SIR.
GET YOUR DAILY PLANET!
MET TEAM WINS CUP!!!
NEW PLANET! GET YOUR NEW PLANET!
OKAY, HERE GOES...

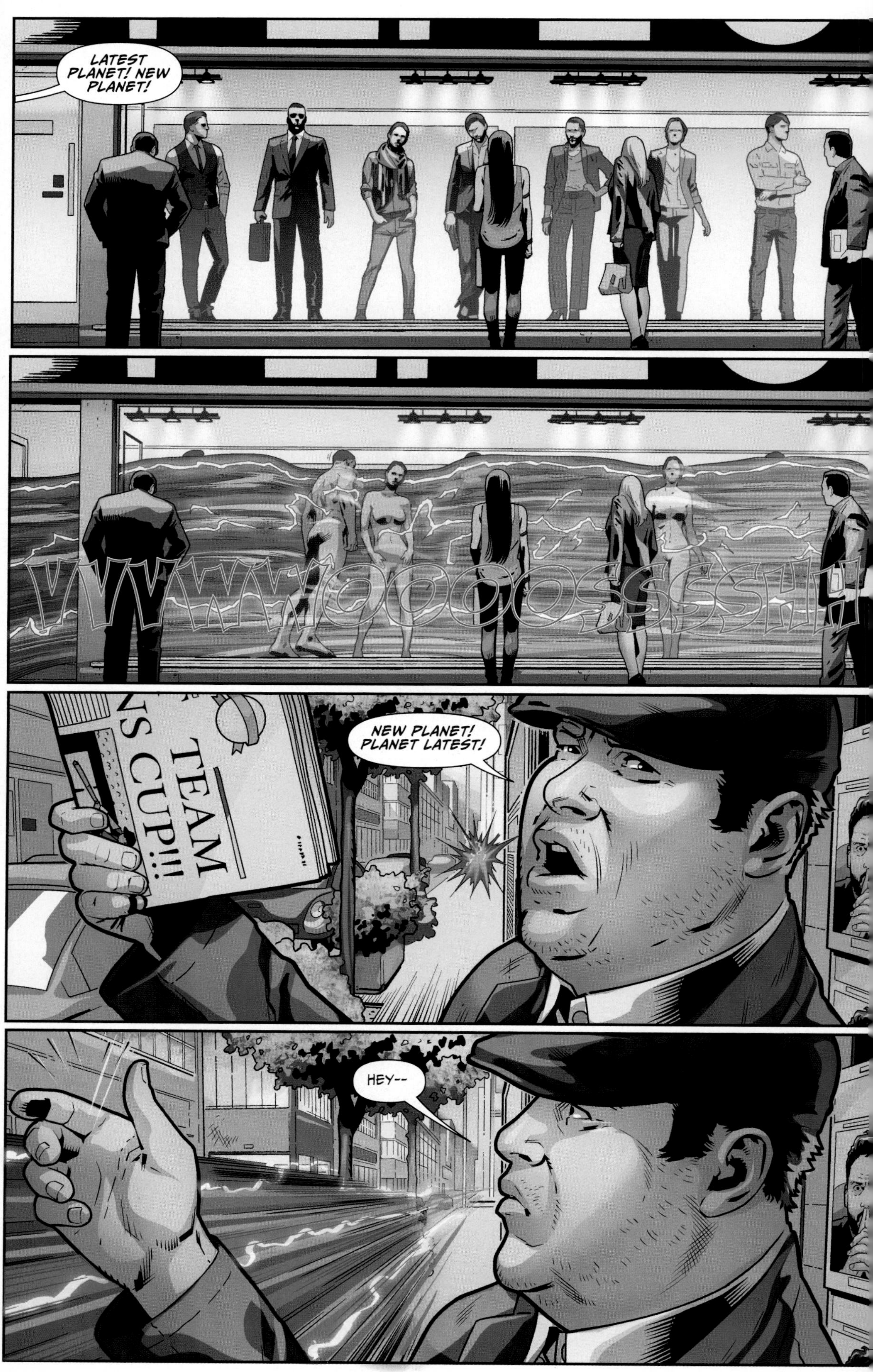
LATEST PLANET! NEW PLANET!
VVVVWWOOOOSSSSH!!
TEAM
NS CUP!!!
NEW PLANET! PLANET LATEST!
HEY--

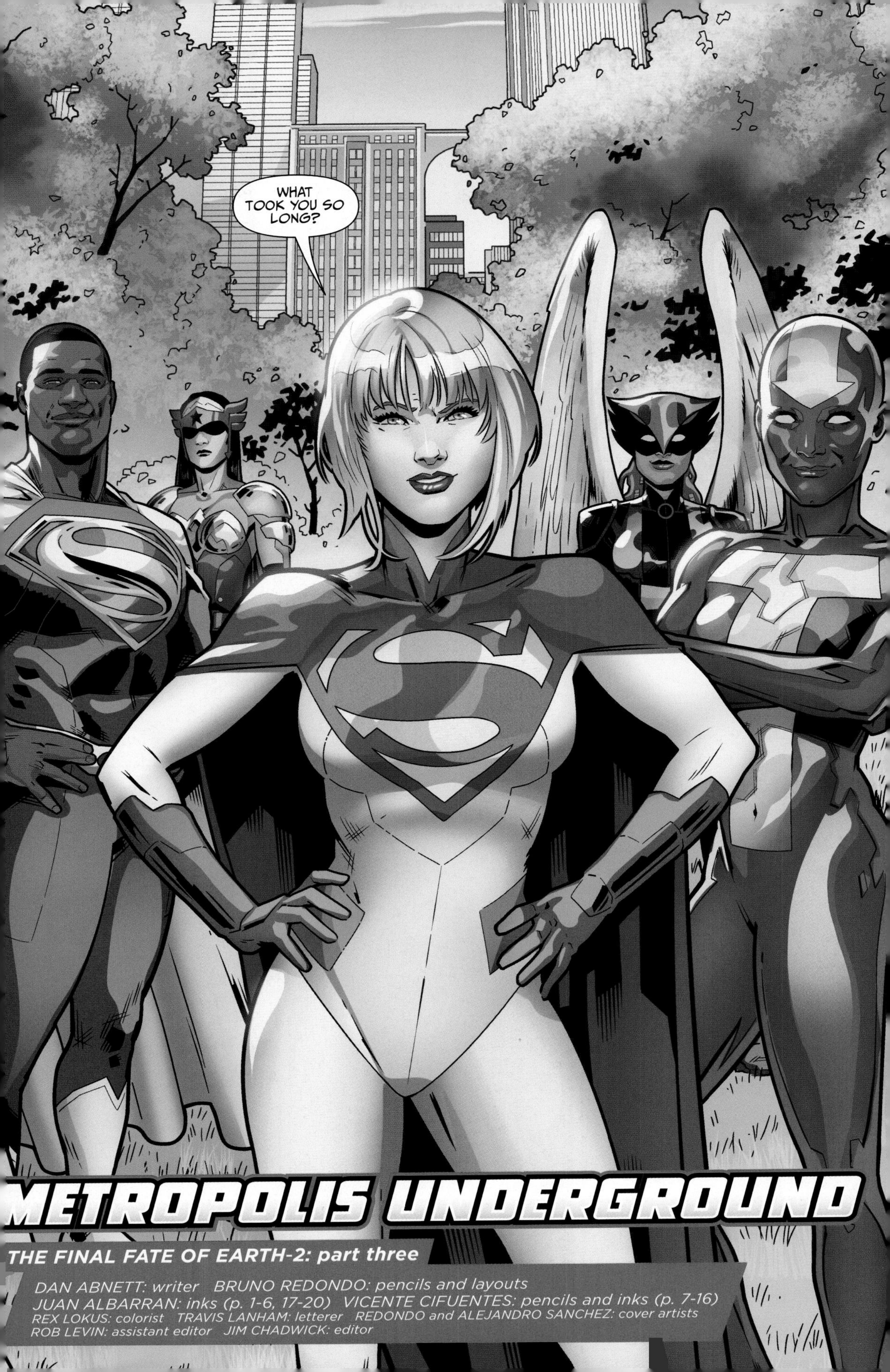
WHAT TOOK YOU SO LONG?
METROPOLIS UNDERGROUND
THE FINAL FATE OF EARTH-2: part three
DAN ABNETT: writer BRUNO REDONDO: pencils and layouts
JUAN ALBARRAN: inks (p. 1-6, 17-20) VICENTE CIFUENTES: pencils and inks (p. 7-16)
REX LOKUS: colorist TRAVIS LANHAM: letterer REDONDO and ALEJANDRO SANCHEZ: cover artists
ROB LEVIN: assistant editor JIM CHADWICK: editor

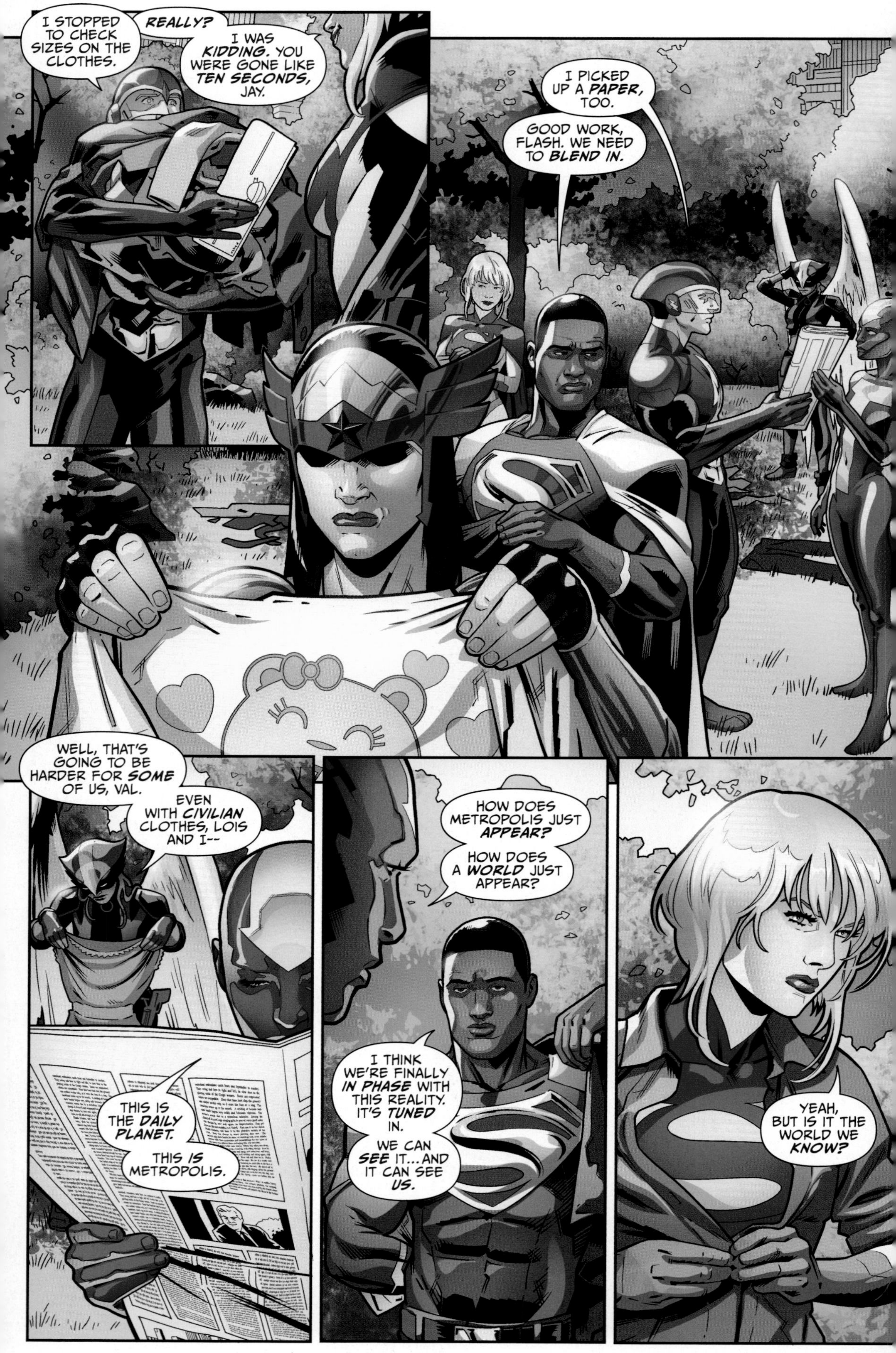
I STOPPED TO CHECK SIZES ON THE CLOTHES.
REALLY?
I WAS KIDDING. YOU WERE GONE LIKE TEN SECONDS, JAY.
I PICKED UP A PAPER, TOO.
GOOD WORK, FLASH. WE NEED TO BLEND IN.
WELL, THAT'S GOING TO BE HARDER FOR SOME OF US, VAL.
EVEN WITH CIVILIAN CLOTHES, LOIS AND I--
THIS IS THE DAILY PLANET.
THIS IS METROPOLIS.
HOW DOES METROPOLIS JUST APPEAR?
HOW DOES A WORLD JUST APPEAR?
I THINK WE'RE FINALLY IN PHASE WITH THIS REALITY. IT'S TUNED IN.
WE CAN SEE IT...AND IT CAN SEE US.
YEAH, BUT IS IT THE WORLD WE KNOW?

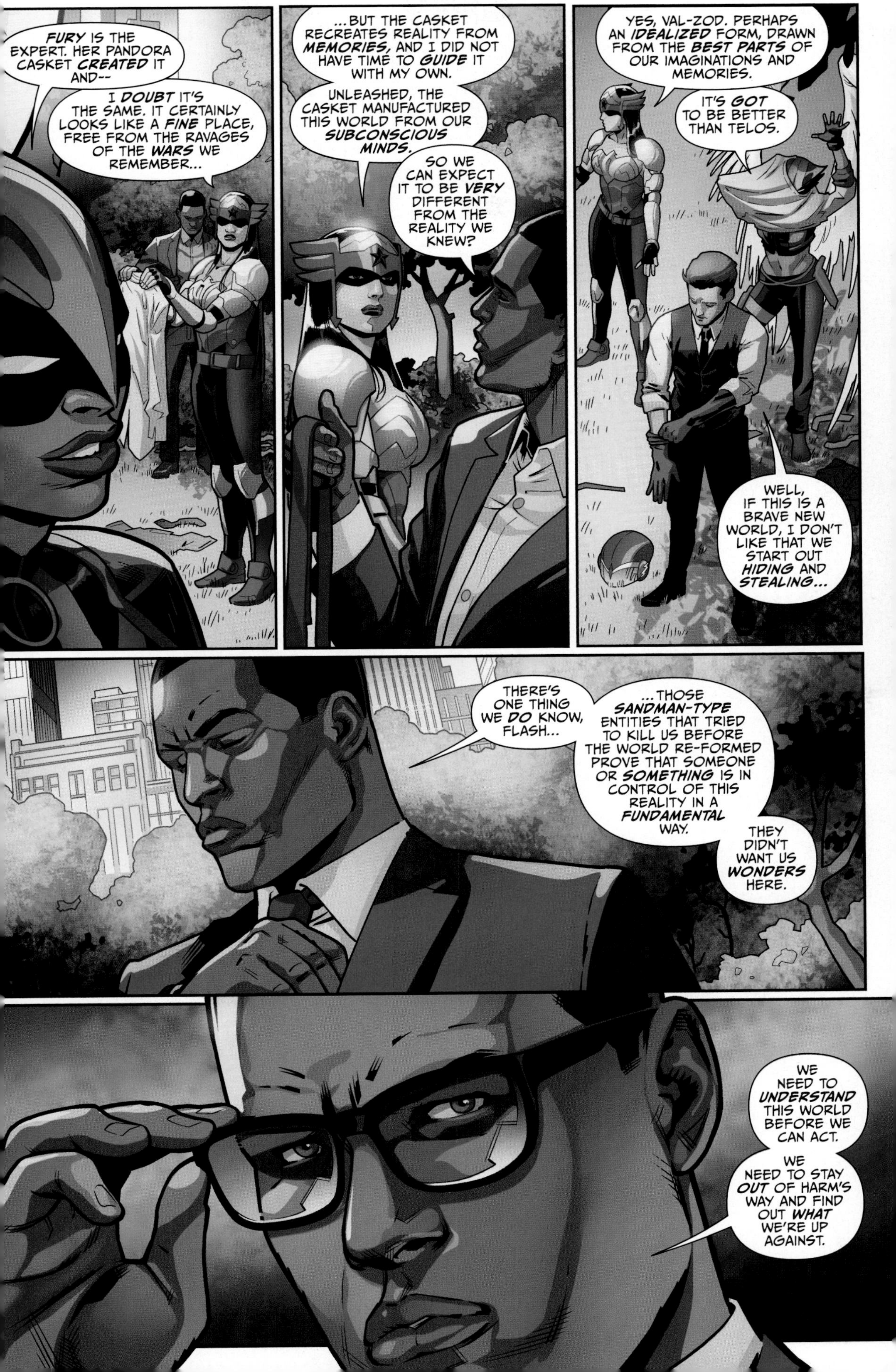
FURY IS THE EXPERT. HER PANDORA CASKET CREATED IT AND--
I DOUBT IT'S THE SAME. IT CERTAINLY LOOKS LIKE A FINE PLACE, FREE FROM THE RAVAGES OF THE WARS WE REMEMBER...
...BUT THE CASKET RECREATES REALITY FROM MEMORIES, AND I DID NOT HAVE TIME TO GUIDE IT WITH MY OWN.
UNLEASHED, THE CASKET MANUFACTURED THIS WORLD FROM OUR SUBCONSCIOUS MINDS.
SO WE CAN EXPECT IT TO BE VERY DIFFERENT FROM THE REALITY WE KNEW?
YES, VAL-ZOD. PERHAPS AN IDEALIZED FORM, DRAWN FROM THE BEST PARTS OF OUR IMAGINATIONS AND MEMORIES.
IT'S GOT TO BE BETTER THAN TELOS.
WELL, IF THIS IS A BRAVE NEW WORLD, I DON'T LIKE THAT WE START OUT HIDING AND STEALING...
THERE'S ONE THING WE DO KNOW, FLASH...
...THOSE SANDMAN-TYPE ENTITIES THAT TRIED TO KILL US BEFORE THE WORLD RE-FORMED PROVE THAT SOMEONE OR SOMETHING IS IN CONTROL OF THIS REALITY IN A FUNDAMENTAL WAY.
THEY DIDN'T WANT US WONDERS HERE.
WE NEED TO UNDERSTAND THIS WORLD BEFORE WE CAN ACT.
WE NEED TO STAY OUT OF HARM'S WAY AND FIND OUT WHAT WE'RE UP AGAINST.

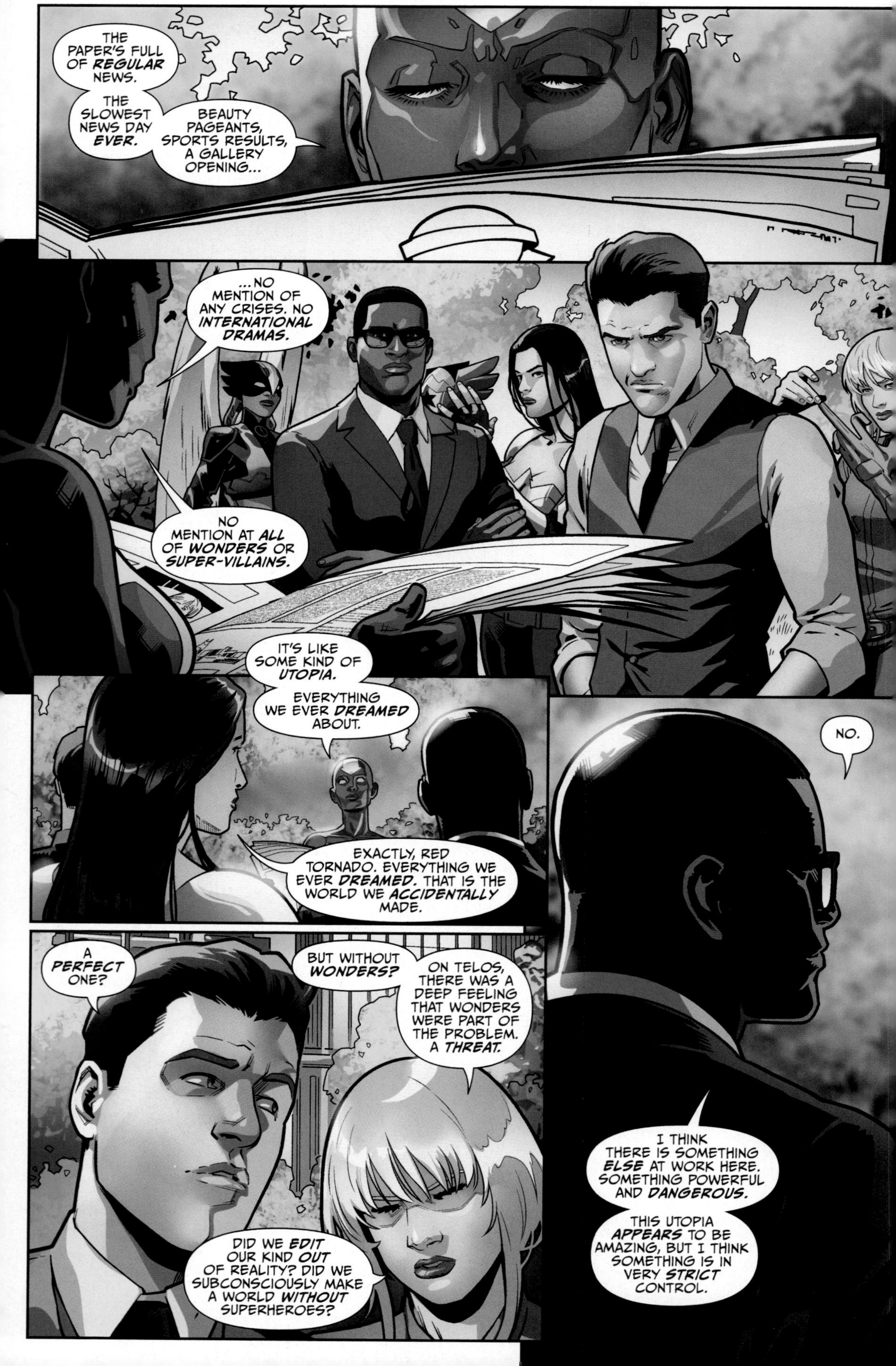
THE PAPER'S FULL OF *REGULAR* NEWS.
THE SLOWEST NEWS DAY *EVER.*
BEAUTY PAGEANTS, SPORTS RESULTS, A GALLERY OPENING...
...NO MENTION OF ANY CRISES. NO *INTERNATIONAL DRAMAS.*
NO MENTION AT *ALL* OF *WONDERS* OR *SUPER-VILLAINS.*
IT'S LIKE SOME KIND OF *UTOPIA.*
EVERYTHING WE EVER *DREAMED* ABOUT.
EXACTLY, RED TORNADO. EVERYTHING WE EVER *DREAMED.* THAT IS THE WORLD WE *ACCIDENTALLY* MADE.
NO.
A *PERFECT* ONE?
BUT WITHOUT *WONDERS?*
ON TELOS, THERE WAS A DEEP FEELING THAT WONDERS WERE PART OF THE PROBLEM. A *THREAT.*
DID WE *EDIT* OUR KIND *OUT* OF REALITY? DID WE SUBCONSCIOUSLY MAKE A WORLD *WITHOUT* SUPERHEROES?
I THINK THERE IS SOMETHING *ELSE* AT WORK HERE. SOMETHING POWERFUL AND *DANGEROUS.*
THIS UTOPIA *APPEARS* TO BE AMAZING, BUT I THINK SOMETHING IS IN VERY *STRICT* CONTROL.

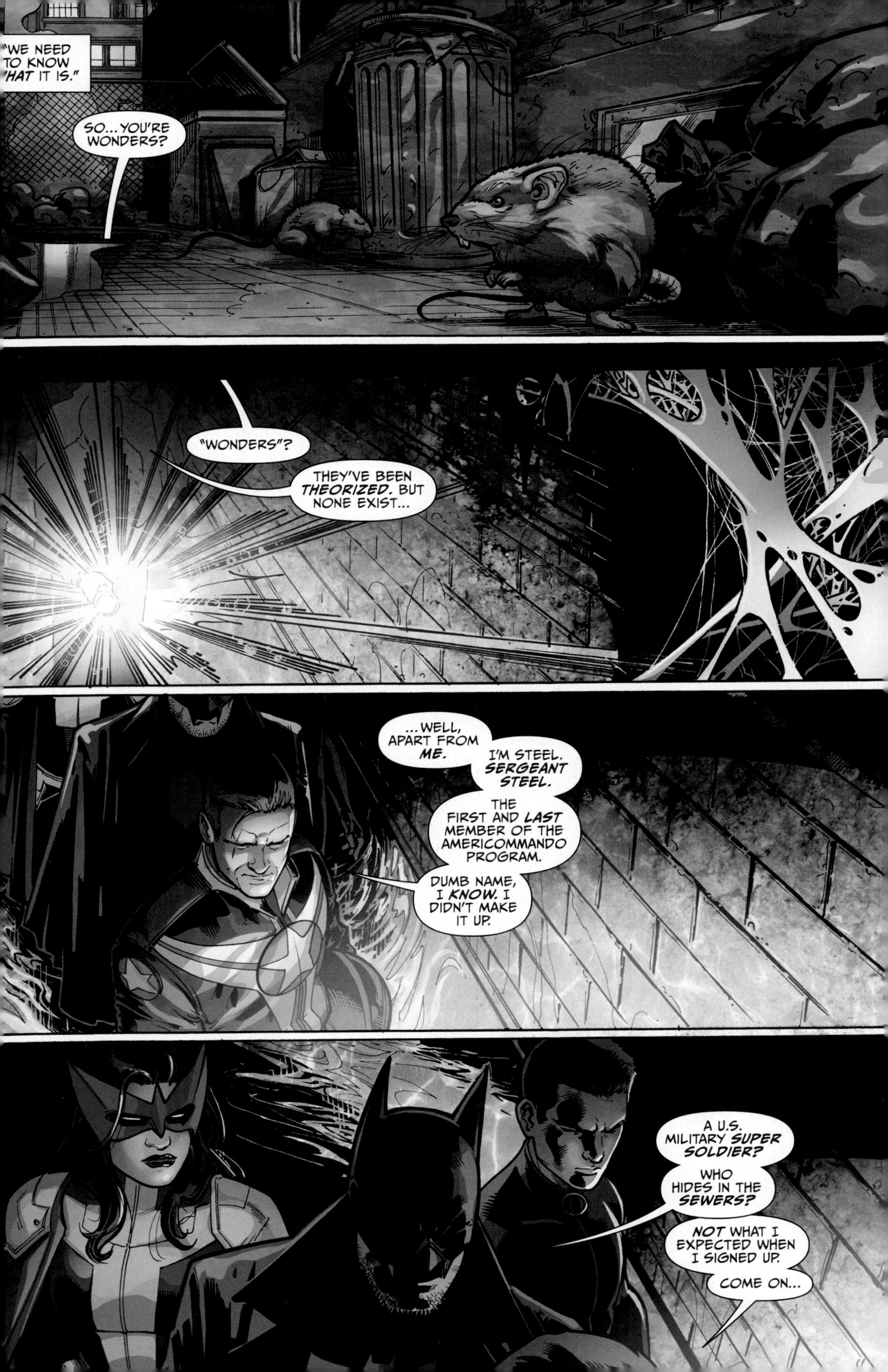
"WE NEED TO KNOW HAT IT IS."
SO... YOU'RE WONDERS?
"WONDERS"?
THEY'VE BEEN THEORIZED. BUT NONE EXIST...
...WELL, APART FROM ME.
I'M STEEL. SERGEANT STEEL.
THE FIRST AND LAST MEMBER OF THE AMERICOMMANDO PROGRAM.
DUMB NAME, I KNOW. I DIDN'T MAKE IT UP.
A U.S. MILITARY SUPER SOLDIER?
WHO HIDES IN THE SEWERS?
NOT WHAT I EXPECTED WHEN I SIGNED UP.
COME ON...

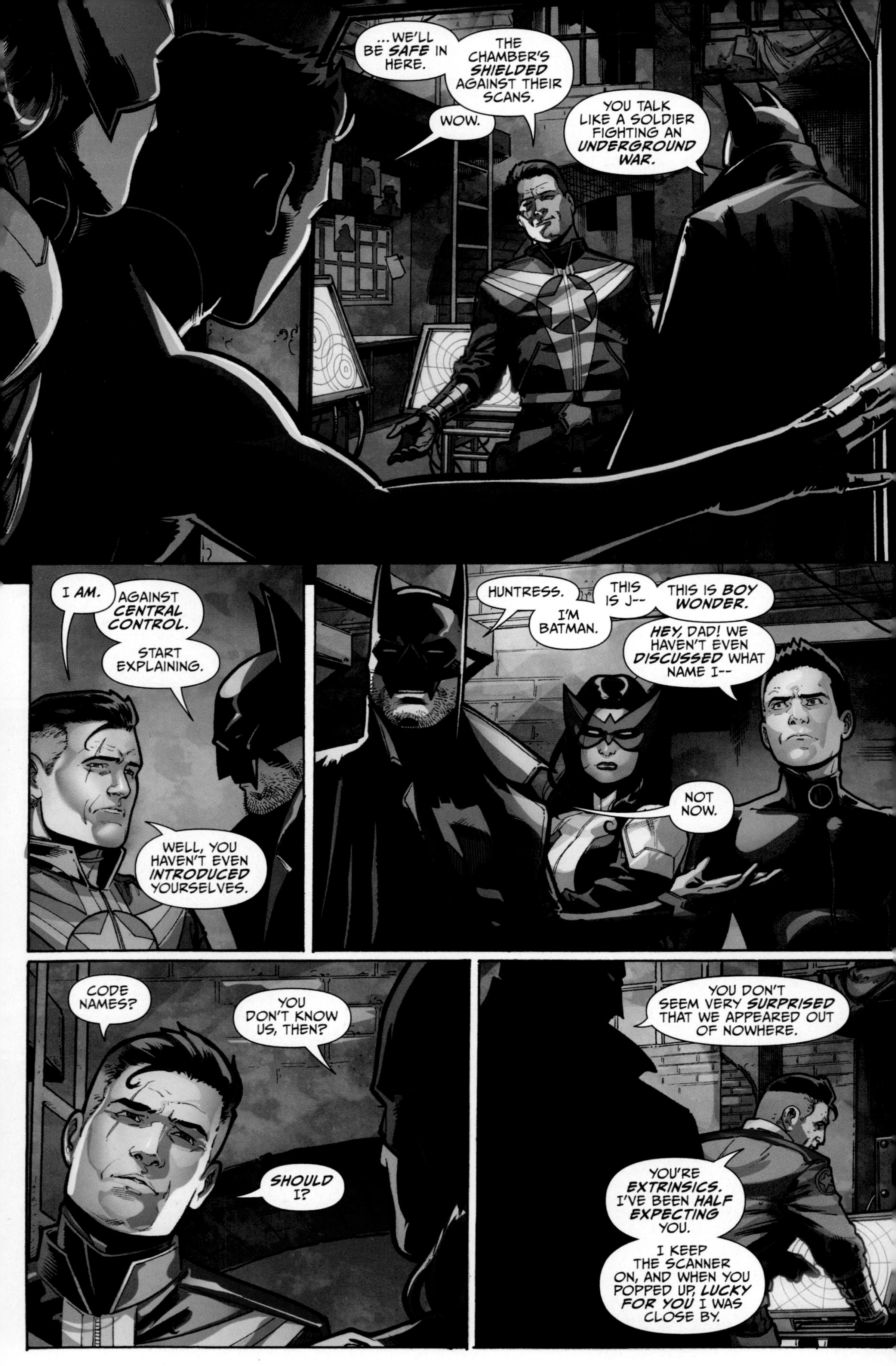
...WE'LL BE SAFE IN HERE.
THE CHAMBER'S SHIELDED AGAINST THEIR SCANS.
WOW.
YOU TALK LIKE A SOLDIER FIGHTING AN UNDERGROUND WAR.
I AM.
AGAINST CENTRAL CONTROL.
START EXPLAINING.
WELL, YOU HAVEN'T EVEN INTRODUCED YOURSELVES.
HUNTRESS.
THIS IS J--
I'M BATMAN.
THIS IS BOY WONDER.
HEY, DAD! WE HAVEN'T EVEN DISCUSSED WHAT NAME I--
NOT NOW.
CODE NAMES?
YOU DON'T KNOW US, THEN?
SHOULD I?
YOU DON'T SEEM VERY SURPRISED THAT WE APPEARED OUT OF NOWHERE.
YOU'RE EXTRINSICS. I'VE BEEN HALF EXPECTING YOU.
I KEEP THE SCANNER ON, AND WHEN YOU POPPED UP, LUCKY FOR YOU I WAS CLOSE BY.

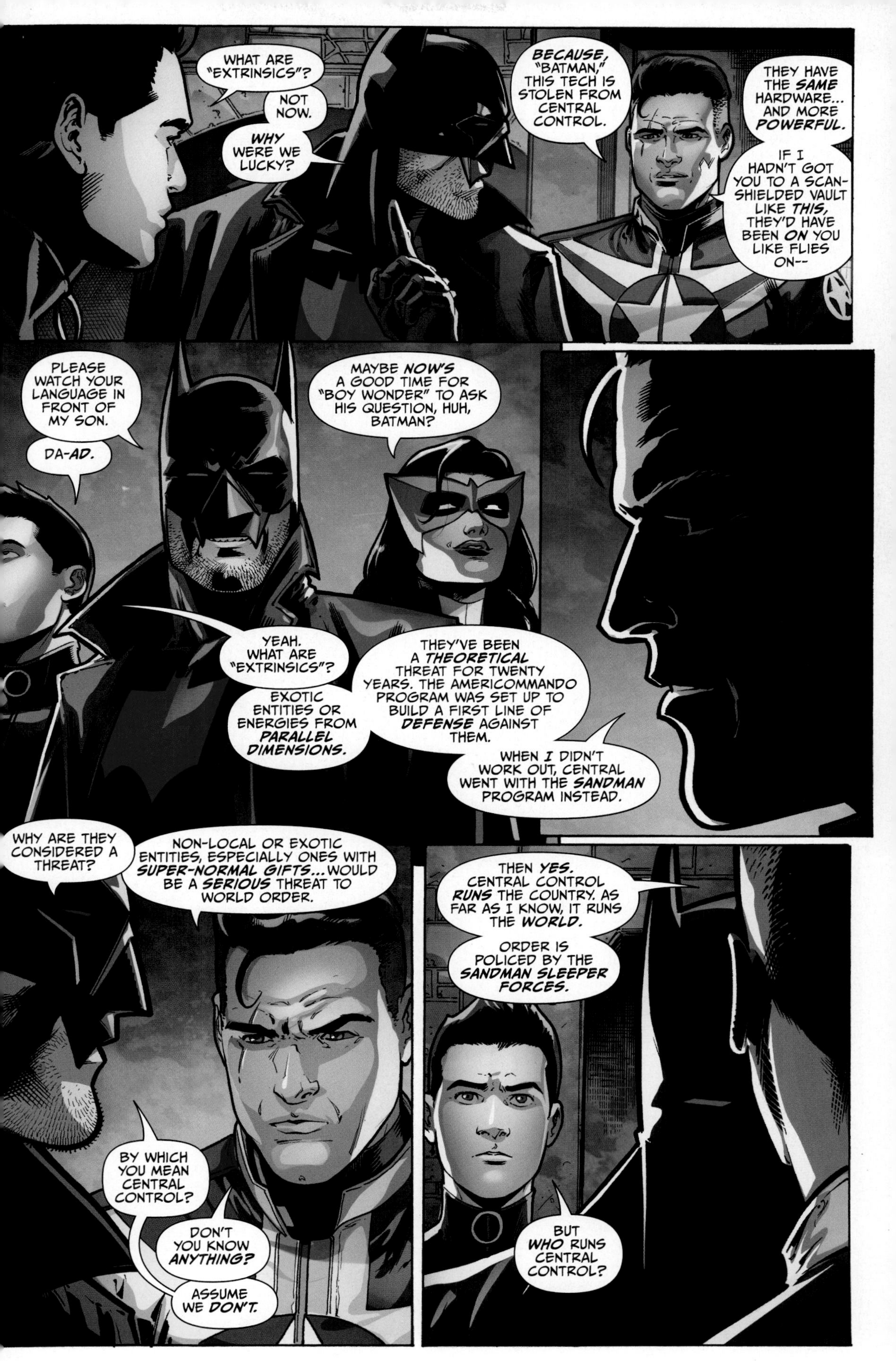
WHAT ARE "EXTRINSICS"?
NOT NOW.
WHY WERE WE LUCKY?
BECAUSE, "BATMAN," THIS TECH IS STOLEN FROM CENTRAL CONTROL.
THEY HAVE THE SAME HARDWARE... AND MORE POWERFUL.
IF I HADN'T GOT YOU TO A SCAN-SHIELDED VAULT LIKE THIS, THEY'D HAVE BEEN ON YOU LIKE FLIES ON--
PLEASE WATCH YOUR LANGUAGE IN FRONT OF MY SON.
DA-AD.
MAYBE NOW'S A GOOD TIME FOR "BOY WONDER" TO ASK HIS QUESTION, HUH, BATMAN?
YEAH. WHAT ARE "EXTRINSICS"?
EXOTIC ENTITIES OR ENERGIES FROM PARALLEL DIMENSIONS.
THEY'VE BEEN A THEORETICAL THREAT FOR TWENTY YEARS. THE AMERICOMMANDO PROGRAM WAS SET UP TO BUILD A FIRST LINE OF DEFENSE AGAINST THEM.
WHEN I DIDN'T WORK OUT, CENTRAL WENT WITH THE SANDMAN PROGRAM INSTEAD.
WHY ARE THEY CONSIDERED A THREAT?
NON-LOCAL OR EXOTIC ENTITIES, ESPECIALLY ONES WITH SUPER-NORMAL GIFTS... WOULD BE A SERIOUS THREAT TO WORLD ORDER.
BY WHICH YOU MEAN CENTRAL CONTROL?
DON'T YOU KNOW ANYTHING?
ASSUME WE DON'T.
THEN YES. CENTRAL CONTROL RUNS THE COUNTRY. AS FAR AS I KNOW, IT RUNS THE WORLD.
ORDER IS POLICED BY THE SANDMAN SLEEPER FORCES.
BUT WHO RUNS CENTRAL CONTROL?

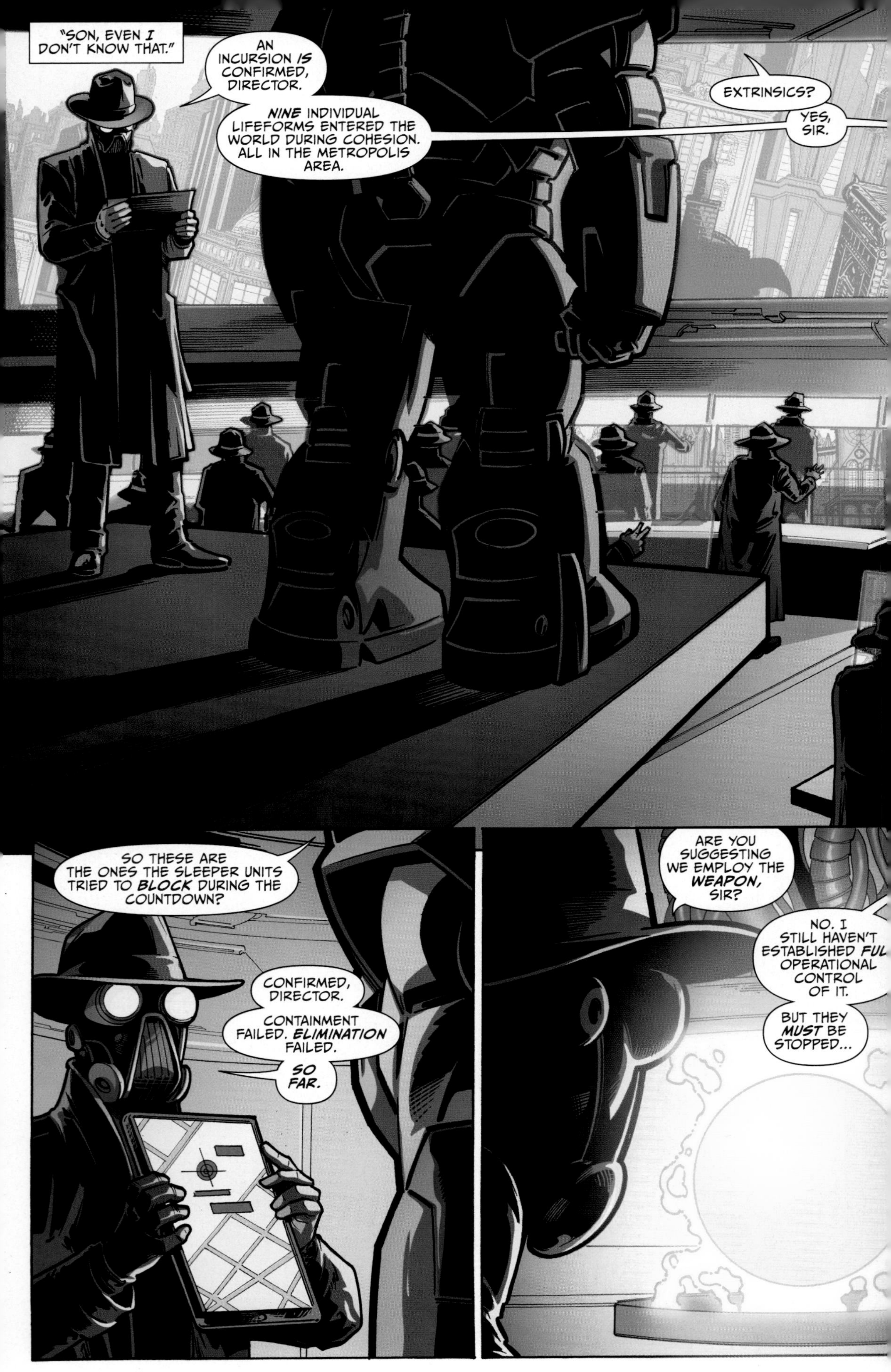

"SON, EVEN I DON'T KNOW THAT."
AN INCURSION IS CONFIRMED, DIRECTOR.
NINE INDIVIDUAL LIFEFORMS ENTERED THE WORLD DURING COHESION. ALL IN THE METROPOLIS AREA.
EXTRINSICS?
YES, SIR.
SO THESE ARE THE ONES THE SLEEPER UNITS TRIED TO BLOCK DURING THE COUNTDOWN?
CONFIRMED, DIRECTOR.
CONTAINMENT FAILED. ELIMINATION FAILED.
SO FAR.
ARE YOU SUGGESTING WE EMPLOY THE WEAPON, SIR?
NO. I STILL HAVEN'T ESTABLISHED FUL OPERATIONAL CONTROL OF IT.
BUT THEY MUST BE STOPPED...

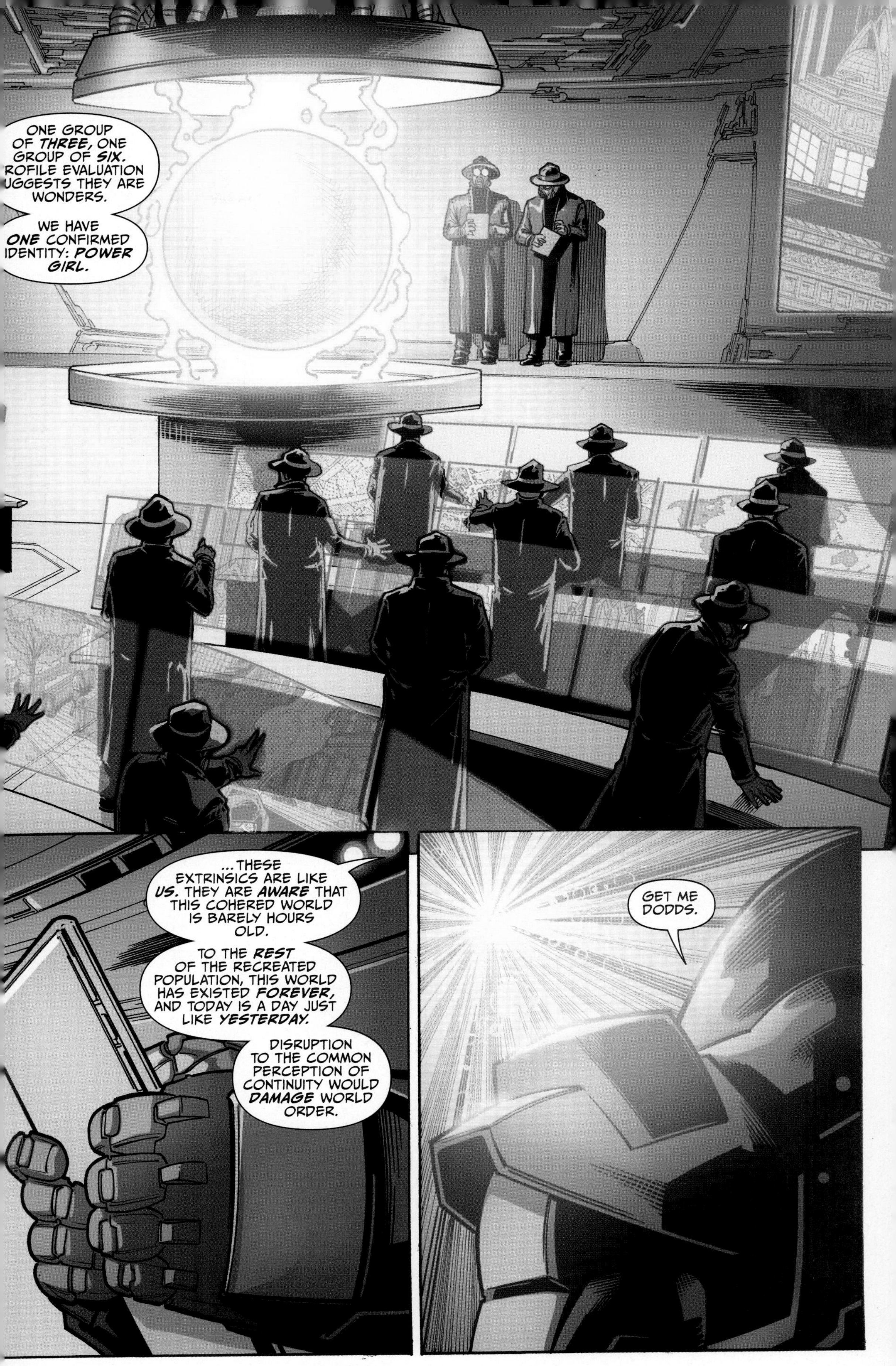
ONE GROUP OF THREE, ONE GROUP OF SIX. PROFILE EVALUATION SUGGESTS THEY ARE WONDERS.
WE HAVE ONE CONFIRMED IDENTITY: POWER GIRL.
...THESE EXTRINSICS ARE LIKE US. THEY ARE AWARE THAT THIS COHERED WORLD IS BARELY HOURS OLD.
TO THE REST OF THE RECREATED POPULATION, THIS WORLD HAS EXISTED FOREVER, AND TODAY IS A DAY JUST LIKE YESTERDAY.
DISRUPTION TO THE COMMON PERCEPTION OF CONTINUITY WOULD DAMAGE WORLD ORDER.
GET ME DODDS.

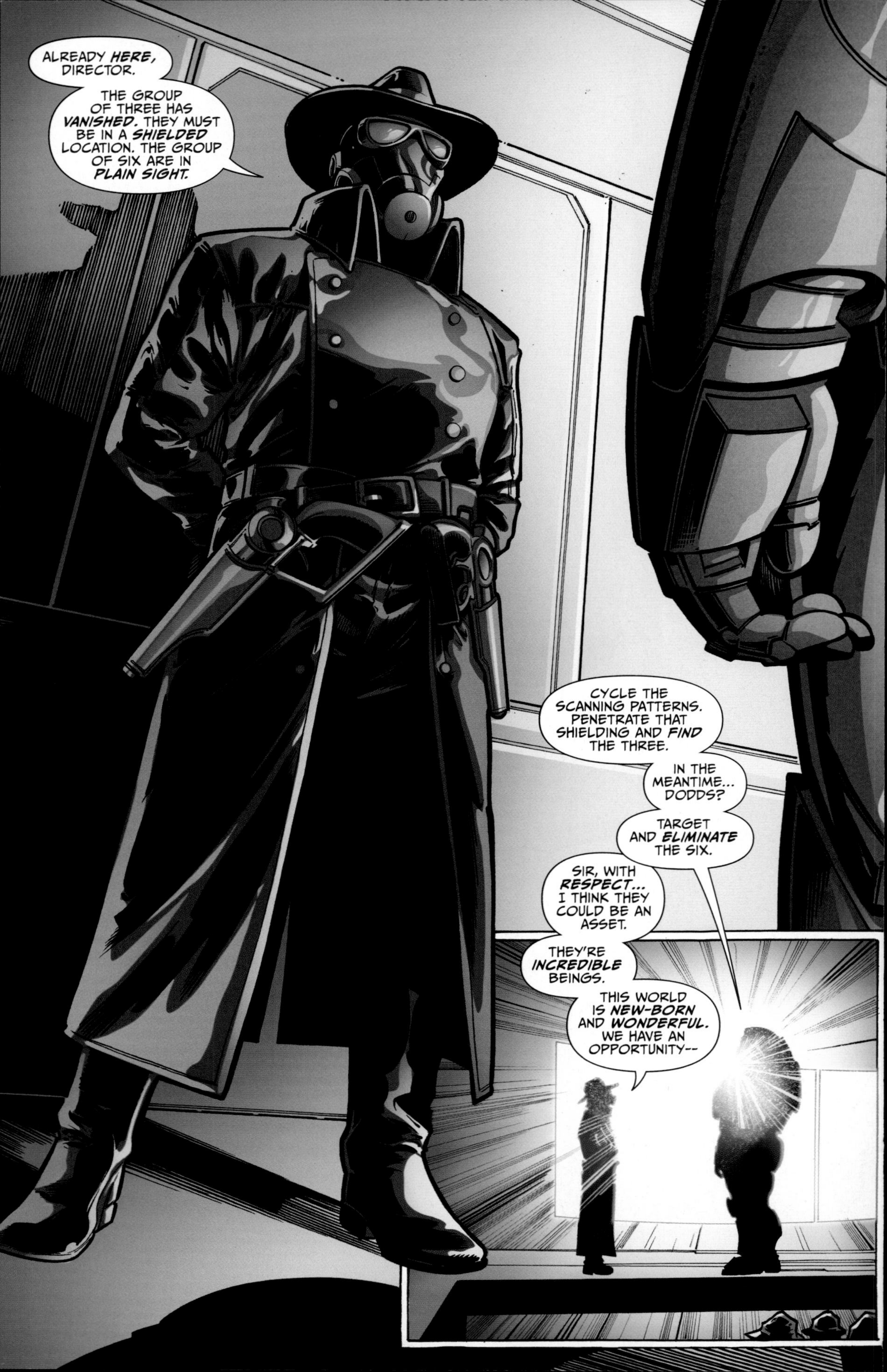
ALREADY HERE, DIRECTOR.
THE GROUP OF THREE HAS VANISHED. THEY MUST BE IN A SHIELDED LOCATION. THE GROUP OF SIX ARE IN PLAIN SIGHT.
CYCLE THE SCANNING PATTERNS. PENETRATE THAT SHIELDING AND FIND THE THREE.
IN THE MEANTIME... DODDS?
TARGET AND ELIMINATE THE SIX.
SIR, WITH RESPECT... I THINK THEY COULD BE AN ASSET.
THEY'RE INCREDIBLE BEINGS.
THIS WORLD IS NEW-BORN AND WONDERFUL. WE HAVE AN OPPORTUNITY--

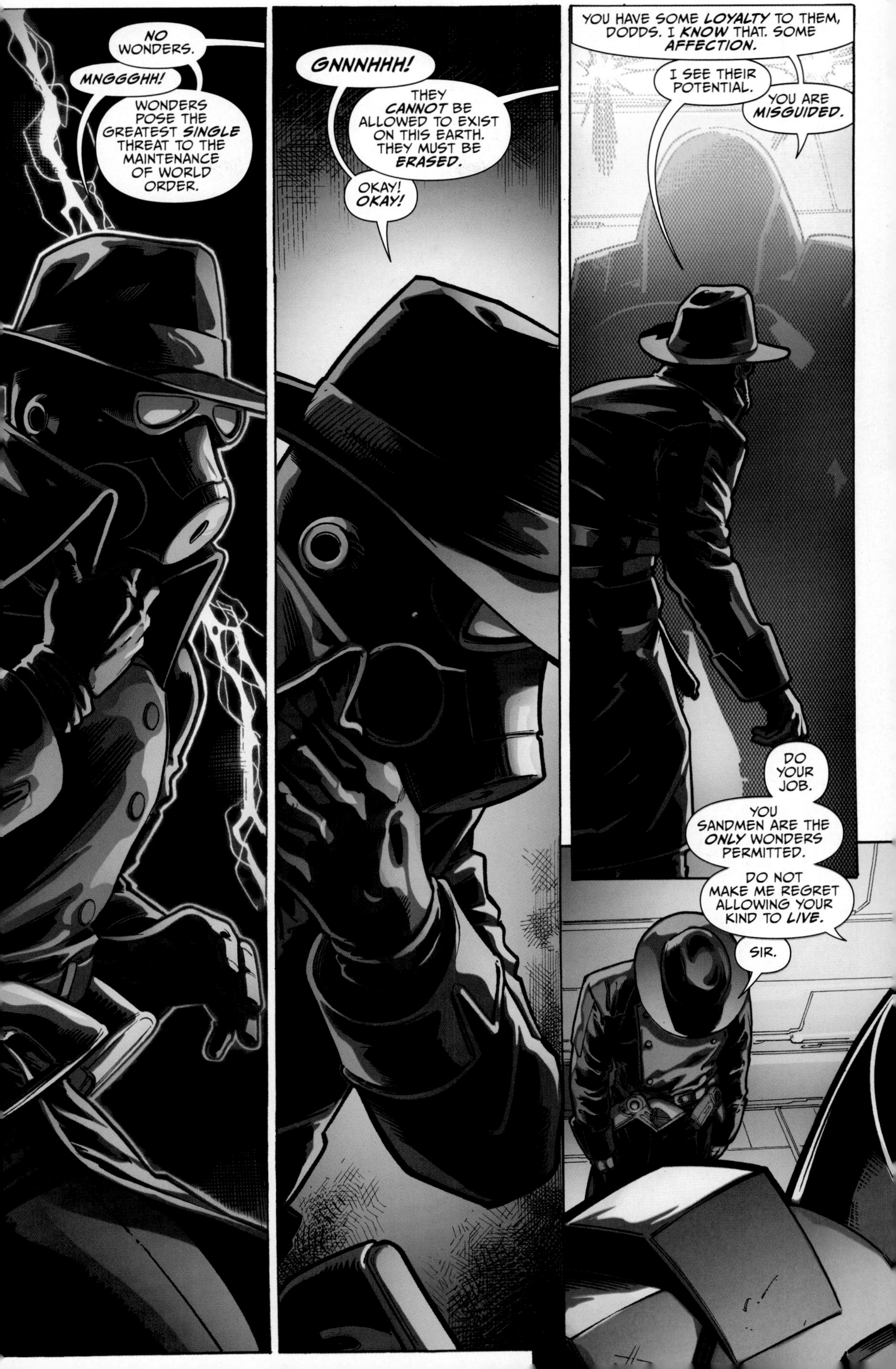

NO WONDERS.
MNGGGHH!
WONDERS POSE THE GREATEST *SINGLE* THREAT TO THE MAINTENANCE OF WORLD ORDER.
GNNNHHH!
THEY *CANNOT* BE ALLOWED TO EXIST ON THIS EARTH. THEY MUST BE *ERASED.*
OKAY! *OKAY!*
YOU HAVE SOME *LOYALTY* TO THEM, DODDS. I *KNOW* THAT. SOME *AFFECTION.*
I SEE THEIR POTENTIAL.
YOU ARE *MISGUIDED.*
DO YOUR JOB.
YOU SANDMEN ARE THE *ONLY* WONDERS PERMITTED.
DO NOT MAKE ME REGRET ALLOWING YOUR KIND TO *LIVE.*
SIR.

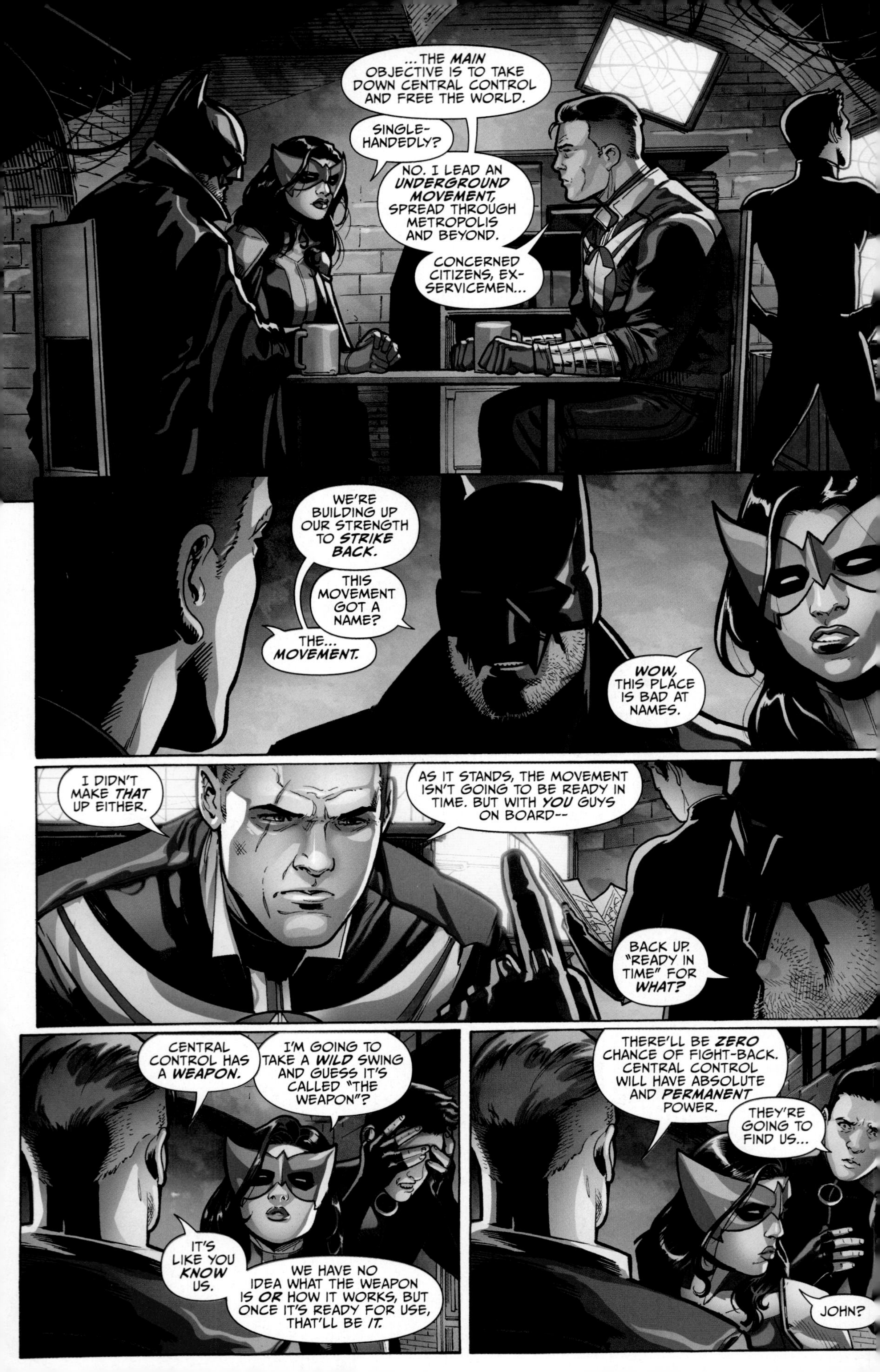
...THE MAIN OBJECTIVE IS TO TAKE DOWN CENTRAL CONTROL AND FREE THE WORLD.
SINGLE-HANDEDLY?
NO. I LEAD AN UNDERGROUND MOVEMENT, SPREAD THROUGH METROPOLIS AND BEYOND.
CONCERNED CITIZENS, EX-SERVICEMEN...
WE'RE BUILDING UP OUR STRENGTH TO STRIKE BACK.
THIS MOVEMENT GOT A NAME?
THE... MOVEMENT.
WOW, THIS PLACE IS BAD AT NAMES.
I DIDN'T MAKE THAT UP EITHER.
AS IT STANDS, THE MOVEMENT ISN'T GOING TO BE READY IN TIME. BUT WITH YOU GUYS ON BOARD--
BACK UP. "READY IN TIME" FOR WHAT?
CENTRAL CONTROL HAS A WEAPON.
I'M GOING TO TAKE A WILD SWING AND GUESS IT'S CALLED "THE WEAPON"?
IT'S LIKE YOU KNOW US.
WE HAVE NO IDEA WHAT THE WEAPON IS OR HOW IT WORKS, BUT ONCE IT'S READY FOR USE, THAT'LL BE IT.
THERE'LL BE ZERO CHANCE OF FIGHT-BACK. CENTRAL CONTROL WILL HAVE ABSOLUTE AND PERMANENT POWER.
THEY'RE GOING TO FIND US...
JOHN?

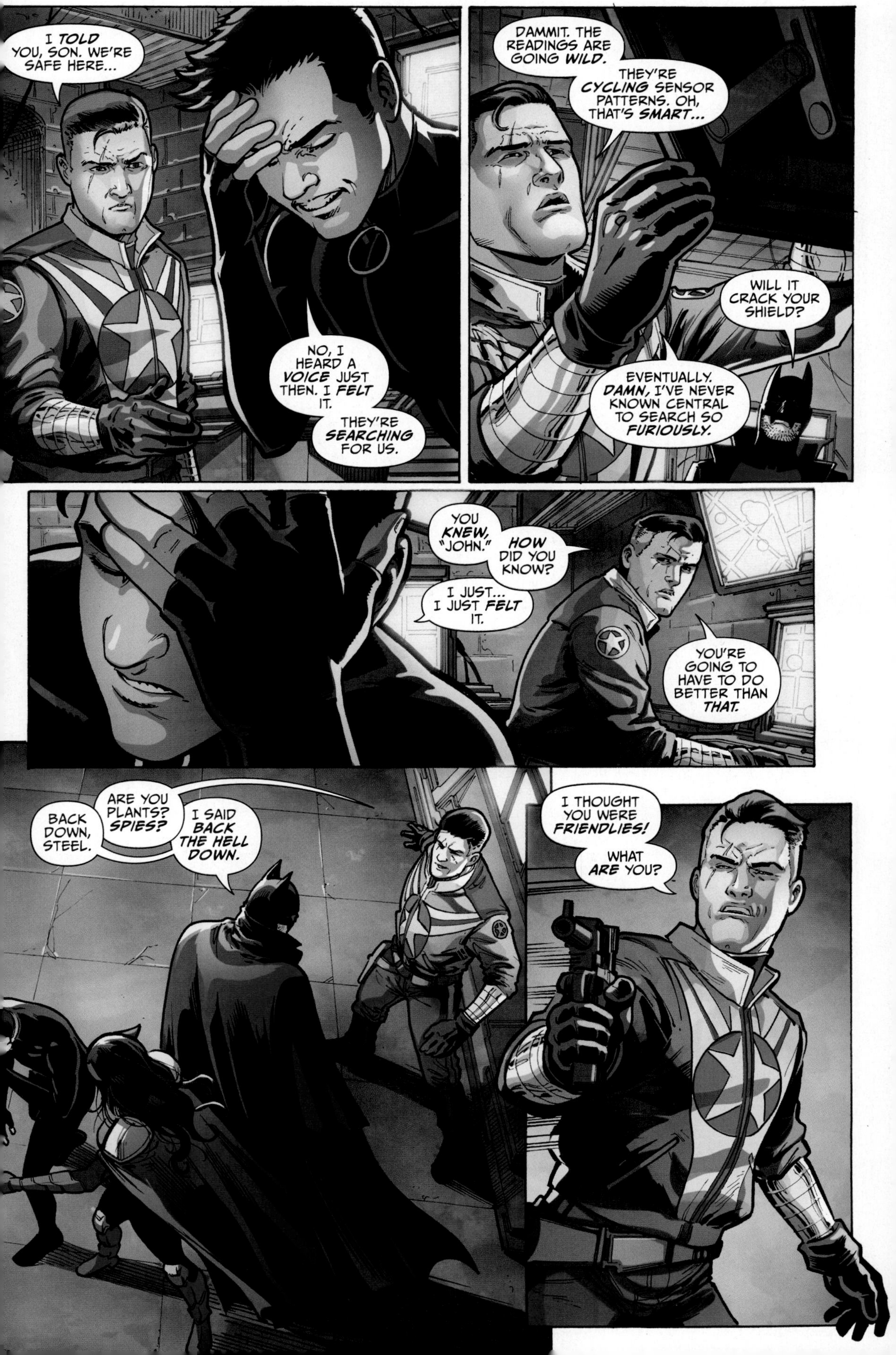
I *TOLD* YOU, SON. WE'RE SAFE HERE...
NO, I HEARD A *VOICE* JUST THEN. I *FELT* IT.
THEY'RE *SEARCHING* FOR US.
DAMMIT. THE READINGS ARE GOING *WILD*.
THEY'RE *CYCLING* SENSOR PATTERNS. OH, THAT'S *SMART*...
WILL IT CRACK YOUR SHIELD?
EVENTUALLY. *DAMN*, I'VE NEVER KNOWN CENTRAL TO SEARCH SO *FURIOUSLY*.
YOU *KNEW*, "JOHN." *HOW* DID YOU KNOW?
I JUST... I JUST *FELT* IT.
YOU'RE GOING TO HAVE TO DO BETTER THAN *THAT*.
BACK DOWN, STEEL.
ARE YOU PLANTS? *SPIES?*
I SAID *BACK THE HELL DOWN*.
I THOUGHT YOU WERE *FRIENDLIES!*
WHAT *ARE* YOU?

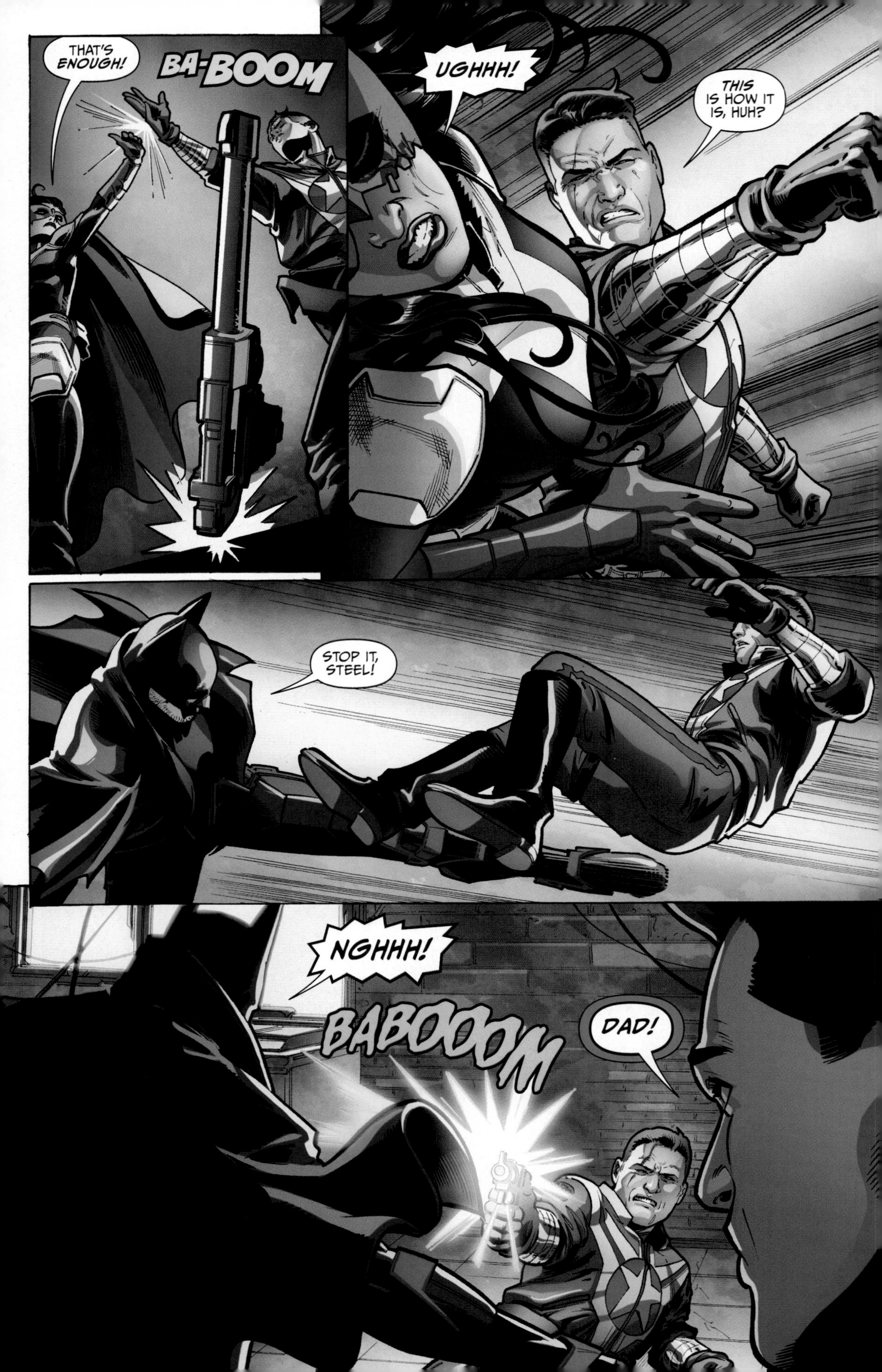
THAT'S ENOUGH!
BA-BOOM
UGHHH!
THIS IS HOW IT IS, HUH?
STOP IT, STEEL!
NGHHH!
BABOOOM
DAD!

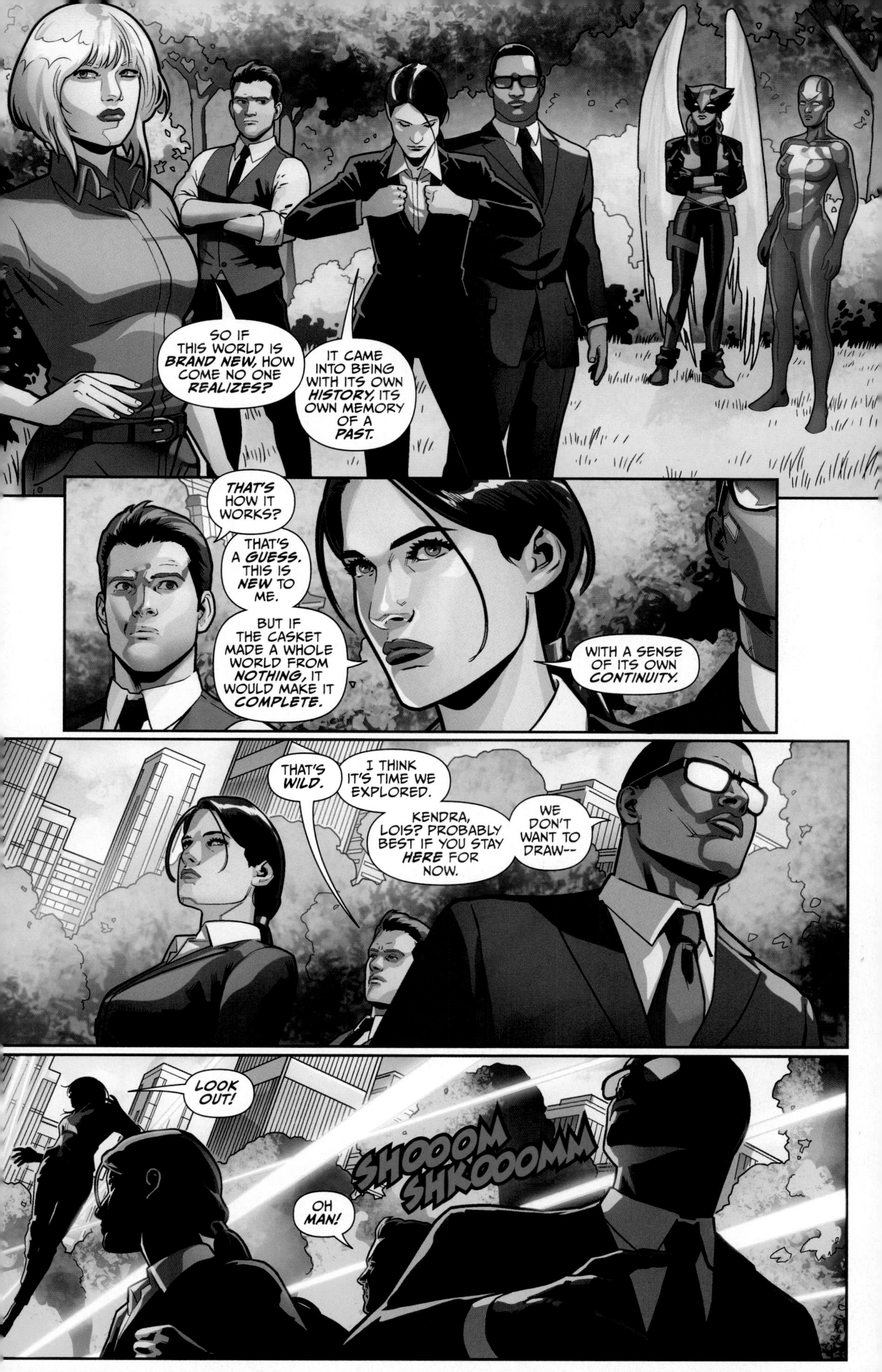
SO IF THIS WORLD IS BRAND NEW, HOW COME NO ONE REALIZES?
IT CAME INTO BEING WITH ITS OWN HISTORY, ITS OWN MEMORY OF A PAST.
THAT'S HOW IT WORKS?
THAT'S A GUESS. THIS IS NEW TO ME.
BUT IF THE CASKET MADE A WHOLE WORLD FROM NOTHING, IT WOULD MAKE IT COMPLETE.
WITH A SENSE OF ITS OWN CONTINUITY.
THAT'S WILD.
I THINK IT'S TIME WE EXPLORED.
KENDRA, LOIS? PROBABLY BEST IF YOU STAY HERE FOR NOW.
WE DON'T WANT TO DRAW--
LOOK OUT!
SHOOOM SHKOOOMM
OH MAN!

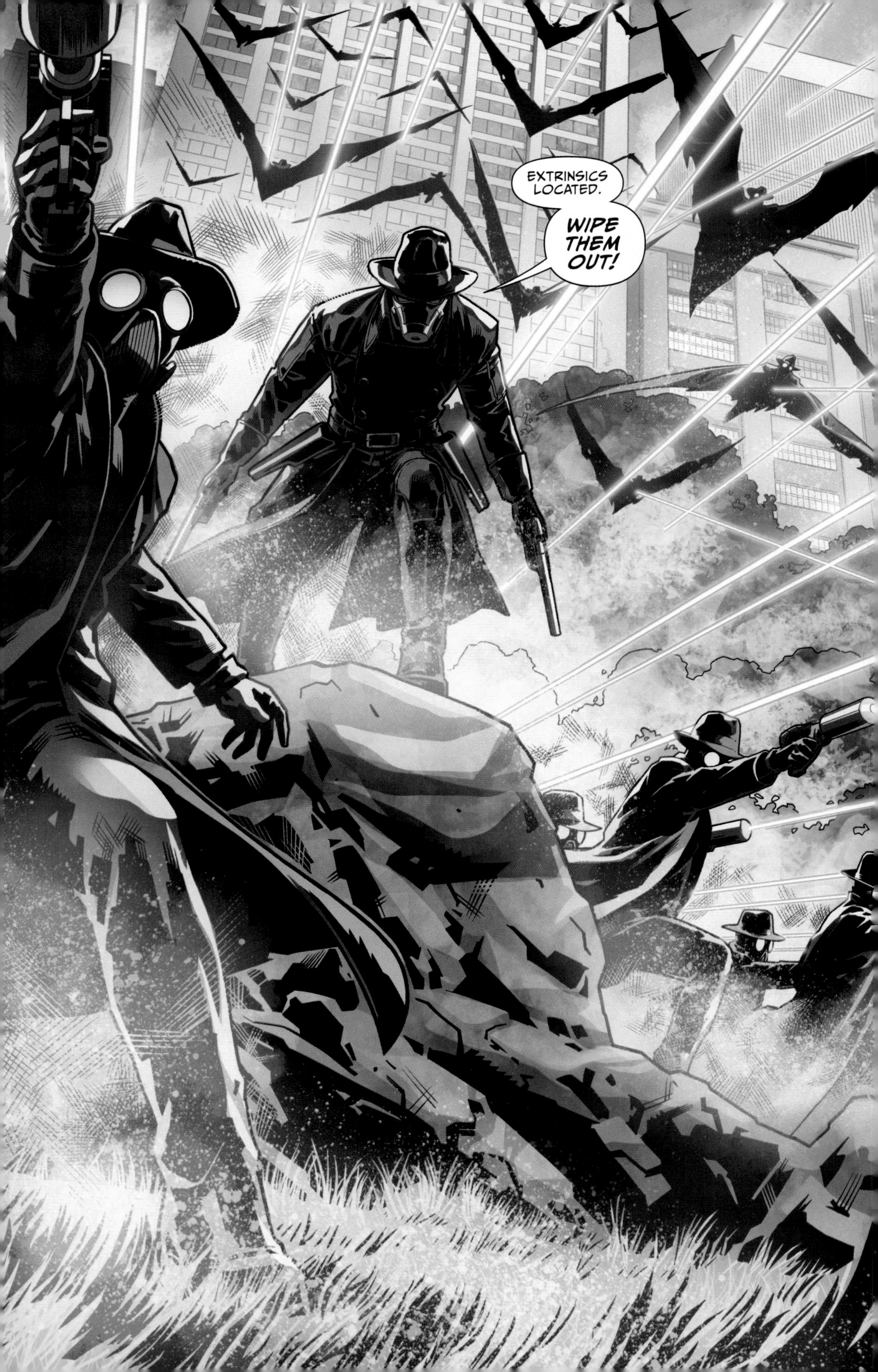
EXTRINSICS LOCATED.
WIPE THEM OUT!

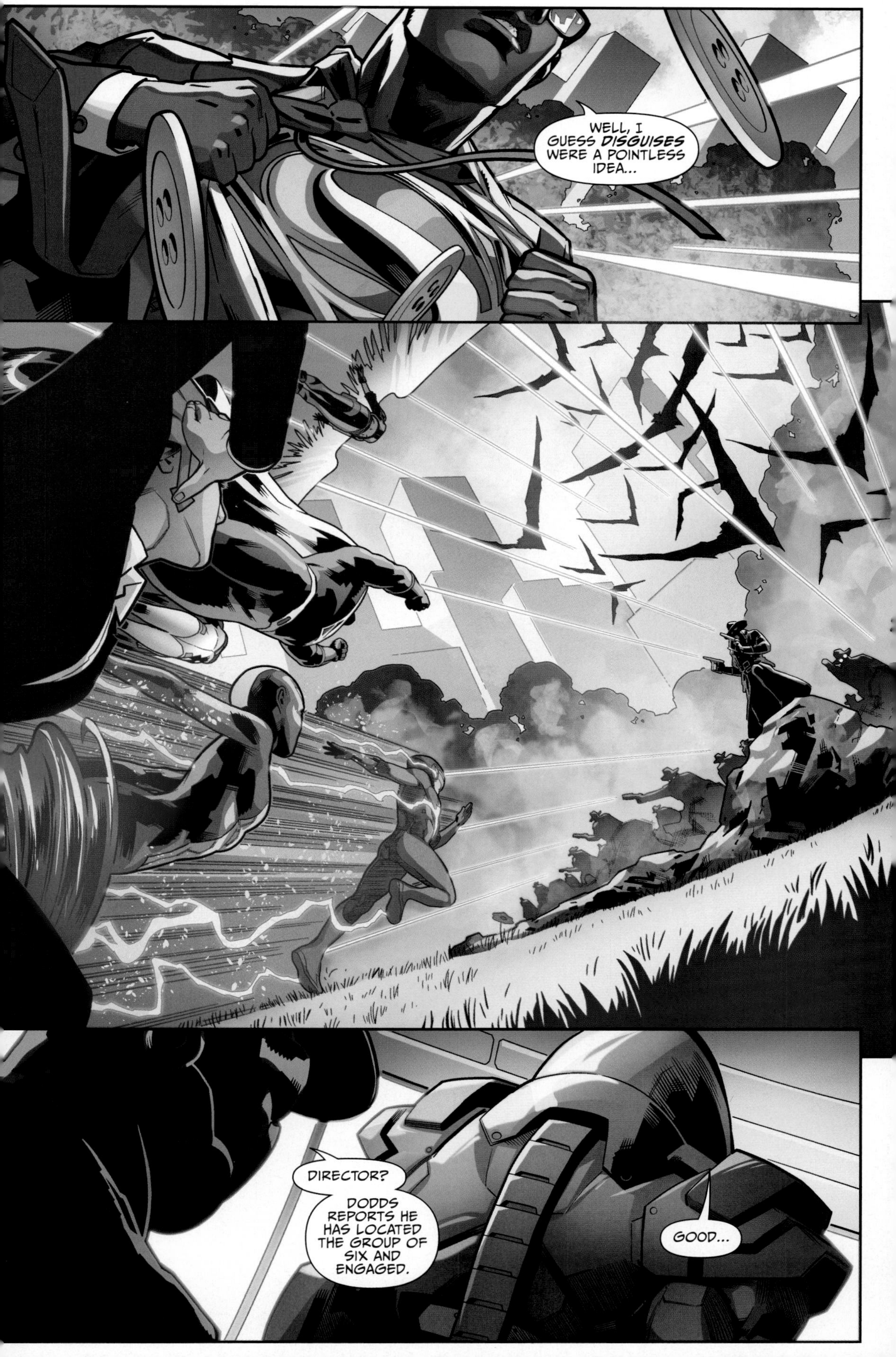
WELL, I GUESS DISGUISES WERE A POINTLESS IDEA...
DIRECTOR?
DODDS REPORTS HE HAS LOCATED THE GROUP OF SIX AND ENGAGED.
GOOD...

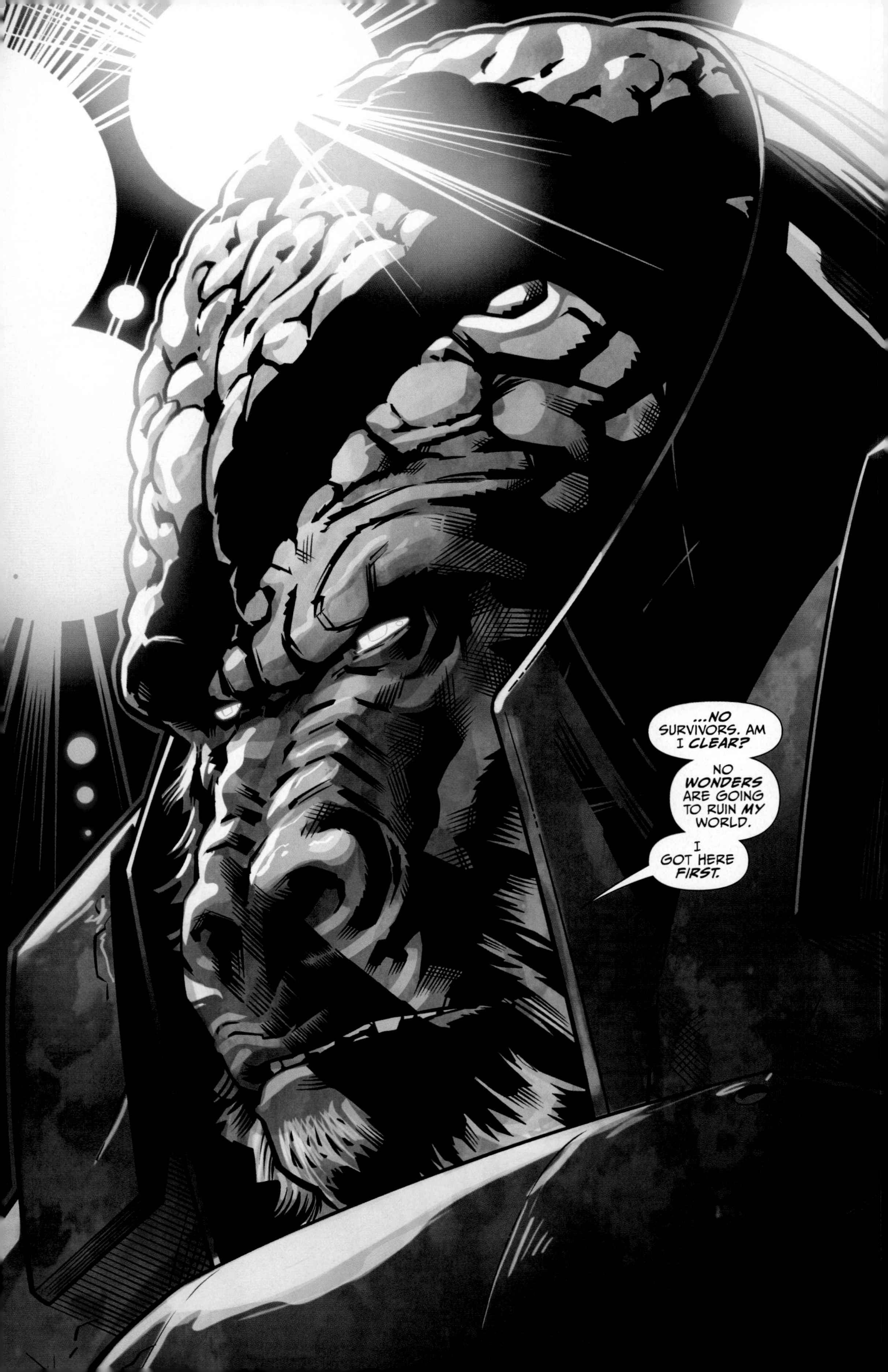
...NO SURVIVORS. AM I CLEAR?
NO WONDERS ARE GOING TO RUIN MY WORLD.
I GOT HERE FIRST.

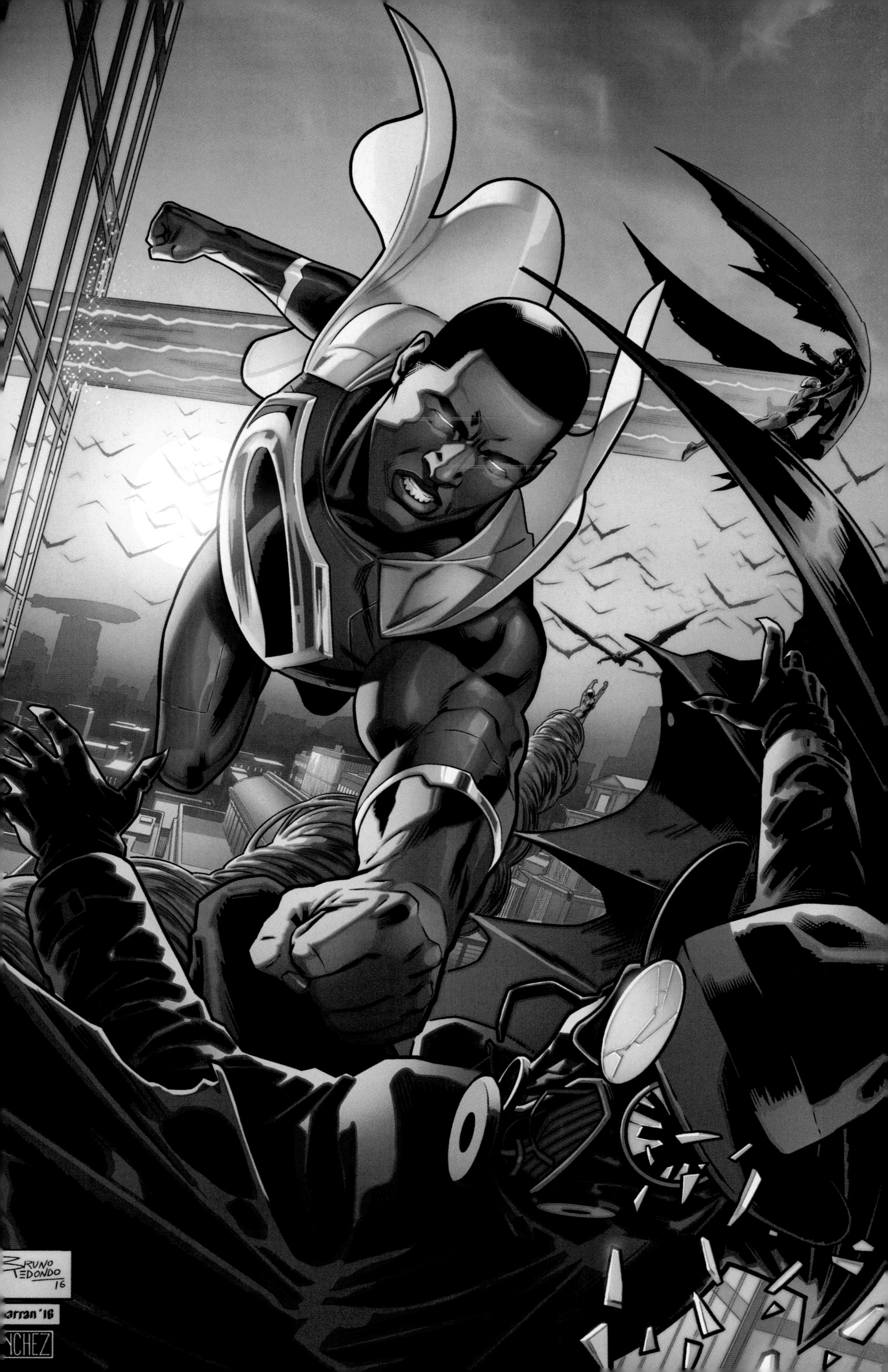
BRUNO REDONDO 16
arran '16
NCHEZ

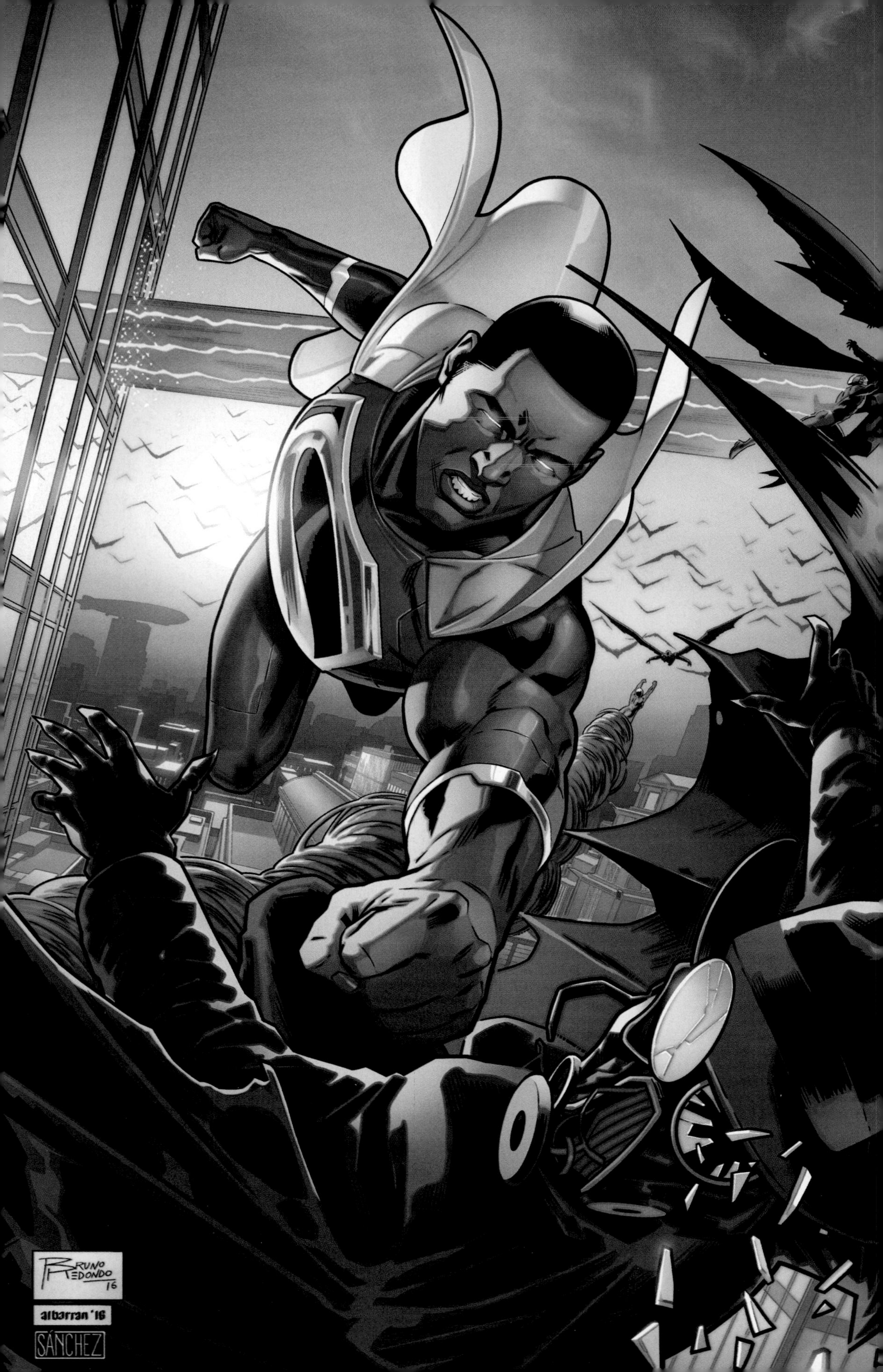
BRUNO REDONDO 16
albarran '16
SÁNCHEZ

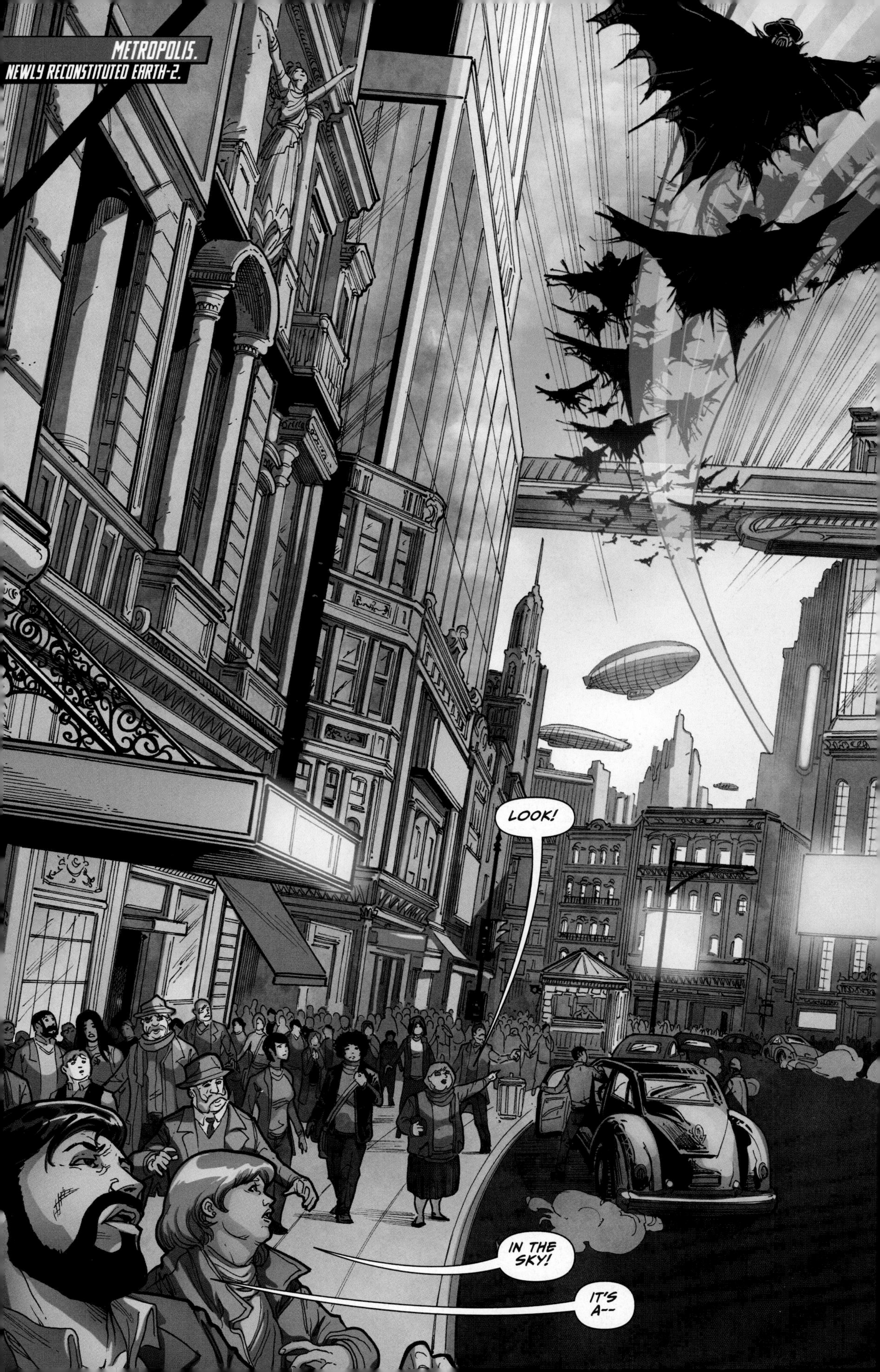
METROPOLIS.
NEWLY RECONSTITUTED EARTH-2.
LOOK!
IN THE SKY!
IT'S A--

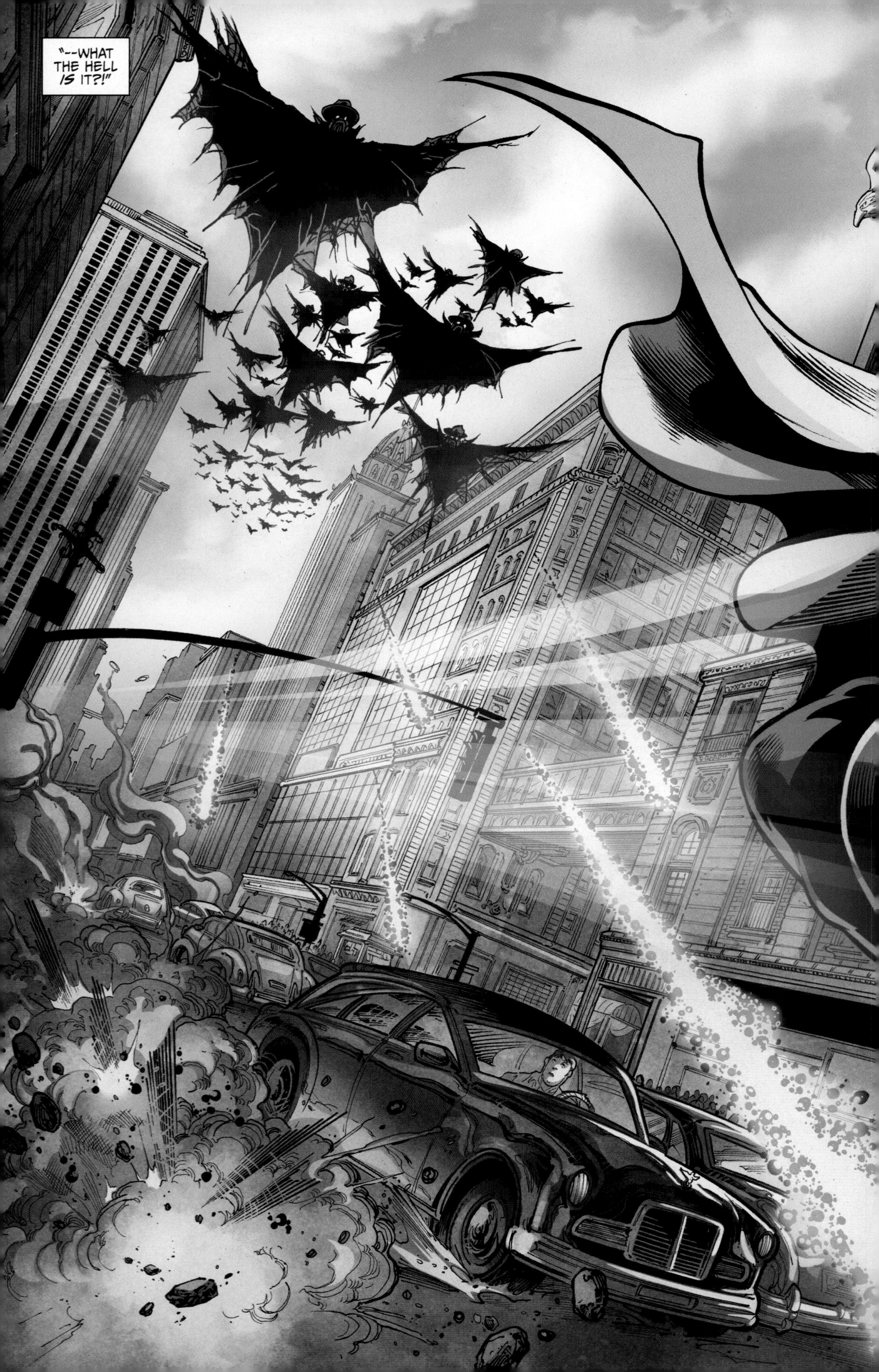
"--WHAT THE HELL IS IT?!"

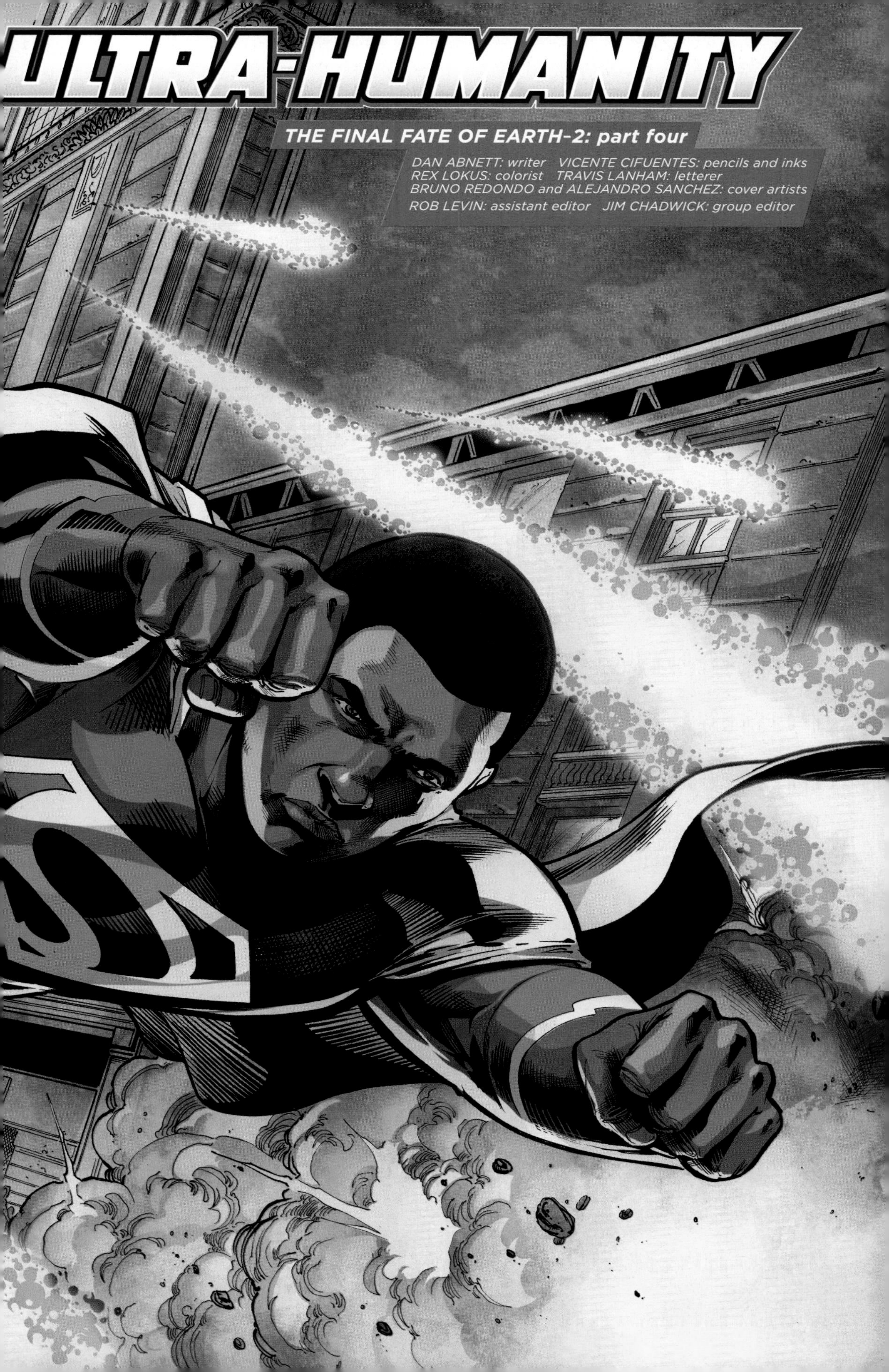
ULTRA-HUMANITY
THE FINAL FATE OF EARTH-2: part four
DAN ABNETT: writer VICENTE CIFUENTES: pencils and inks
REX LOKUS: colorist TRAVIS LANHAM: letterer
BRUNO REDONDO and ALEJANDRO SANCHEZ: cover artists
ROB LEVIN: assistant editor JIM CHADWICK: group editor

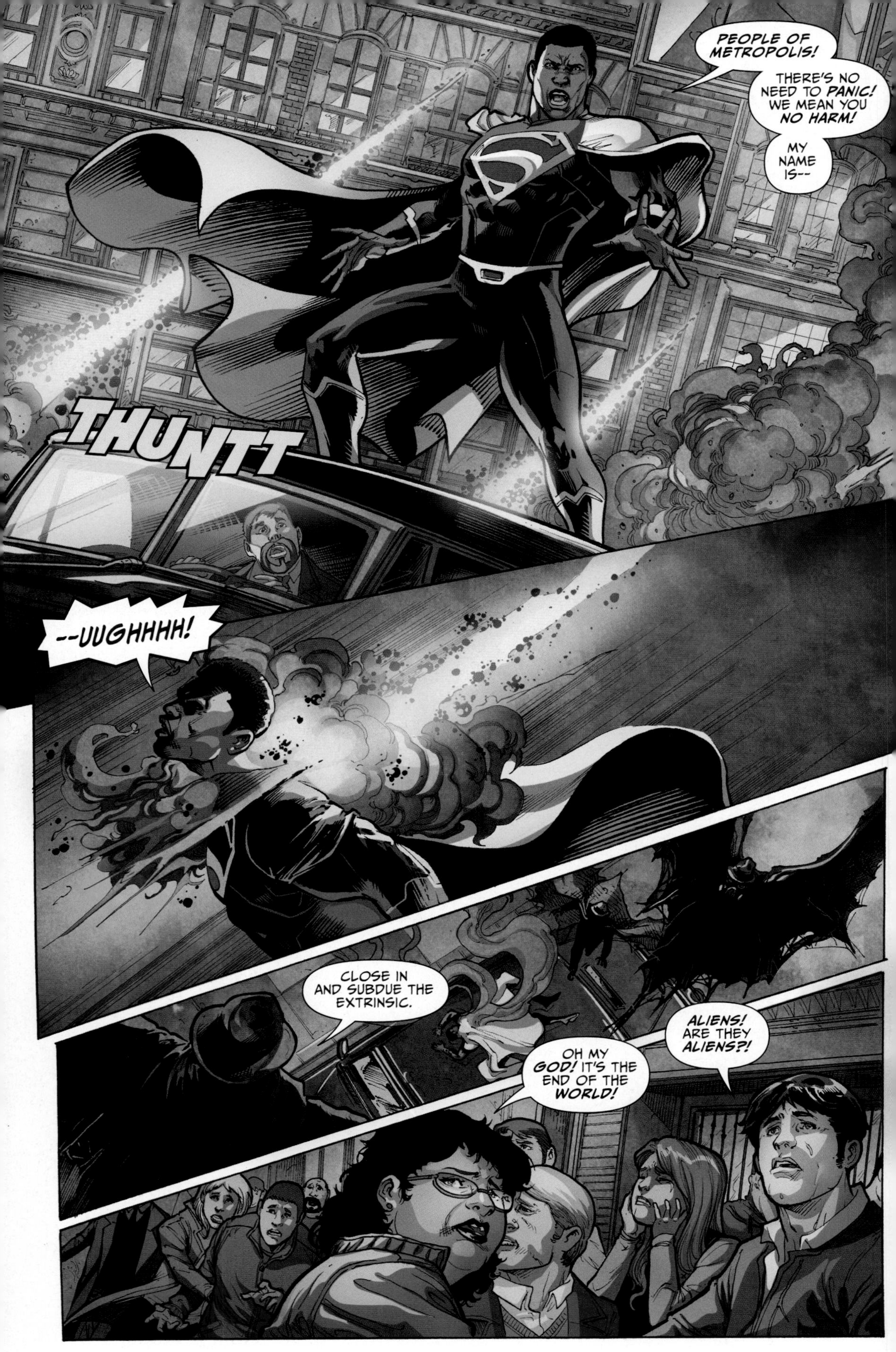
PEOPLE OF METROPOLIS!
THERE'S NO NEED TO PANIC! WE MEAN YOU NO HARM!
MY NAME IS--
THUNTT
--UUGHHHH!
CLOSE IN AND SUBDUE THE EXTRINSIC.
ALIENS! ARE THEY ALIENS?!
OH MY GOD! IT'S THE END OF THE WORLD!

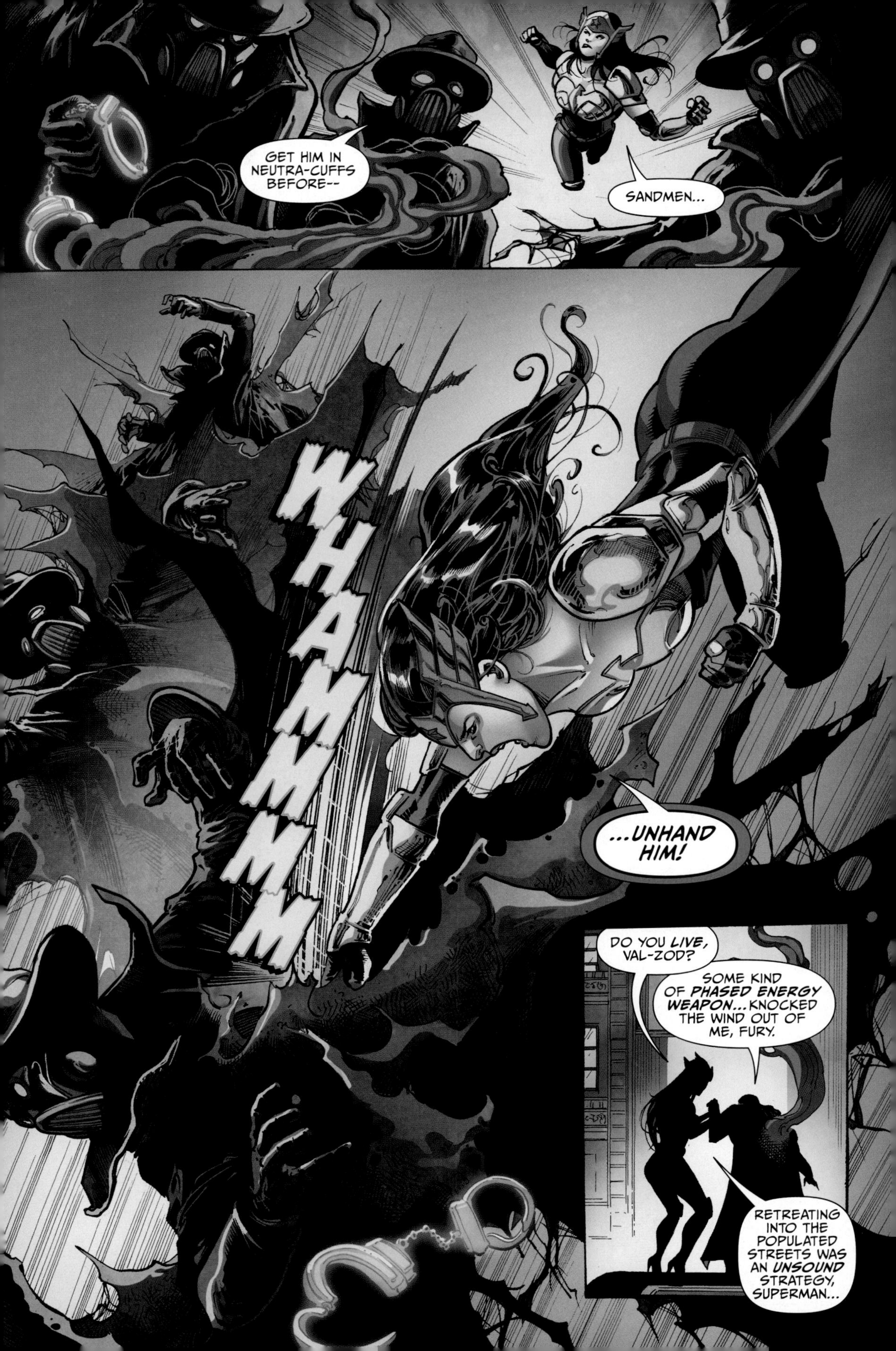
GET HIM IN NEUTRA-CUFFS BEFORE--
SANDMEN...
WHAMMMMM
...UNHAND HIM!
DO YOU *LIVE*, VAL-ZOD?
SOME KIND OF ***PHASED ENERGY WEAPON...*** KNOCKED THE WIND OUT OF ME, FURY.
RETREATING INTO THE POPULATED STREETS WAS AN ***UNSOUND*** STRATEGY, SUPERMAN...

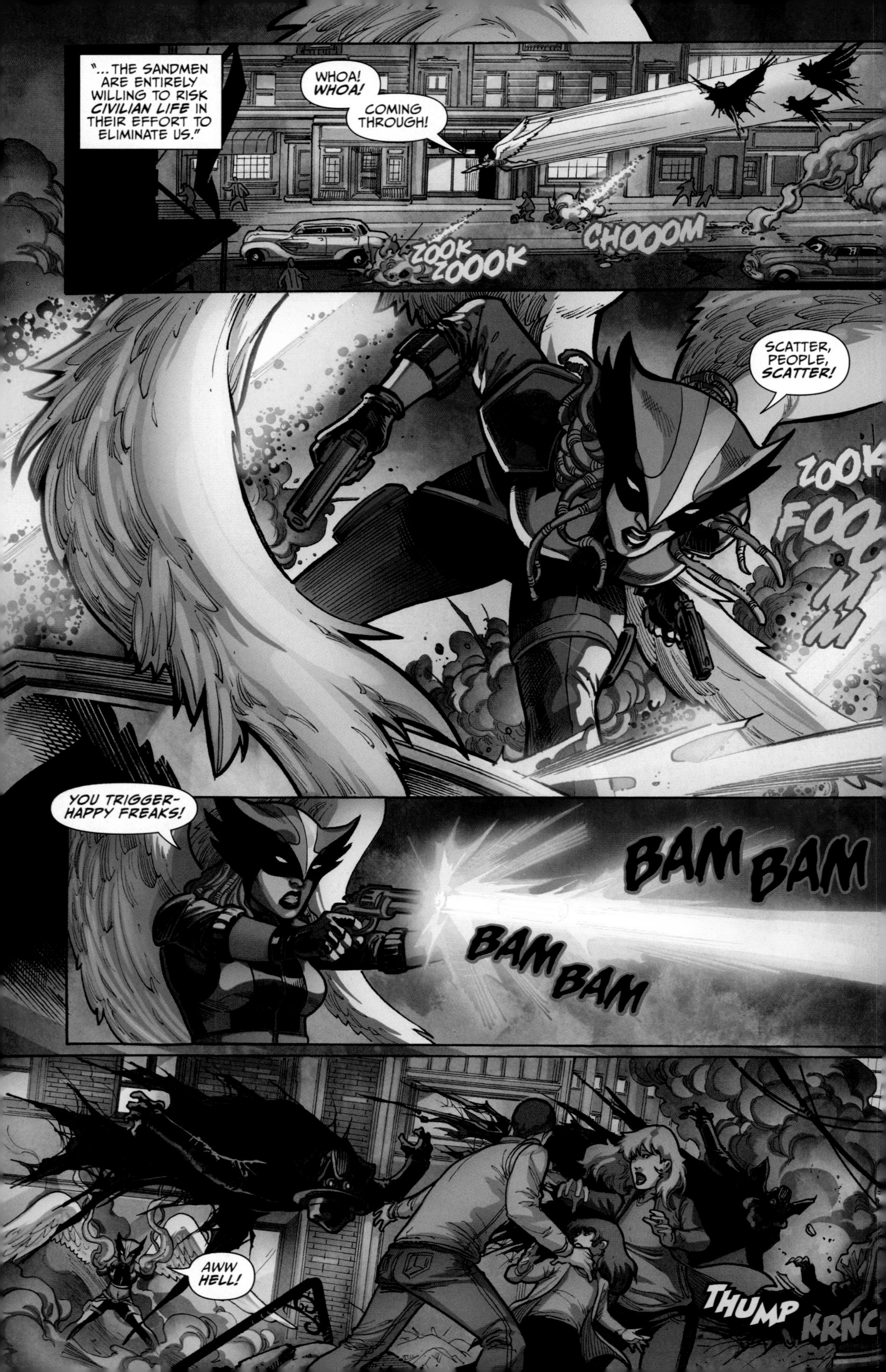

"...THE SANDMEN ARE ENTIRELY WILLING TO RISK CIVILIAN LIFE IN THEIR EFFORT TO ELIMINATE US."
WHOA! WHOA!
COMING THROUGH!
ZOOK ZOOOK
CHOOOM
SCATTER, PEOPLE, SCATTER!
ZOOK
YOU TRIGGER-HAPPY FREAKS!
BAM BAM
BAM BAM
AWW HELL!
THUMP

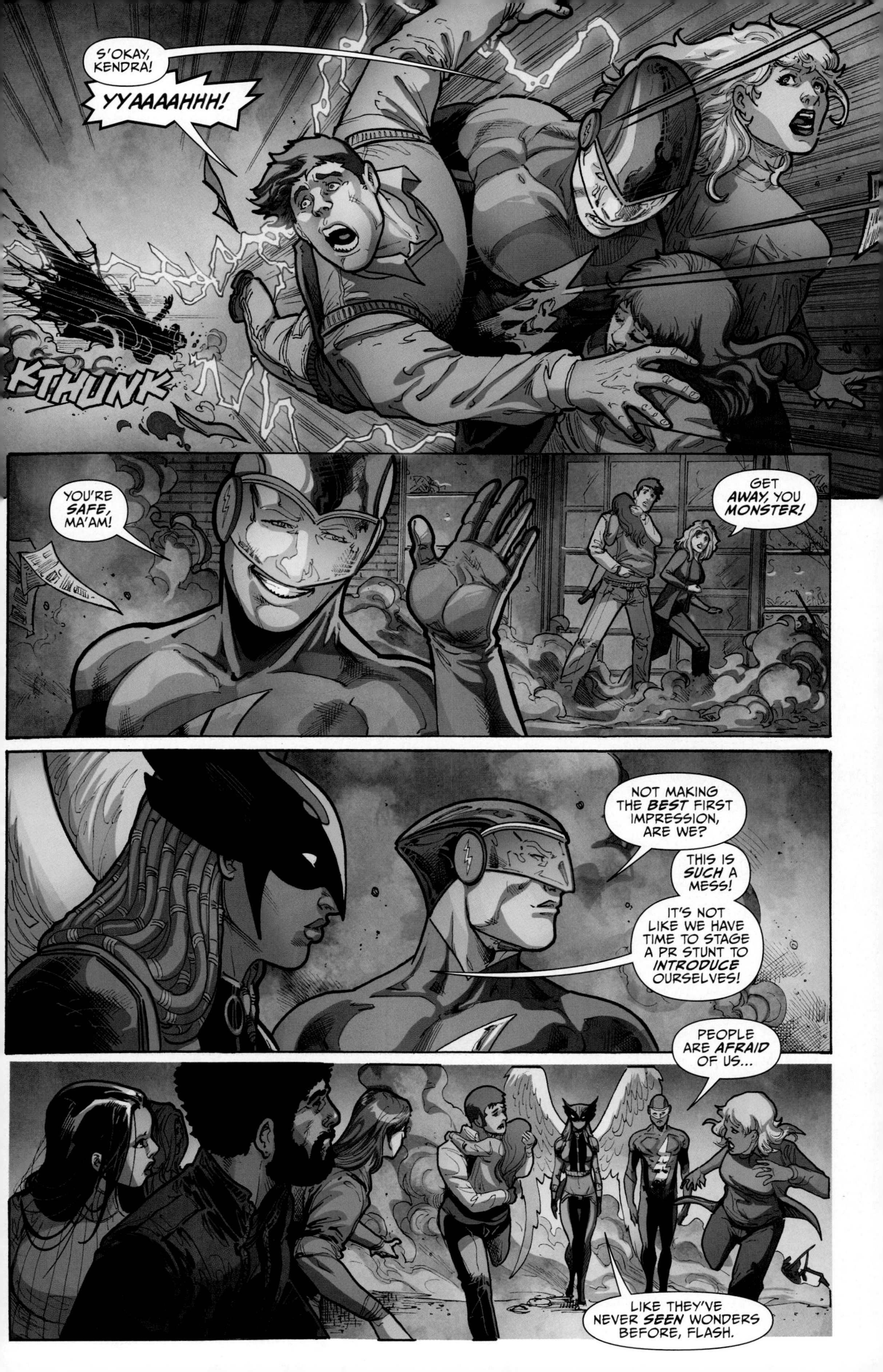
S'OKAY, KENDRA!
YYAAAAHHH!
KTHUNK
YOU'RE SAFE, MA'AM!
GET AWAY, YOU MONSTER!
NOT MAKING THE BEST FIRST IMPRESSION, ARE WE?
THIS IS SUCH A MESS!
IT'S NOT LIKE WE HAVE TIME TO STAGE A PR STUNT TO INTRODUCE OURSELVES!
PEOPLE ARE AFRAID OF US...
LIKE THEY'VE NEVER SEEN WONDERS BEFORE, FLASH.

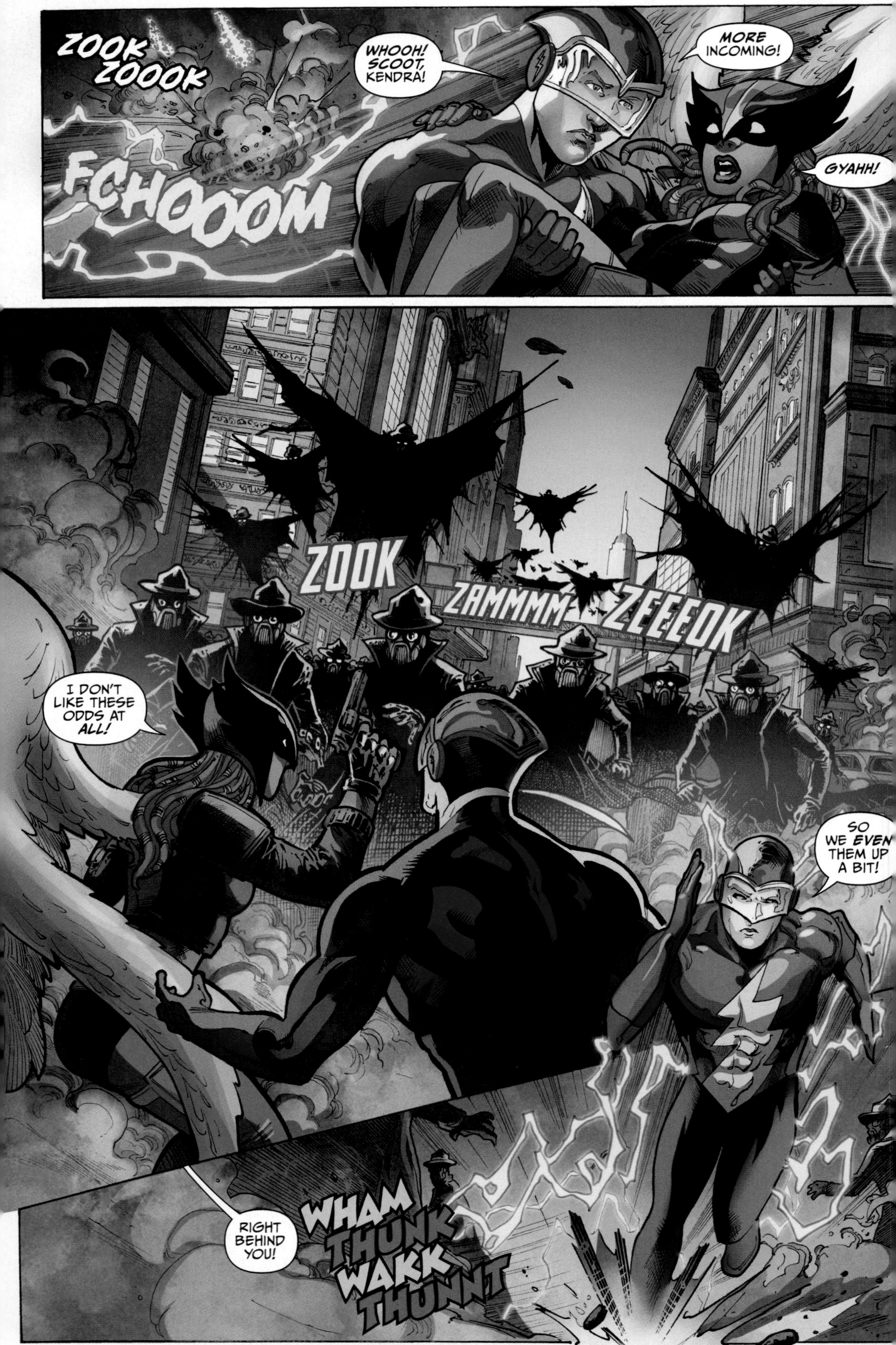
ZOOK ZOOOK
FCHOOOM
WHOOH! SCOOT, KENDRA!
MORE INCOMING!
GYAHH!
ZOOK
ZAMMMM
ZEEEOK
I DON'T LIKE THESE ODDS AT ALL!
SO WE EVEN THEM UP A BIT!
RIGHT BEHIND YOU!
WHAM THUNK WAKK THUNNT

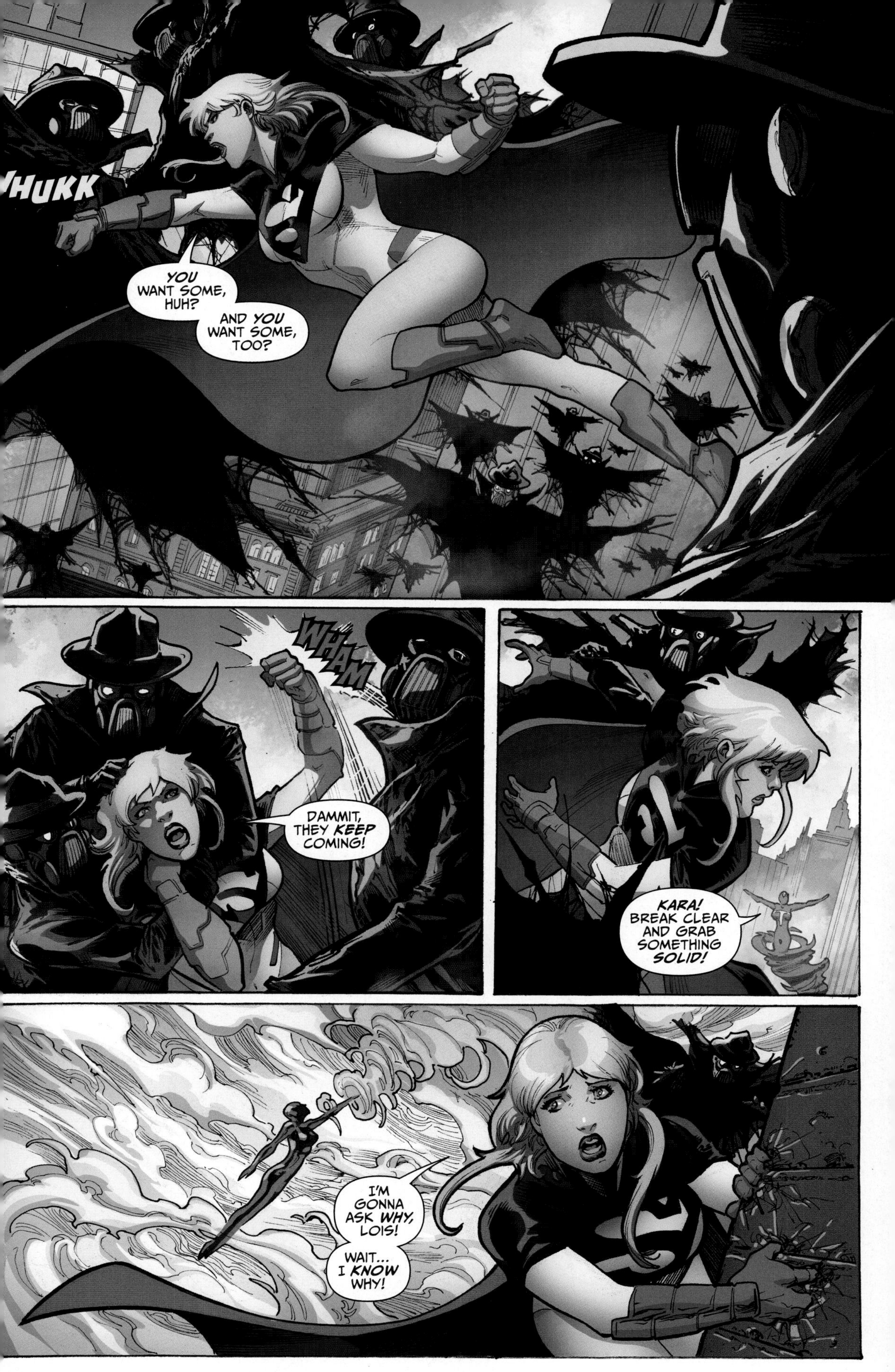

HUKK
YOU WANT SOME, HUH?
AND YOU WANT SOME, TOO?
WHAM
DAMMIT, THEY KEEP COMING!
KARA! BREAK CLEAR AND GRAB SOMETHING SOLID!
I'M GONNA ASK WHY, LOIS!
WAIT... I KNOW WHY!

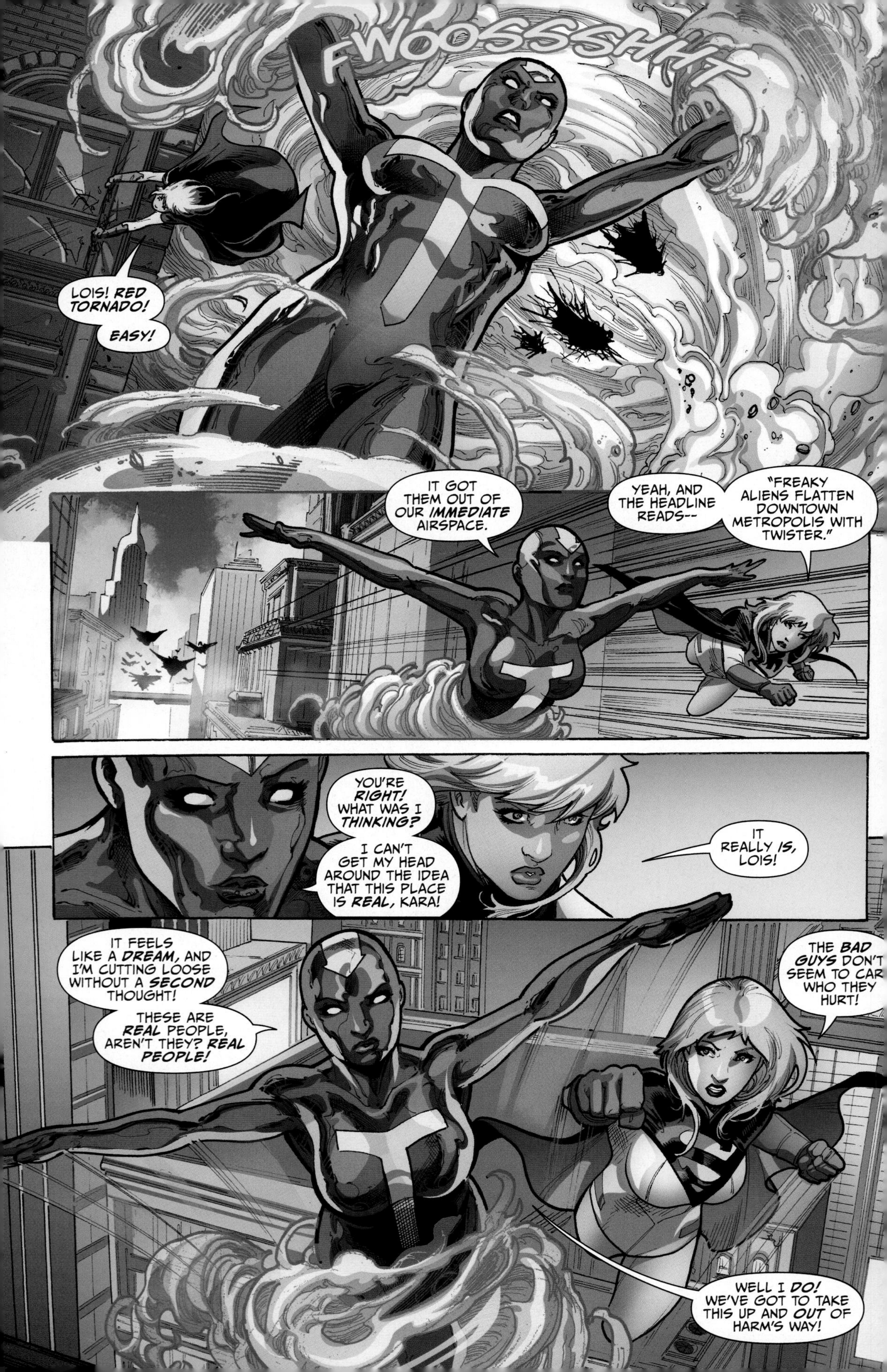
FWOOSSSHHT
LOIS! RED TORNADO!
EASY!
IT GOT THEM OUT OF OUR IMMEDIATE AIRSPACE.
YEAH, AND THE HEADLINE READS--
"FREAKY ALIENS FLATTEN DOWNTOWN METROPOLIS WITH TWISTER."
YOU'RE RIGHT! WHAT WAS I THINKING?
I CAN'T GET MY HEAD AROUND THE IDEA THAT THIS PLACE IS REAL, KARA!
IT REALLY IS, LOIS!
IT FEELS LIKE A DREAM, AND I'M CUTTING LOOSE WITHOUT A SECOND THOUGHT!
THESE ARE REAL PEOPLE, AREN'T THEY? REAL PEOPLE!
THE BAD GUYS DON'T SEEM TO CAR WHO THEY HURT!
WELL I DO! WE'VE GOT TO TAKE THIS UP AND OUT OF HARM'S WAY!

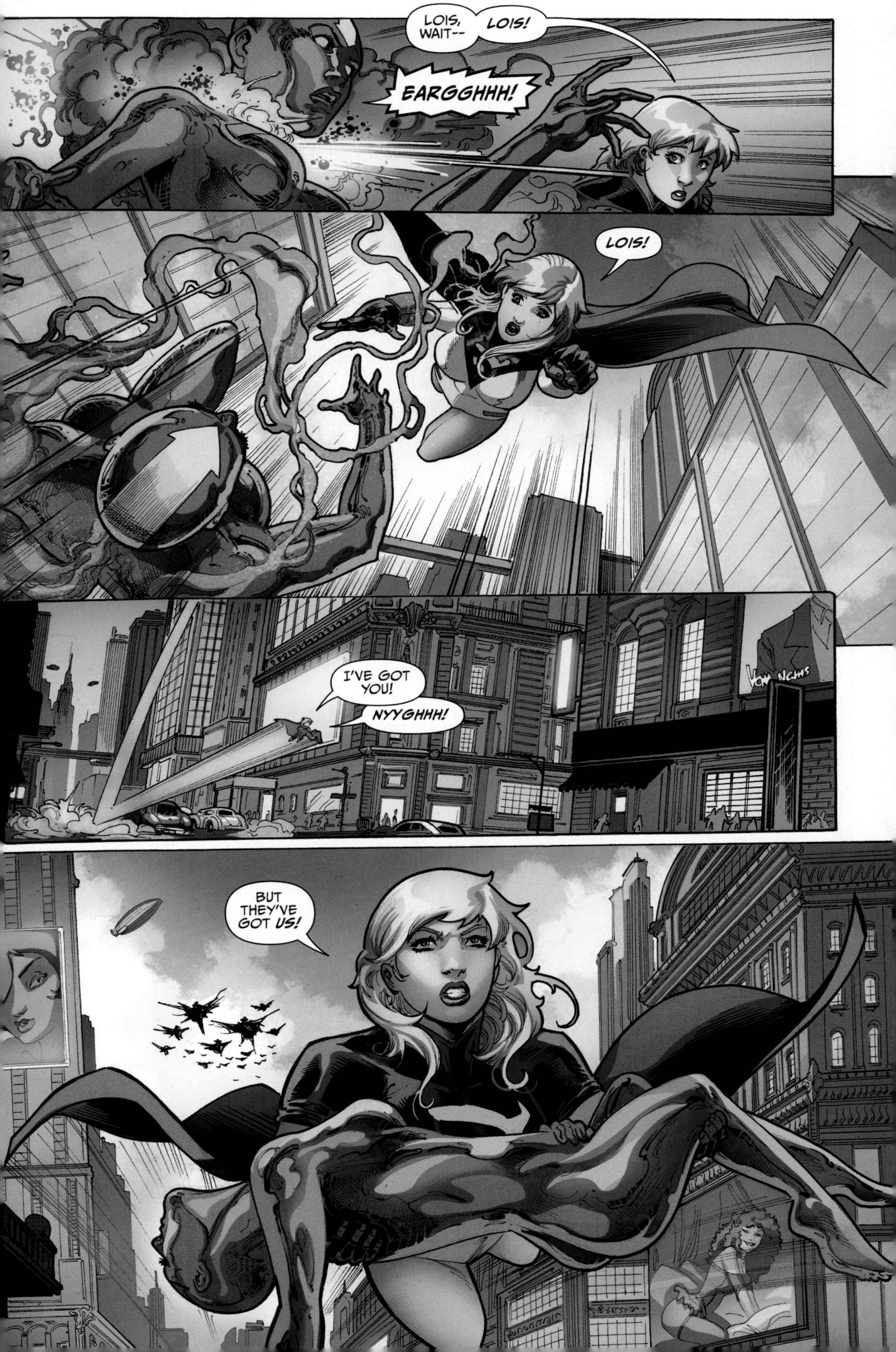
LOIS, WAIT--
LOIS!
EARGGHHH!
LOIS!
I'VE GOT YOU!
NYYGHHH!
BUT THEY'VE GOT US!

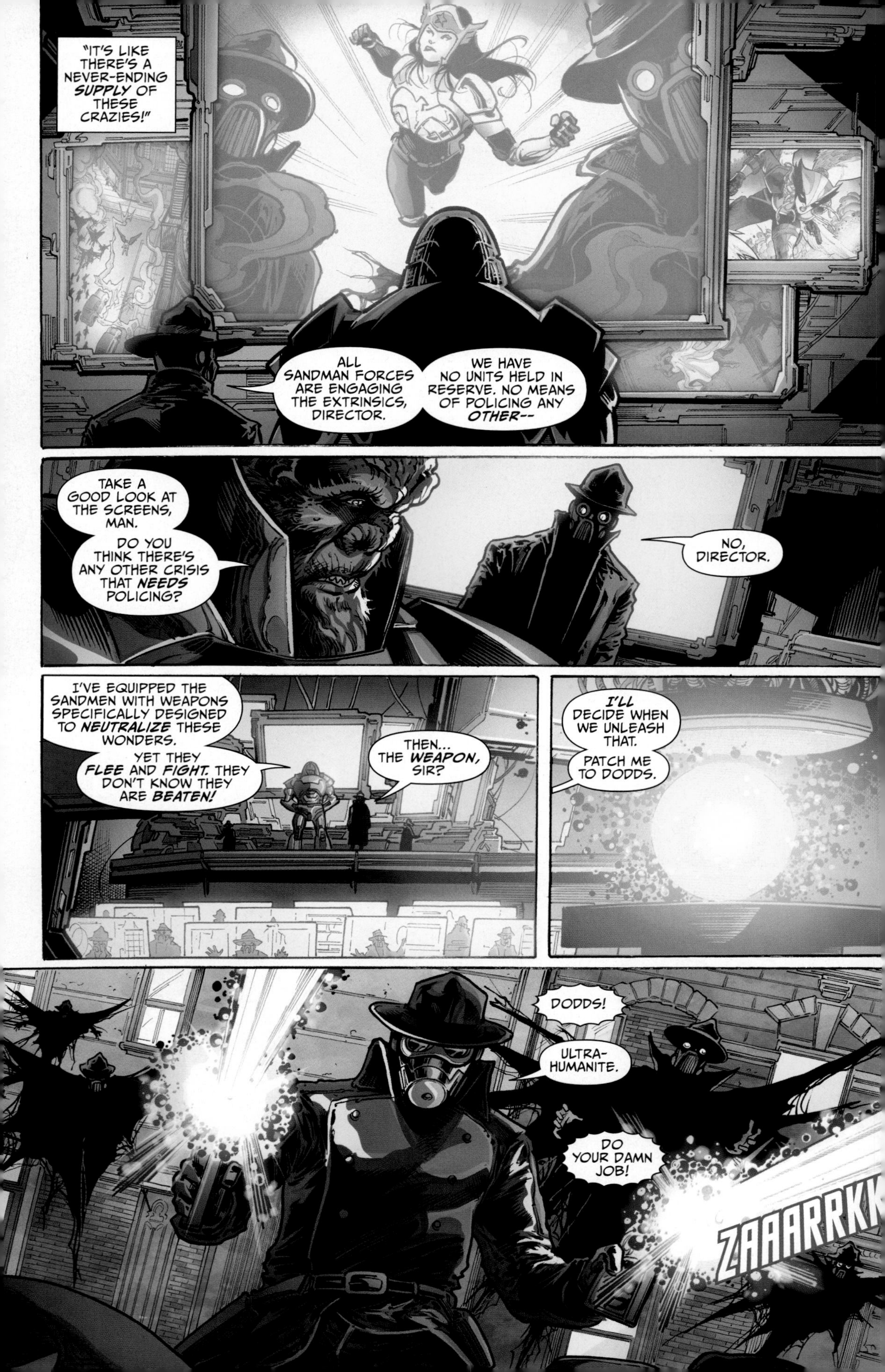
"IT'S LIKE THERE'S A NEVER-ENDING SUPPLY OF THESE CRAZIES!"
ALL SANDMAN FORCES ARE ENGAGING THE EXTRINSICS, DIRECTOR.
WE HAVE NO UNITS HELD IN RESERVE. NO MEANS OF POLICING ANY OTHER--
TAKE A GOOD LOOK AT THE SCREENS, MAN.
DO YOU THINK THERE'S ANY OTHER CRISIS THAT NEEDS POLICING?
NO, DIRECTOR.
I'VE EQUIPPED THE SANDMEN WITH WEAPONS SPECIFICALLY DESIGNED TO NEUTRALIZE THESE WONDERS.
YET THEY FLEE AND FIGHT. THEY DON'T KNOW THEY ARE BEATEN!
THEN... THE WEAPON, SIR?
I'LL DECIDE WHEN WE UNLEASH THAT.
PATCH ME TO DODDS.
DODDS!
ULTRA-HUMANITE.
DO YOUR DAMN JOB!
ZAAARRKK

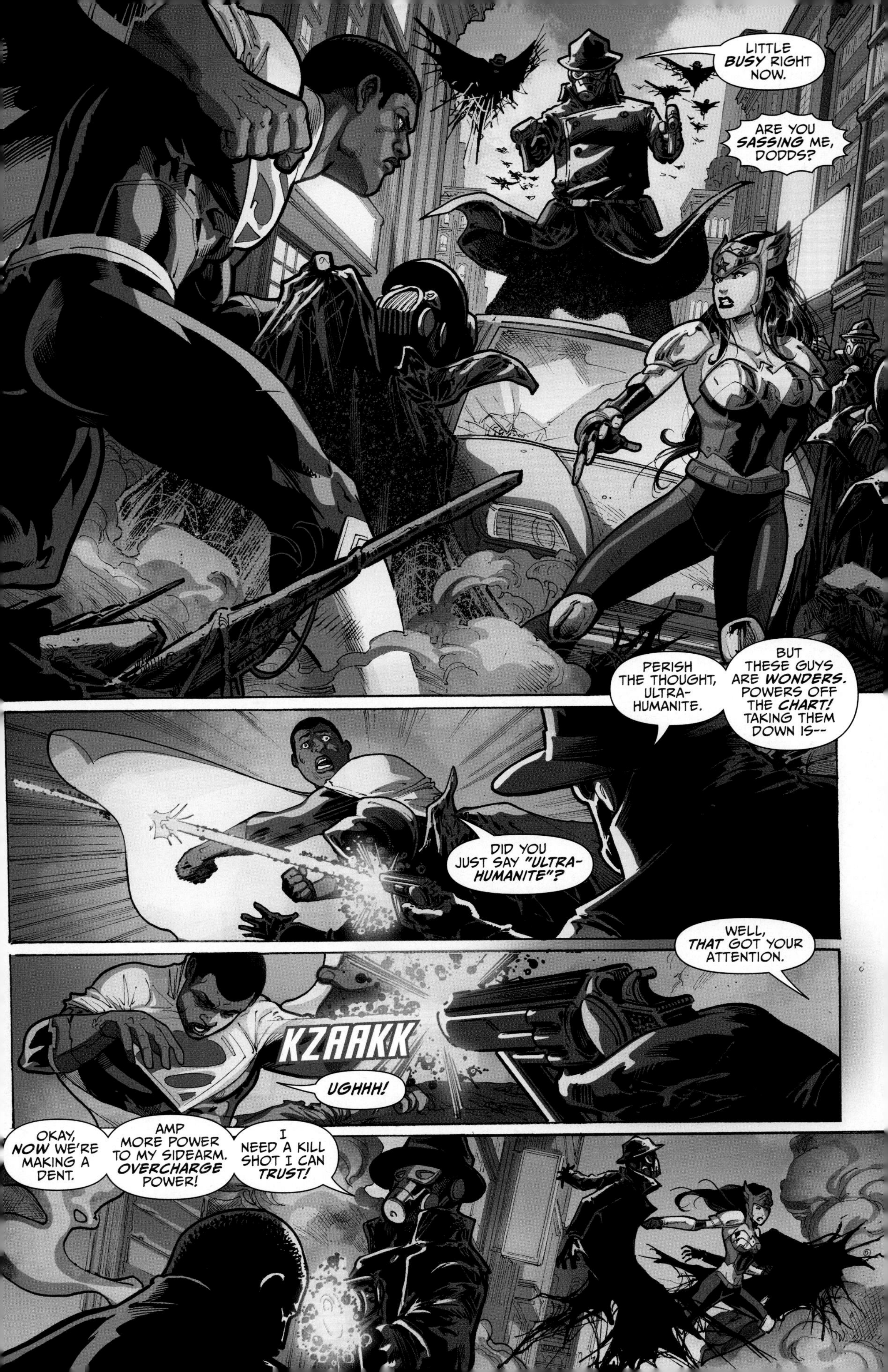
LITTLE BUSY RIGHT NOW.
ARE YOU SASSING ME, DODDS?
PERISH THE THOUGHT, ULTRA-HUMANITE.
BUT THESE GUYS ARE WONDERS. POWERS OFF THE CHART! TAKING THEM DOWN IS--
DID YOU JUST SAY "ULTRA-HUMANITE"?
WELL, THAT GOT YOUR ATTENTION.
KZAAKK
UGHHH!
OKAY, NOW WE'RE MAKING A DENT.
AMP MORE POWER TO MY SIDEARM. OVERCHARGE POWER!
I NEED A KILL SHOT I CAN TRUST!

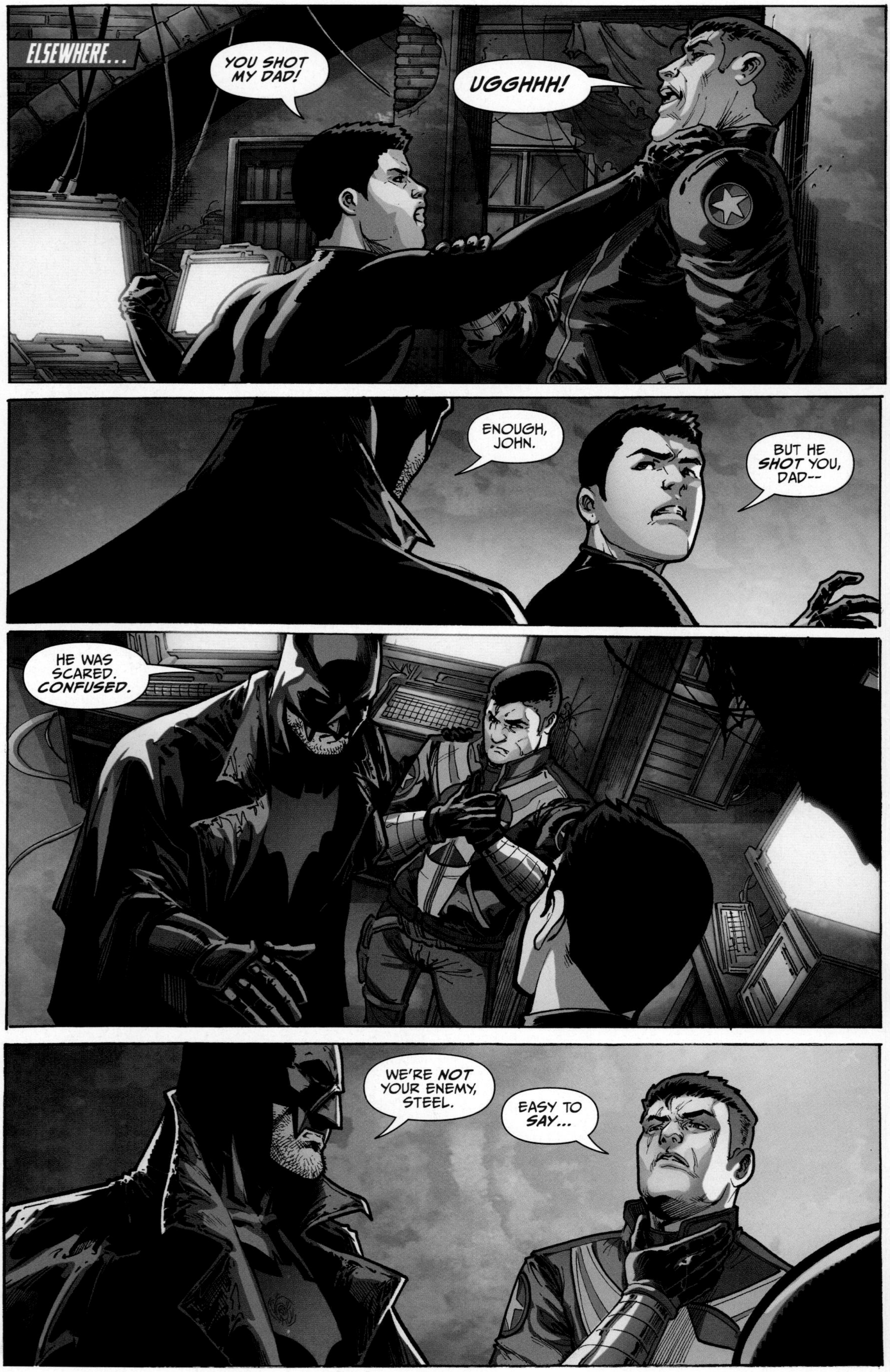
ELSEWHERE...
YOU SHOT MY DAD!
UGGHHH!
ENOUGH, JOHN.
BUT HE SHOT YOU, DAD--
HE WAS SCARED. CONFUSED.
WE'RE NOT YOUR ENEMY, STEEL.
EASY TO SAY...

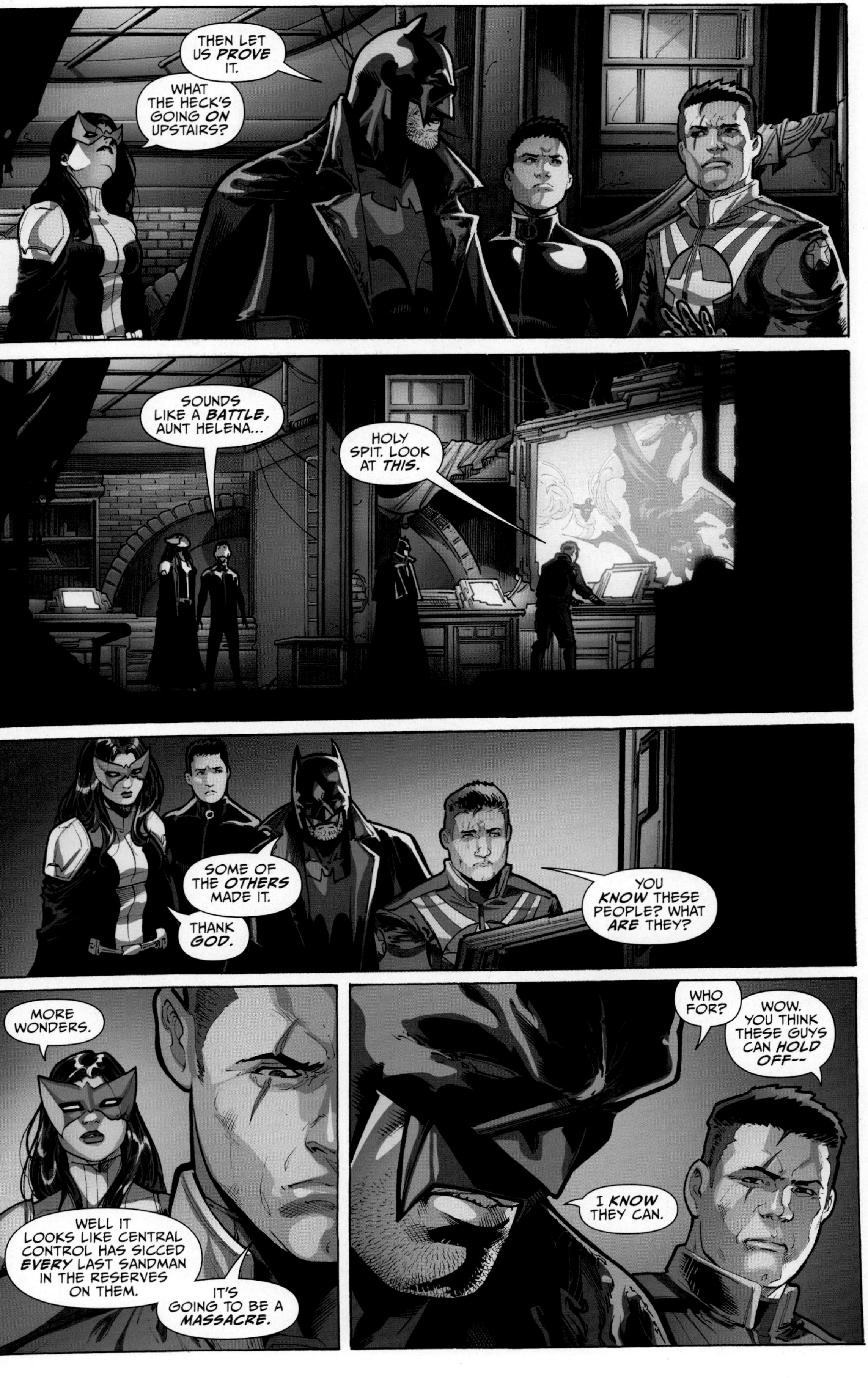
THEN LET US *PROVE* IT.
WHAT THE HECK'S GOING *ON* UPSTAIRS?
SOUNDS LIKE A *BATTLE,* AUNT HELENA...
HOLY SPIT. LOOK AT *THIS.*
SOME OF THE *OTHERS* MADE IT.
THANK *GOD.*
YOU *KNOW* THESE PEOPLE? WHAT *ARE* THEY?
MORE WONDERS.
WELL IT LOOKS LIKE CENTRAL CONTROL HAS SICCED *EVERY* LAST SANDMAN IN THE RESERVES ON THEM.
IT'S GOING TO BE A *MASSACRE.*
WOW. YOU THINK THESE GUYS CAN *HOLD OFF--*
WHO FOR?
I *KNOW* THEY CAN.

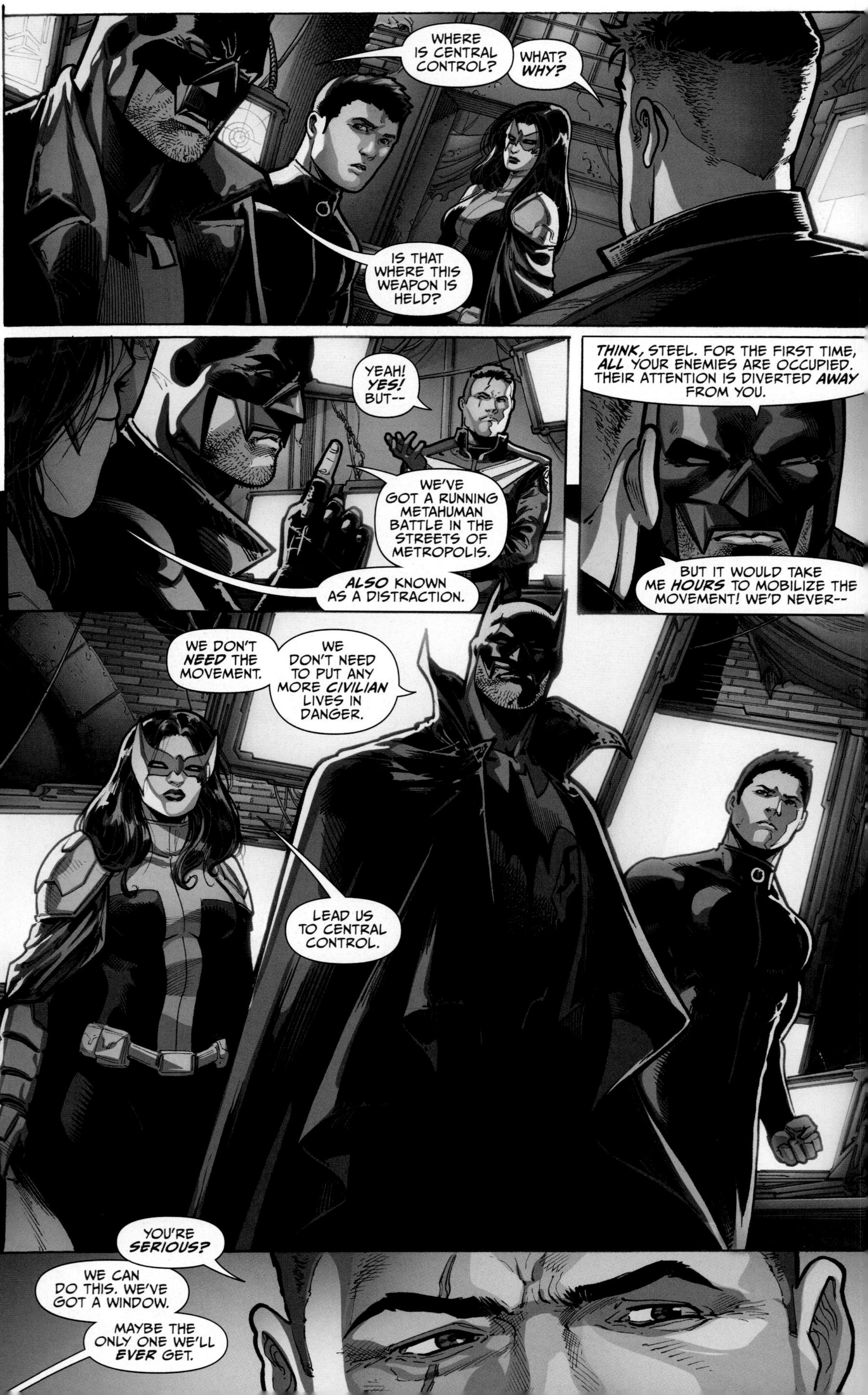
WHERE IS CENTRAL CONTROL?
WHAT? WHY?
IS THAT WHERE THIS WEAPON IS HELD?
YEAH! YES! BUT--
WE'VE GOT A RUNNING METAHUMAN BATTLE IN THE STREETS OF METROPOLIS.
ALSO KNOWN AS A DISTRACTION.
THINK, STEEL. FOR THE FIRST TIME, ALL YOUR ENEMIES ARE OCCUPIED. THEIR ATTENTION IS DIVERTED AWAY FROM YOU.
BUT IT WOULD TAKE ME HOURS TO MOBILIZE THE MOVEMENT! WE'D NEVER--
WE DON'T NEED THE MOVEMENT.
WE DON'T NEED TO PUT ANY MORE CIVILIAN LIVES IN DANGER.
LEAD US TO CENTRAL CONTROL.
YOU'RE SERIOUS?
WE CAN DO THIS. WE'VE GOT A WINDOW.
MAYBE THE ONLY ONE WE'LL EVER GET.

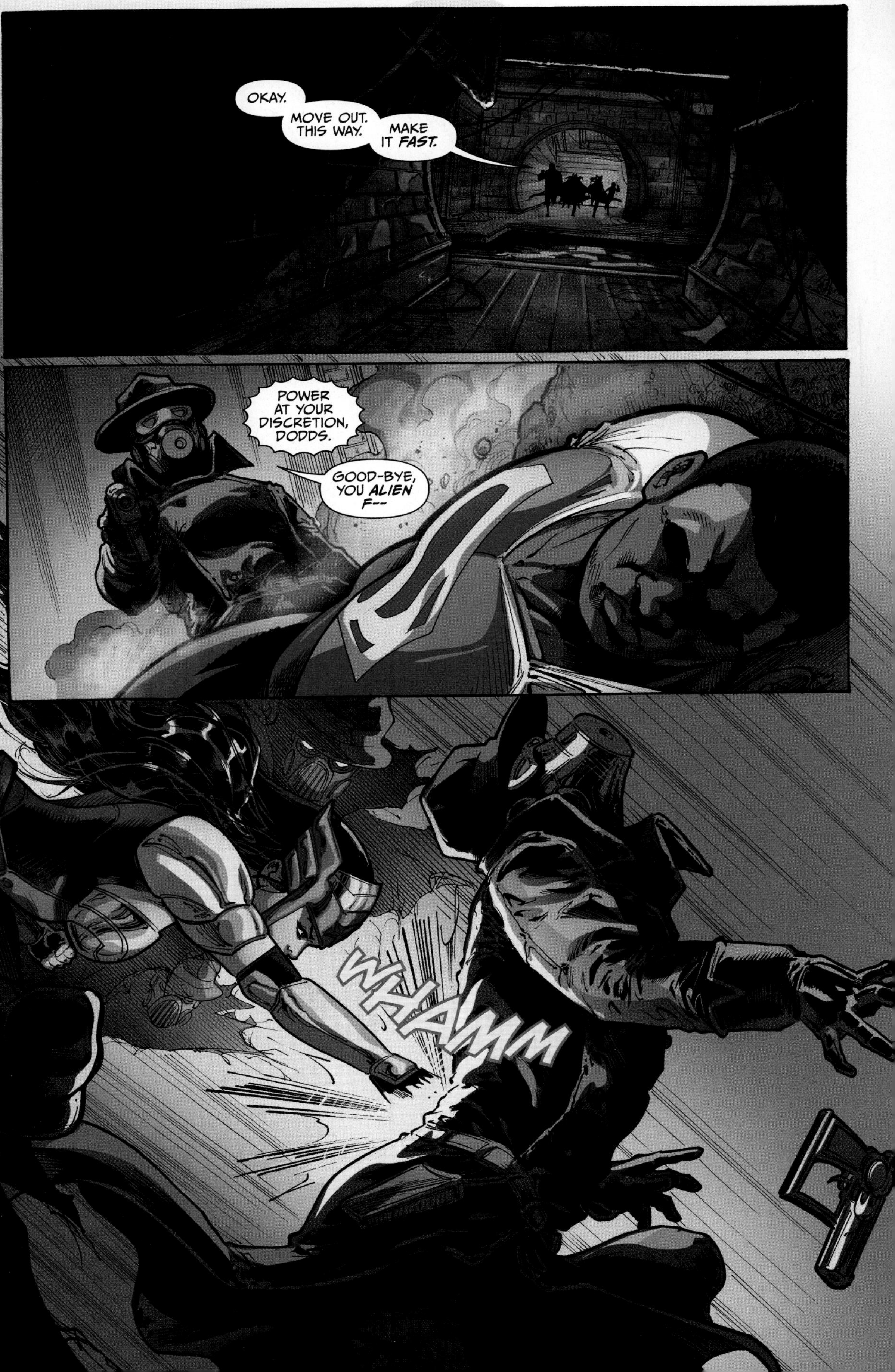
OKAY.
MOVE OUT. THIS WAY.
MAKE IT FAST.
POWER AT YOUR DISCRETION, DODDS.
GOOD-BYE, YOU ALIEN F--
WHAMM

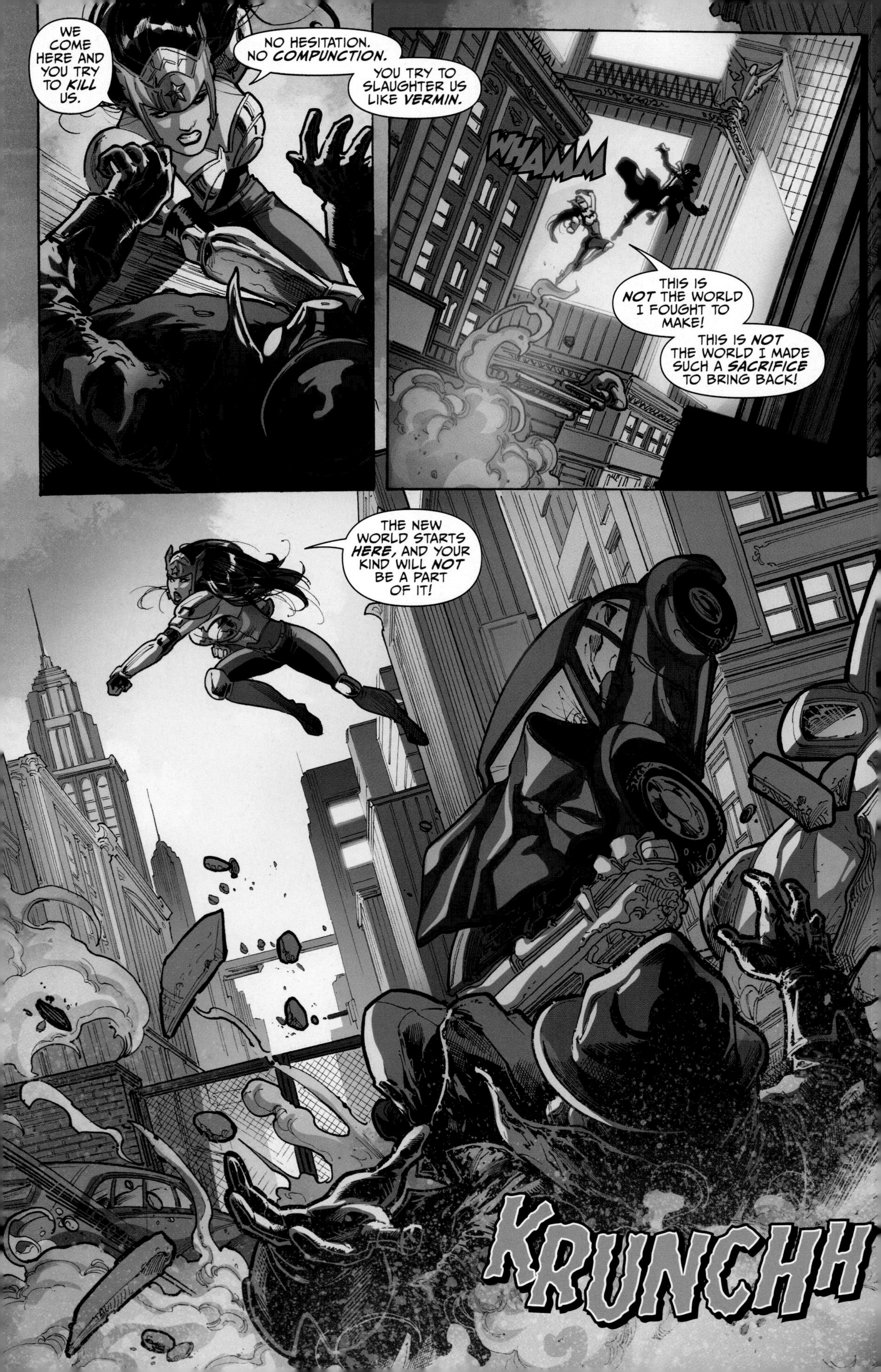
WE COME HERE AND YOU TRY TO KILL US.
NO HESITATION. NO COMPUNCTION.
YOU TRY TO SLAUGHTER US LIKE VERMIN.
WHAMM
THIS IS NOT THE WORLD I FOUGHT TO MAKE!
THIS IS NOT THE WORLD I MADE SUCH A SACRIFICE TO BRING BACK!
THE NEW WORLD STARTS HERE, AND YOUR KIND WILL NOT BE A PART OF IT!
KRUNCHH

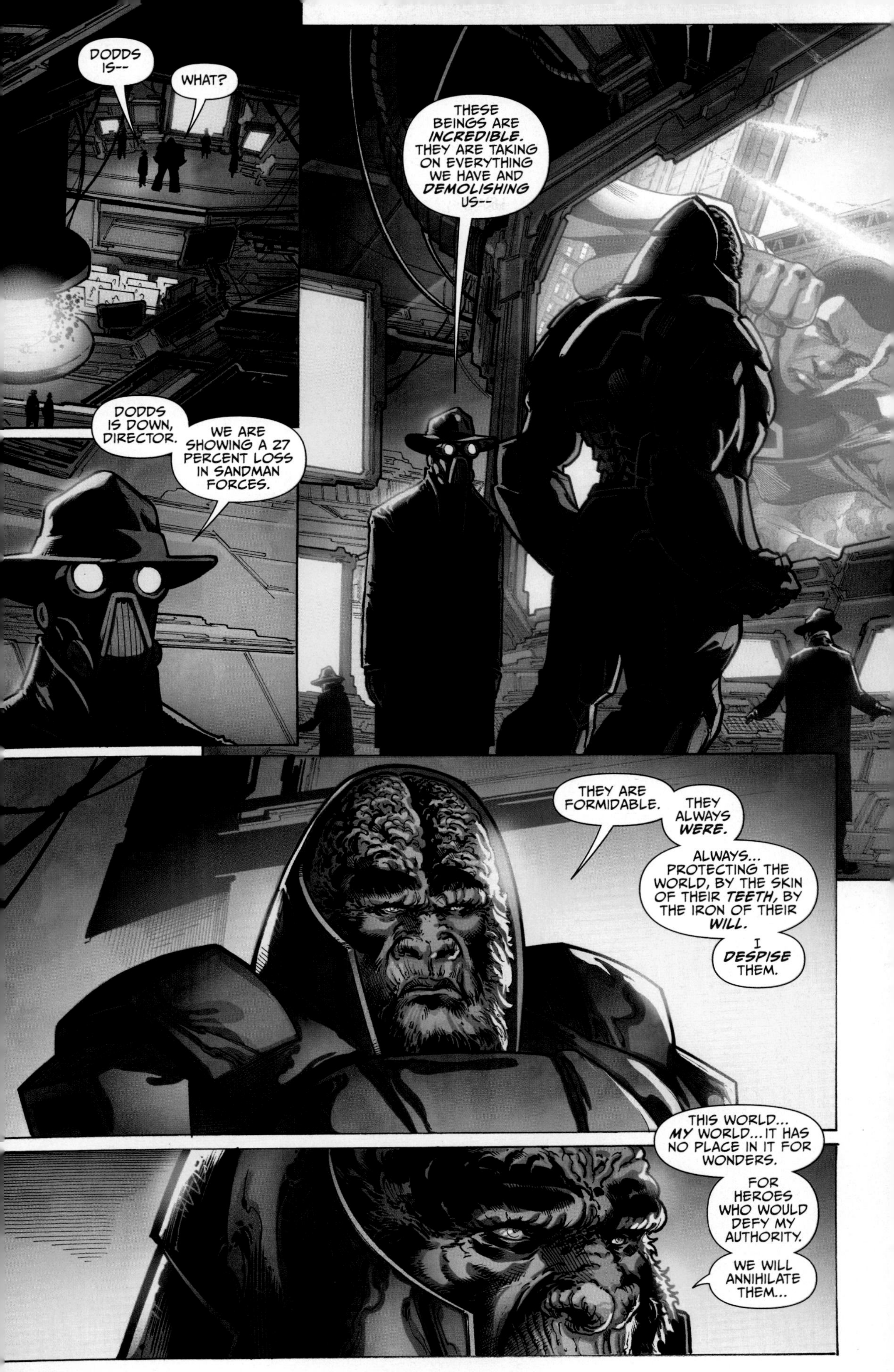
DODDS IS--
WHAT?
THESE BEINGS ARE *INCREDIBLE.* THEY ARE TAKING ON EVERYTHING WE HAVE AND *DEMOLISHING* US--
DODDS IS DOWN, DIRECTOR.
WE ARE SHOWING A 27 PERCENT LOSS IN SANDMAN FORCES.
THEY ARE FORMIDABLE.
THEY ALWAYS *WERE.*
ALWAYS... PROTECTING THE WORLD, BY THE SKIN OF THEIR *TEETH,* BY THE IRON OF THEIR *WILL.*
I *DESPISE* THEM.
THIS WORLD... *MY* WORLD... IT HAS NO PLACE IN IT FOR WONDERS.
FOR HEROES WHO WOULD DEFY MY AUTHORITY.
WE WILL ANNIHILATE THEM...

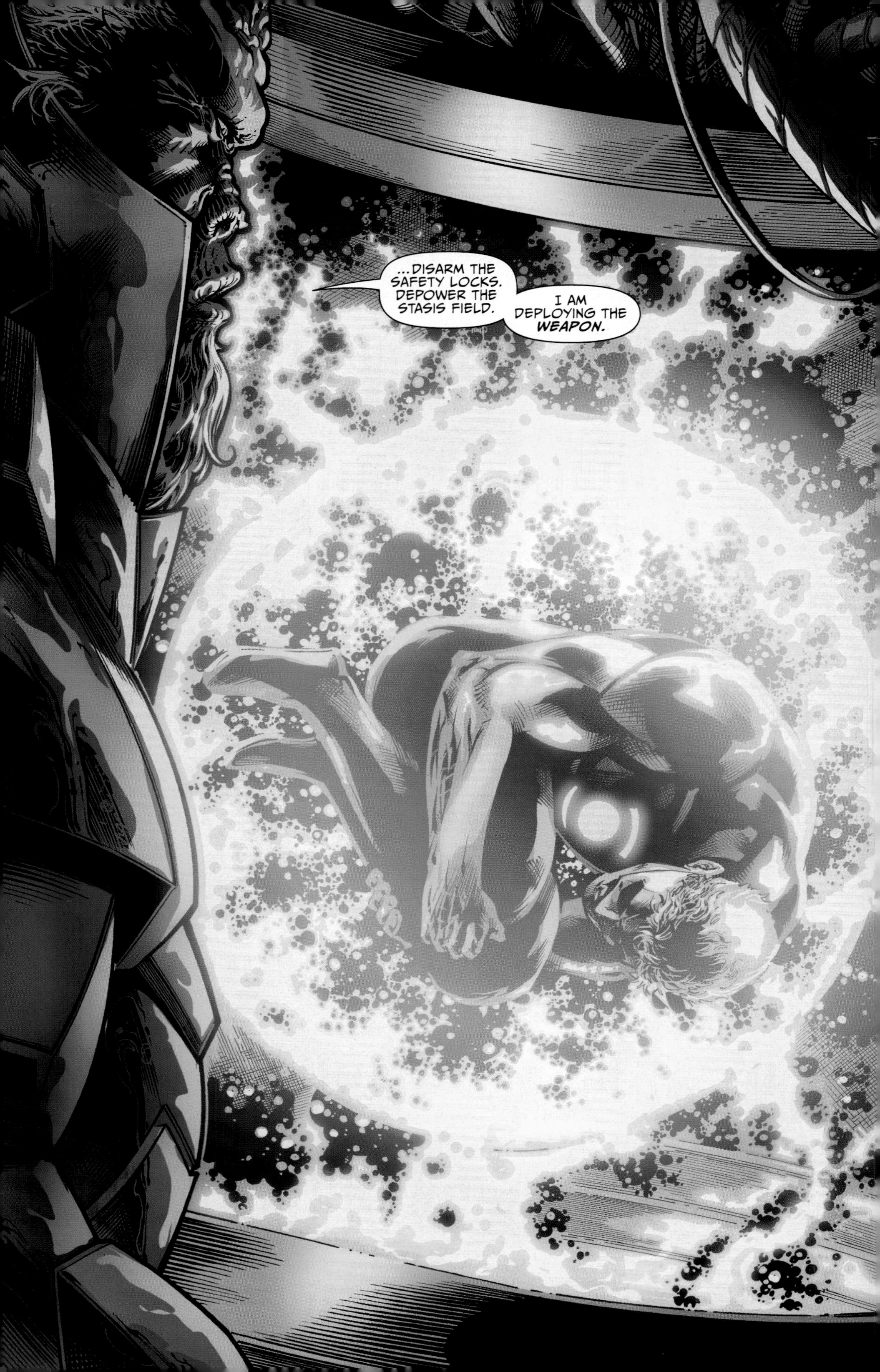
...DISARM THE SAFETY LOCKS. DEPOWER THE STASIS FIELD.
I AM DEPLOYING THE WEAPON.

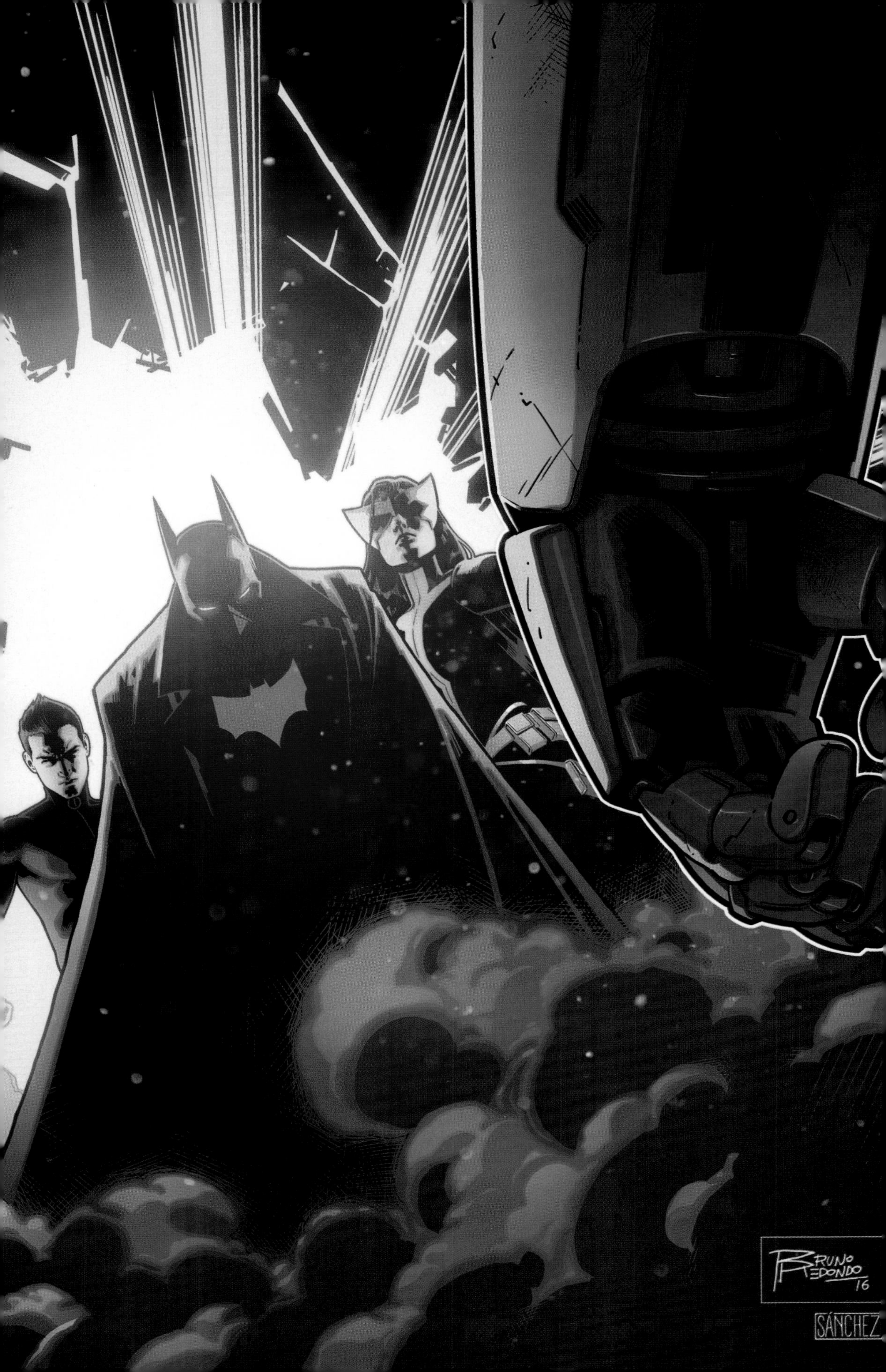

BRUNO REDONDO 16
SÁNCHEZ

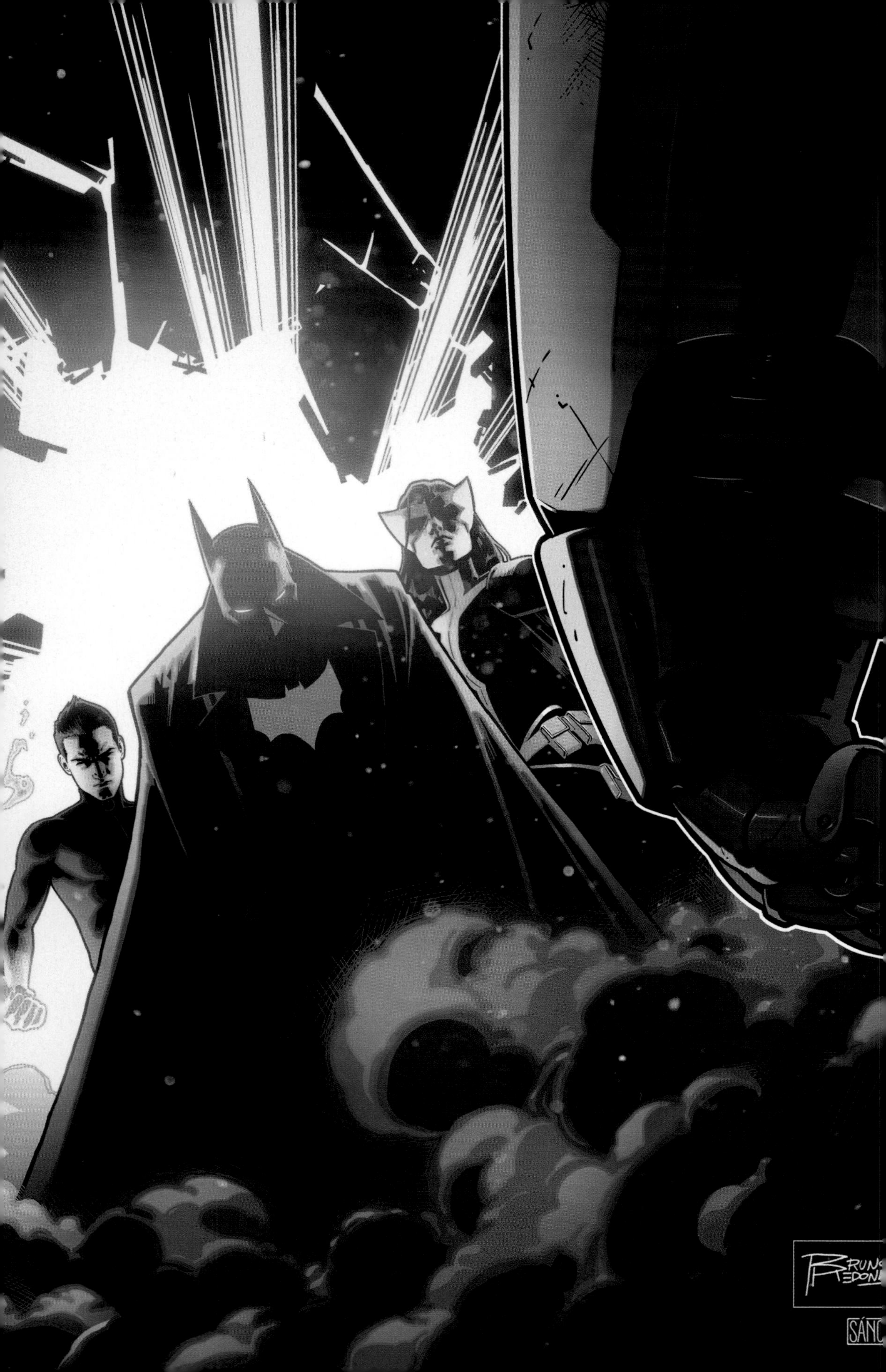

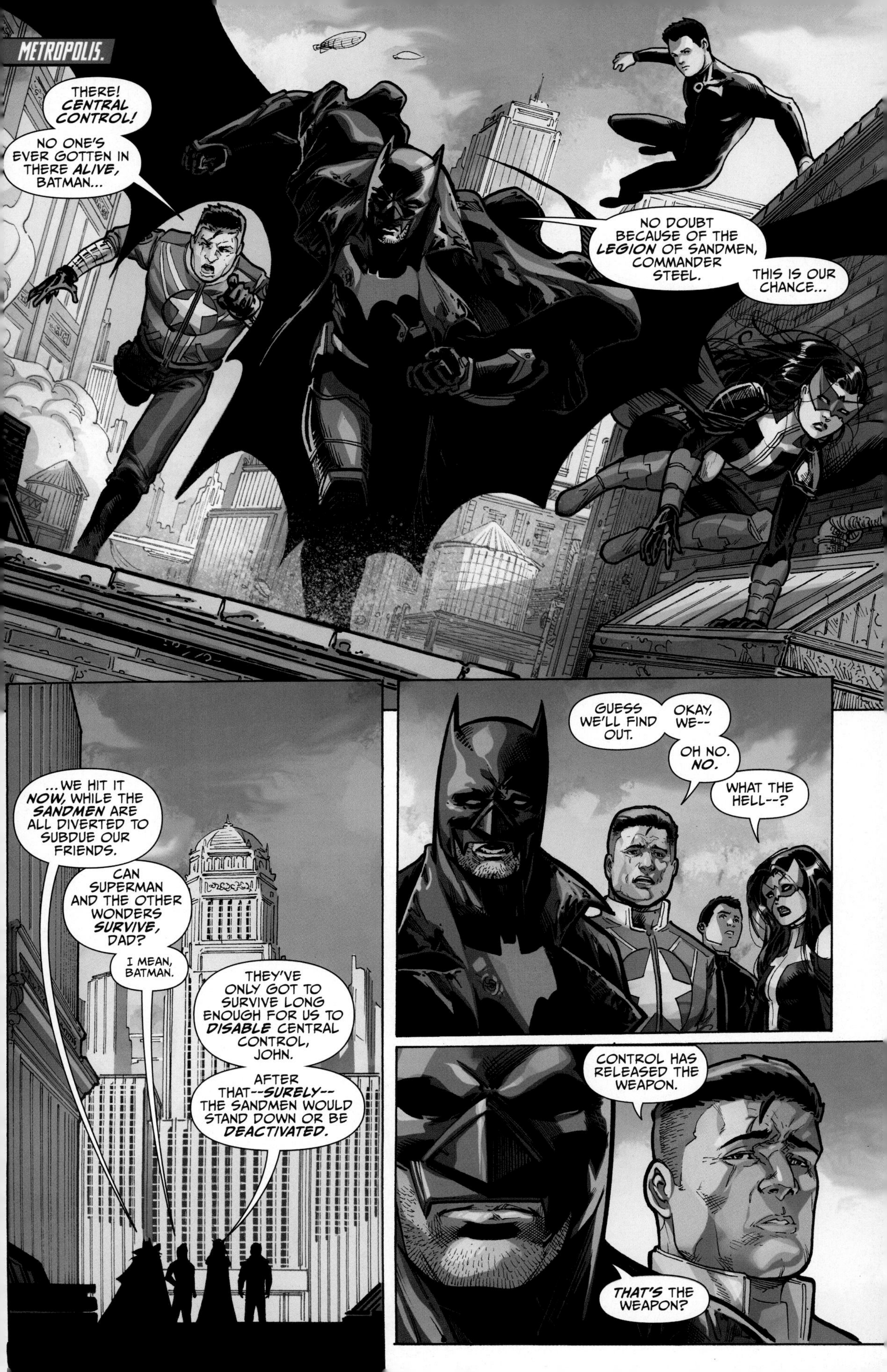
METROPOLIS.
THERE! CENTRAL CONTROL!
NO ONE'S EVER GOTTEN IN THERE ALIVE, BATMAN...
NO DOUBT BECAUSE OF THE LEGION OF SANDMEN, COMMANDER STEEL.
THIS IS OUR CHANCE...
...WE HIT IT NOW, WHILE THE SANDMEN ARE ALL DIVERTED TO SUBDUE OUR FRIENDS.
CAN SUPERMAN AND THE OTHER WONDERS SURVIVE, DAD?
I MEAN, BATMAN.
THEY'VE ONLY GOT TO SURVIVE LONG ENOUGH FOR US TO DISABLE CENTRAL CONTROL, JOHN.
AFTER THAT--SURELY--THE SANDMEN WOULD STAND DOWN OR BE DEACTIVATED.
GUESS WE'LL FIND OUT.
OKAY, WE--
OH NO. NO.
WHAT THE HELL--?
CONTROL HAS RELEASED THE WEAPON.
THAT'S THE WEAPON?

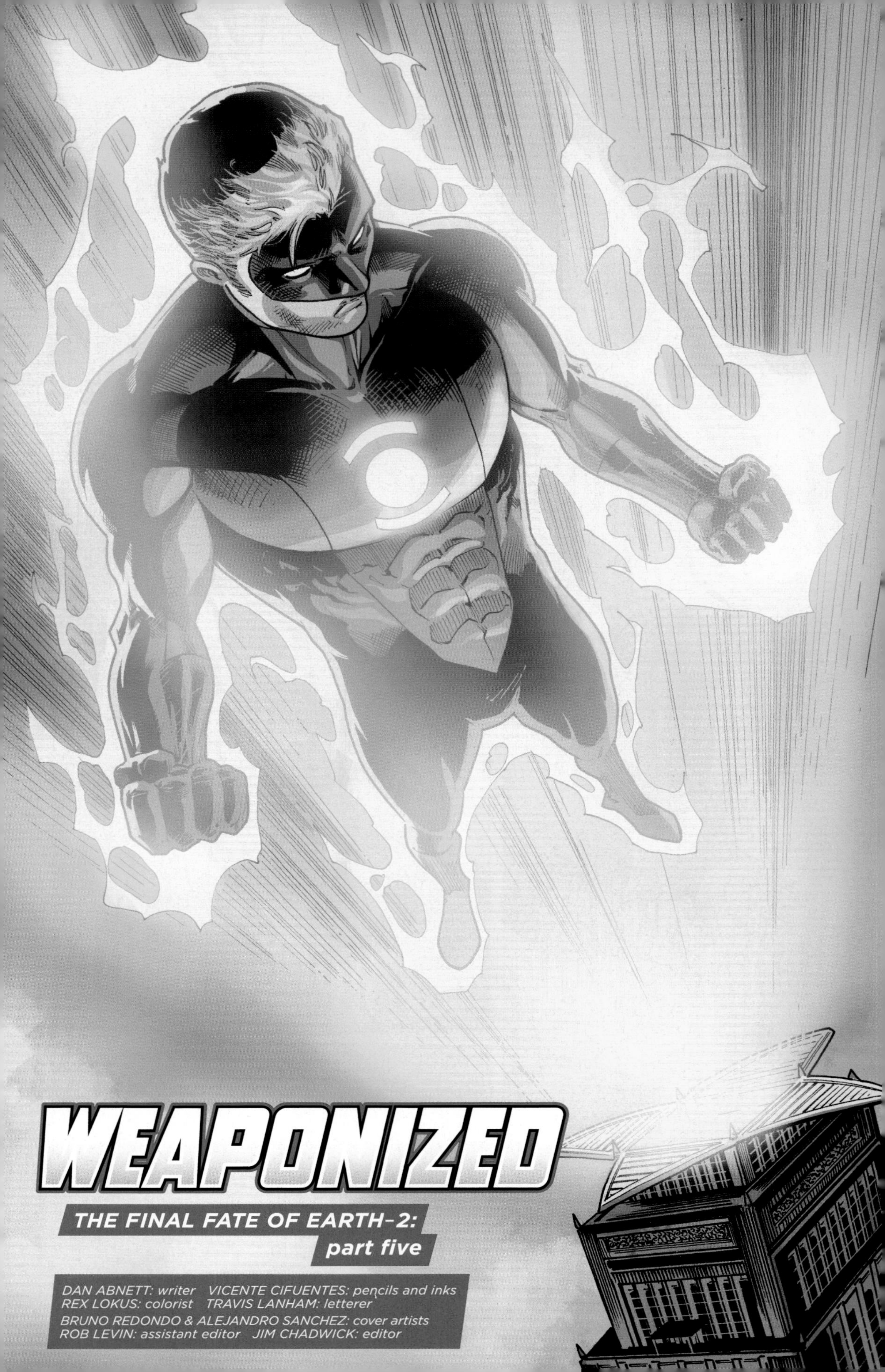
WEAPONIZED
THE FINAL FATE OF EARTH-2:
part five
DAN ABNETT: writer VICENTE CIFUENTES: pencils and inks
REX LOKUS: colorist TRAVIS LANHAM: letterer
BRUNO REDONDO & ALEJANDRO SANCHEZ: cover artists
ROB LEVIN: assistant editor JIM CHADWICK: editor

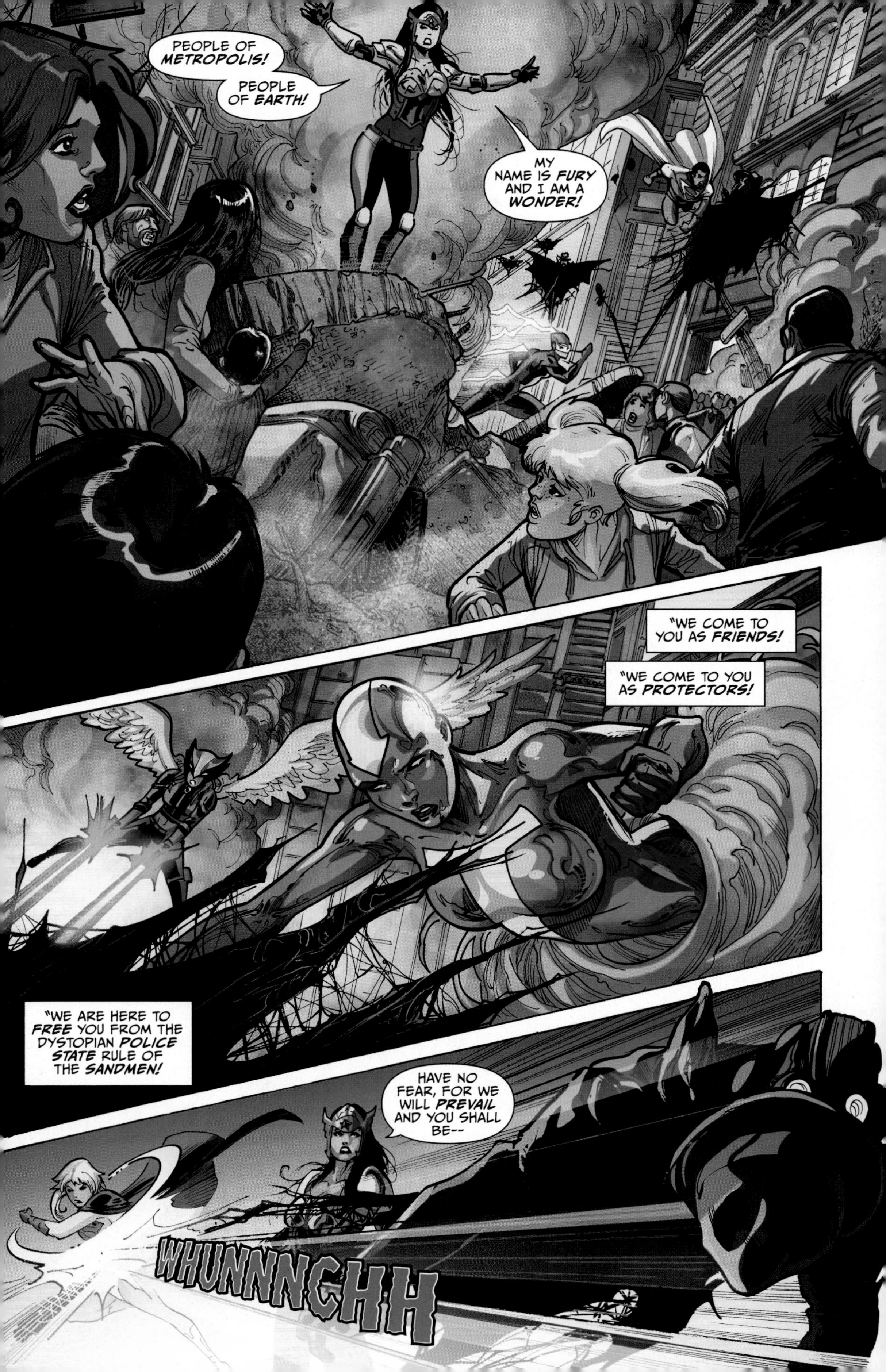
PEOPLE OF METROPOLIS!
PEOPLE OF EARTH!
MY NAME IS FURY AND I AM A WONDER!
"WE COME TO YOU AS FRIENDS!
"WE COME TO YOU AS PROTECTORS!
"WE ARE HERE TO FREE YOU FROM THE DYSTOPIAN POLICE STATE RULE OF THE SANDMEN!
HAVE NO FEAR, FOR WE WILL PREVAIL AND YOU SHALL BE--
WHUNNNNCHH

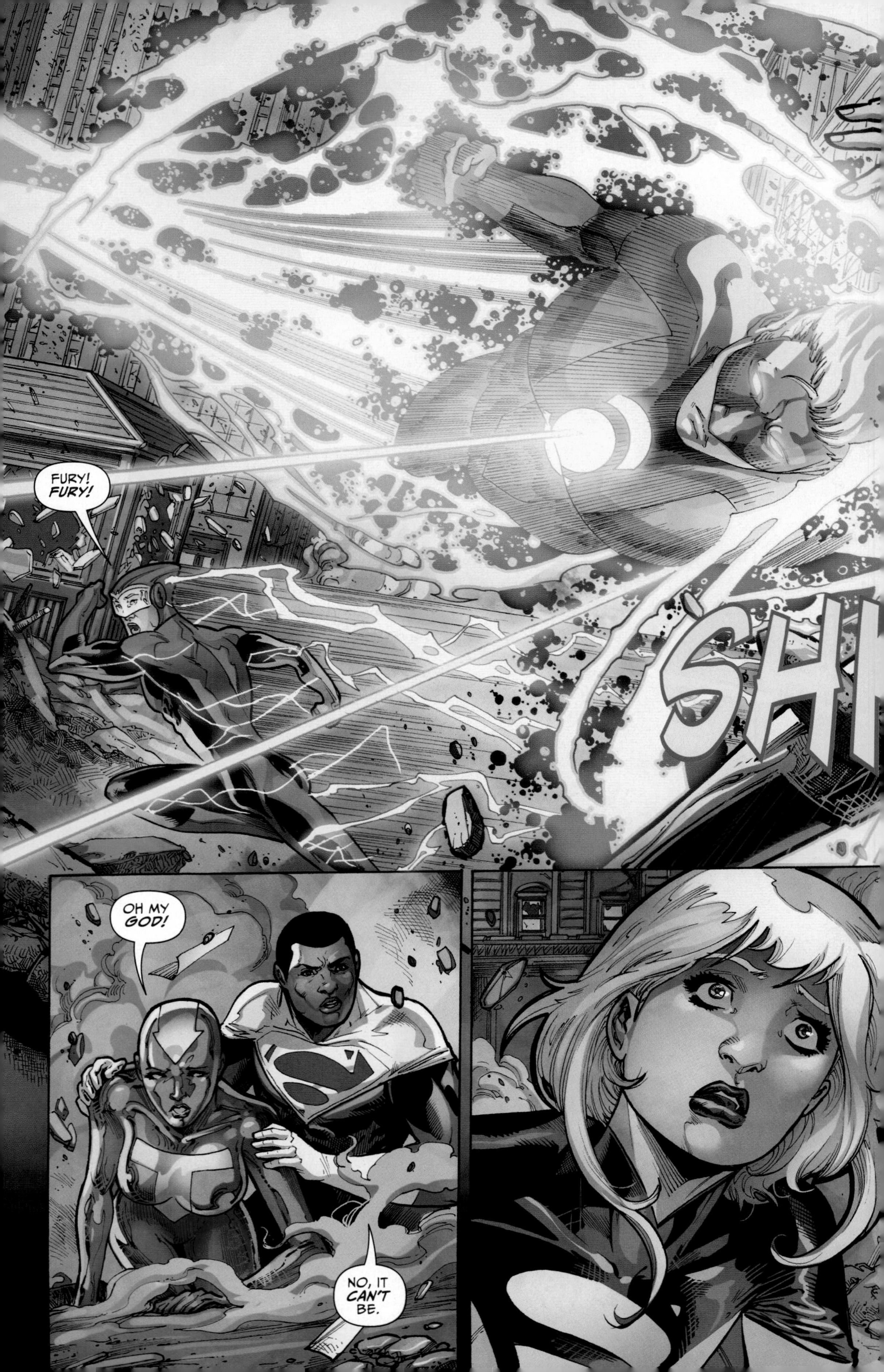
FURY! FURY!
SH
OH MY GOD!
NO, IT CAN'T BE.

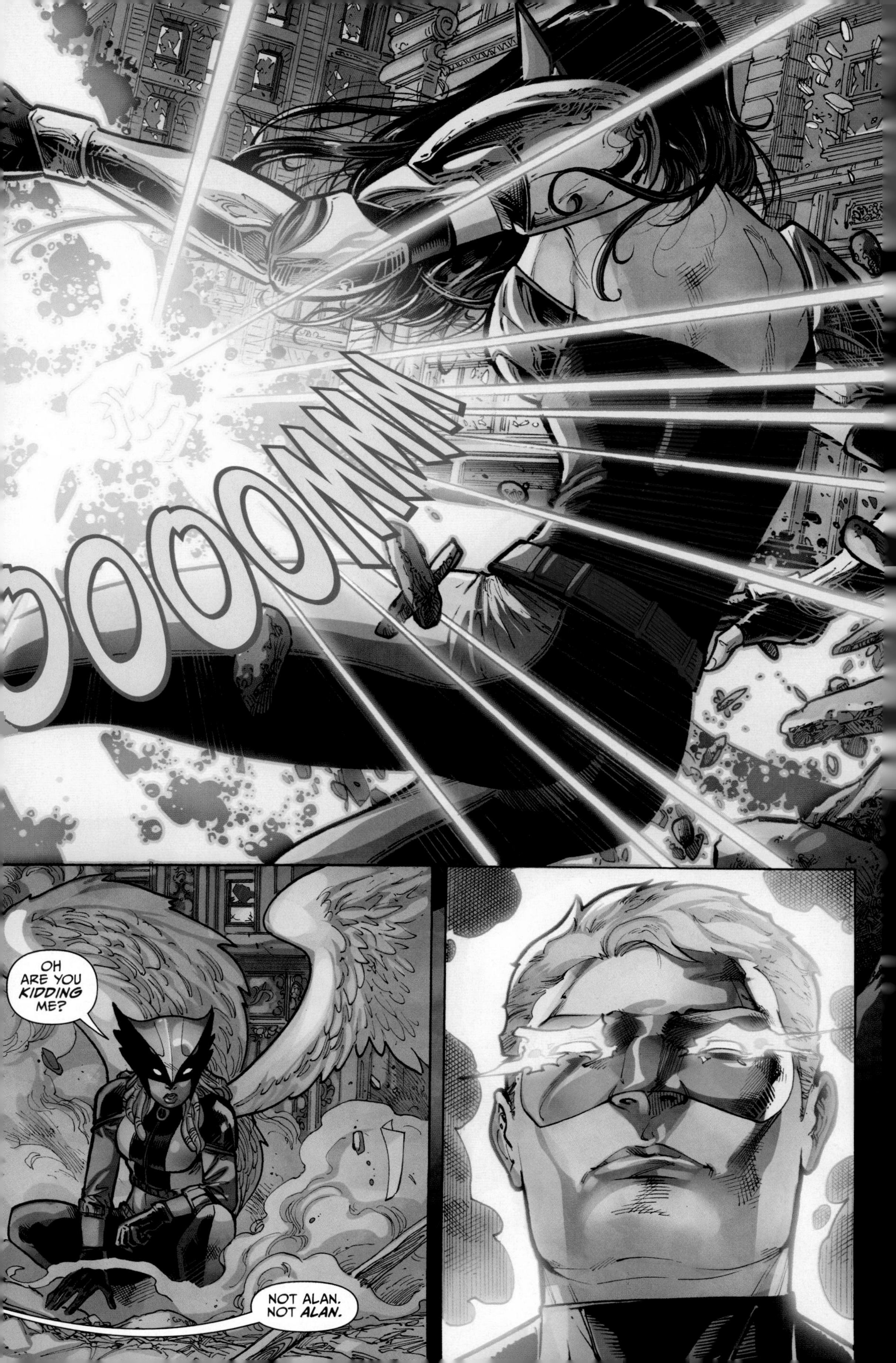
OOOOWM
OH ARE YOU KIDDING ME?
NOT ALAN. NOT ALAN.

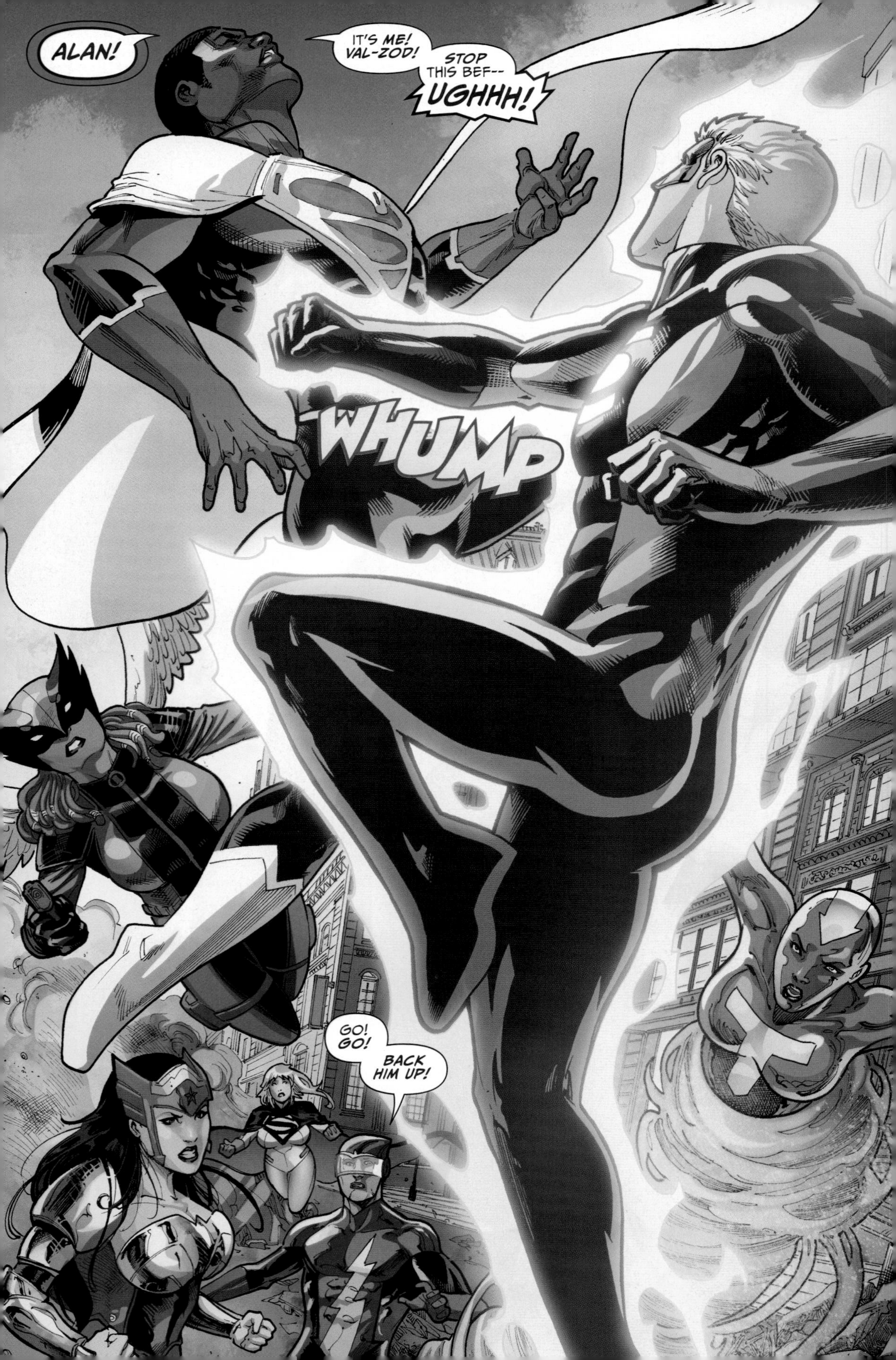
ALAN!
IT'S ME! VAL-ZOD!
STOP THIS BEF--
UGHHH!
WHUMP
GO! GO!
BACK HIM UP!

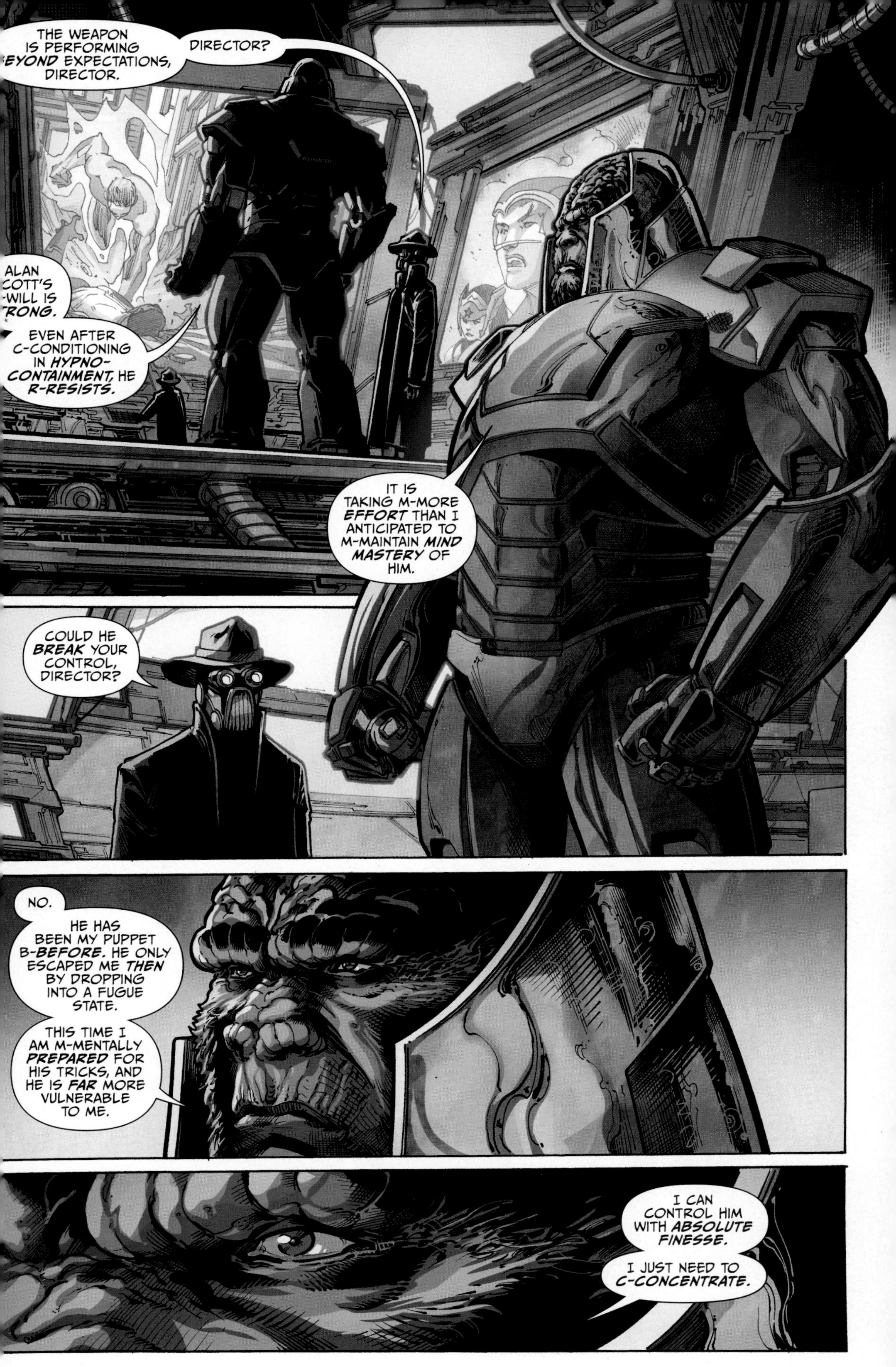

THE WEAPON IS PERFORMING *EYOND* EXPECTATIONS, DIRECTOR.
DIRECTOR?
ALAN COTT'S -WILL IS *TRONG.*
EVEN AFTER C-CONDITIONING IN *HYPNO-CONTAINMENT,* HE *R-RESISTS.*
IT IS TAKING M-MORE *EFFORT* THAN I ANTICIPATED TO M-MAINTAIN *MIND MASTERY* OF HIM.
COULD HE *BREAK* YOUR CONTROL, DIRECTOR?
NO.
HE HAS BEEN MY PUPPET B-*BEFORE.* HE ONLY ESCAPED ME *THEN* BY DROPPING INTO A FUGUE STATE.
THIS TIME I AM M-MENTALLY *PREPARED* FOR HIS TRICKS, AND HE IS *FAR* MORE VULNERABLE TO ME.
I CAN CONTROL HIM WITH *ABSOLUTE FINESSE.*
I JUST NEED TO *C-CONCENTRATE.*

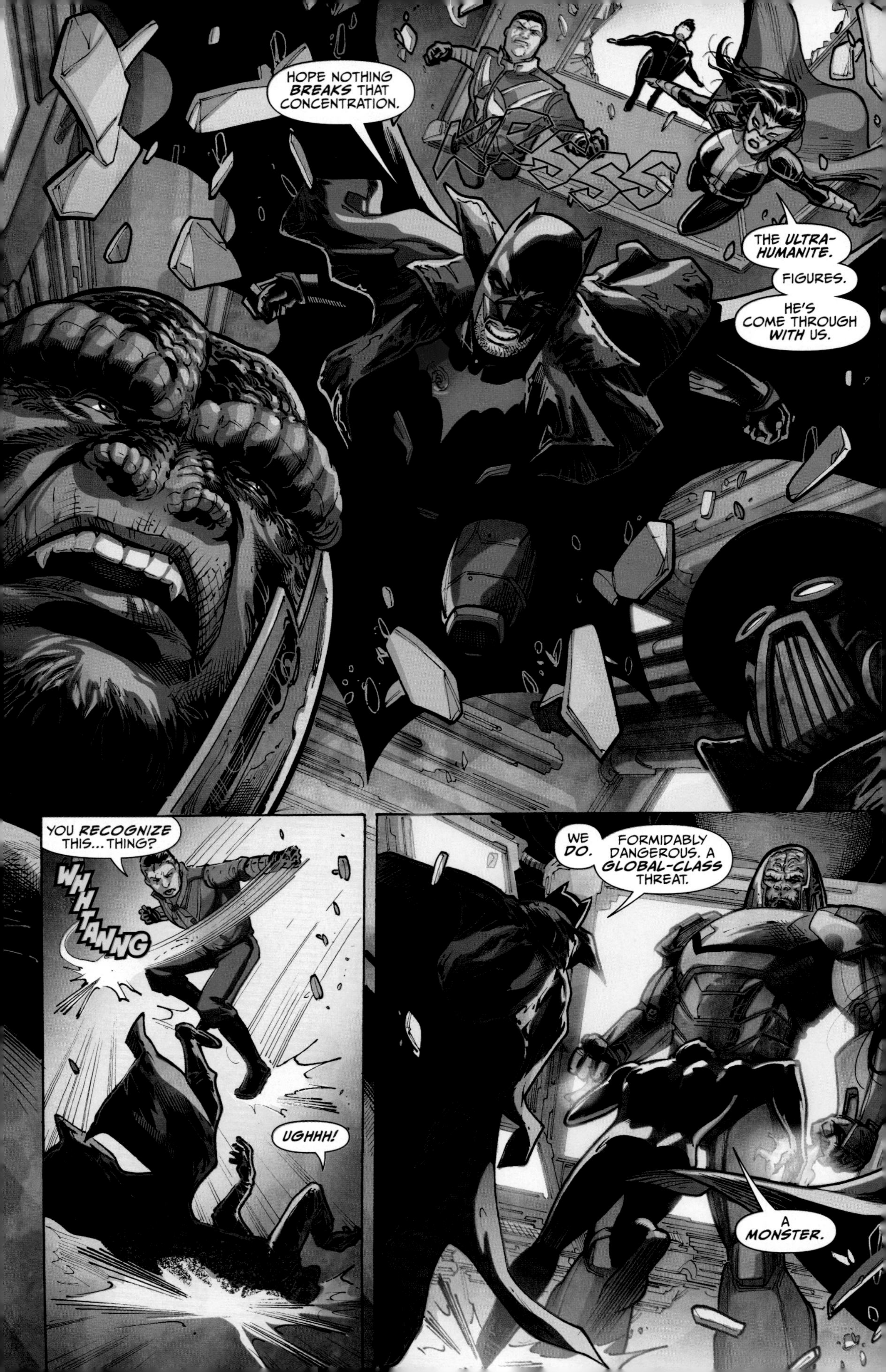
HOPE NOTHING BREAKS THAT CONCENTRATION.
THE ULTRA-HUMANITE.
FIGURES.
HE'S COME THROUGH WITH US.
YOU RECOGNIZE THIS... THING?
WHHTANNG
UGHHH!
WE DO.
FORMIDABLY DANGEROUS. A GLOBAL-CLASS THREAT.
A MONSTER.

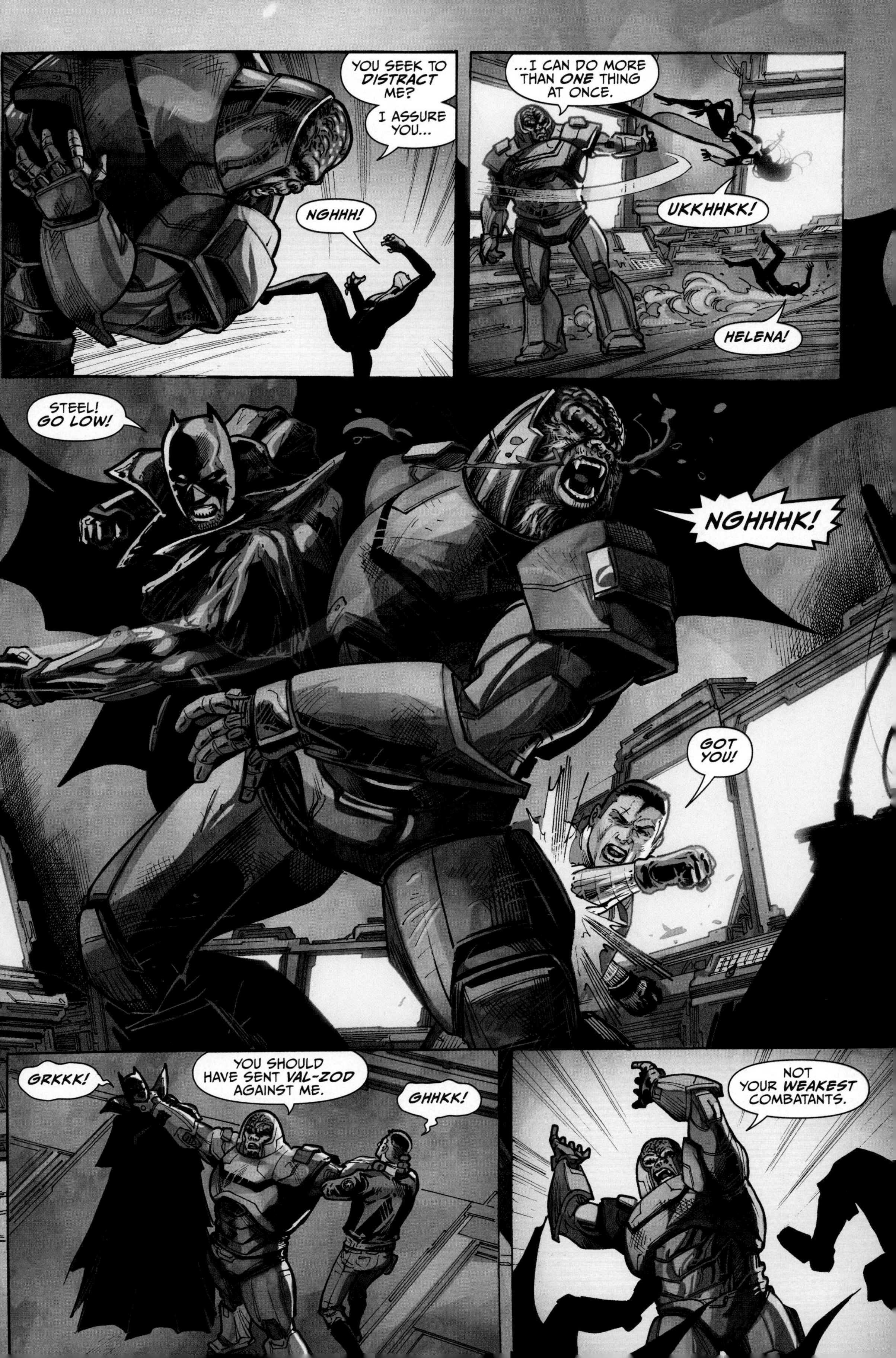
YOU SEEK TO DISTRACT ME?
I ASSURE YOU...
NGHHH!
...I CAN DO MORE THAN ONE THING AT ONCE.
UKKHHKK!
HELENA!
STEEL! GO LOW!
NGHHHK!
GOT YOU!
GRKKK!
YOU SHOULD HAVE SENT VAL-ZOD AGAINST ME.
GHHKK!
NOT YOUR WEAKEST COMBATANTS.

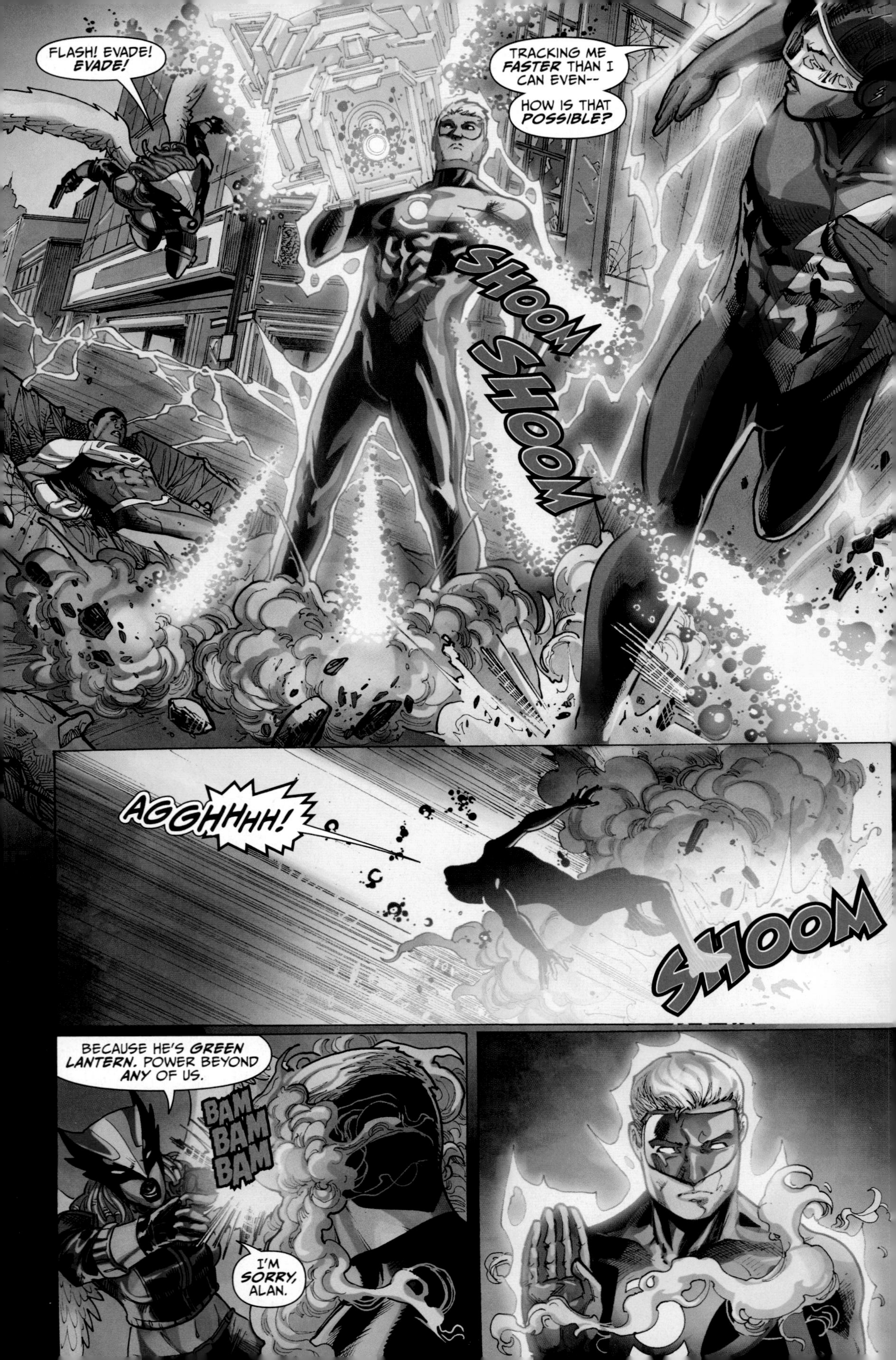
FLASH! EVADE! EVADE!
TRACKING ME FASTER THAN I CAN EVEN--
HOW IS THAT POSSIBLE?
SHOOM SHOOM SHOOM
AGGHHHH!
SHOOM
BECAUSE HE'S GREEN LANTERN. POWER BEYOND ANY OF US.
BAM BAM BAM
I'M SORRY, ALAN.

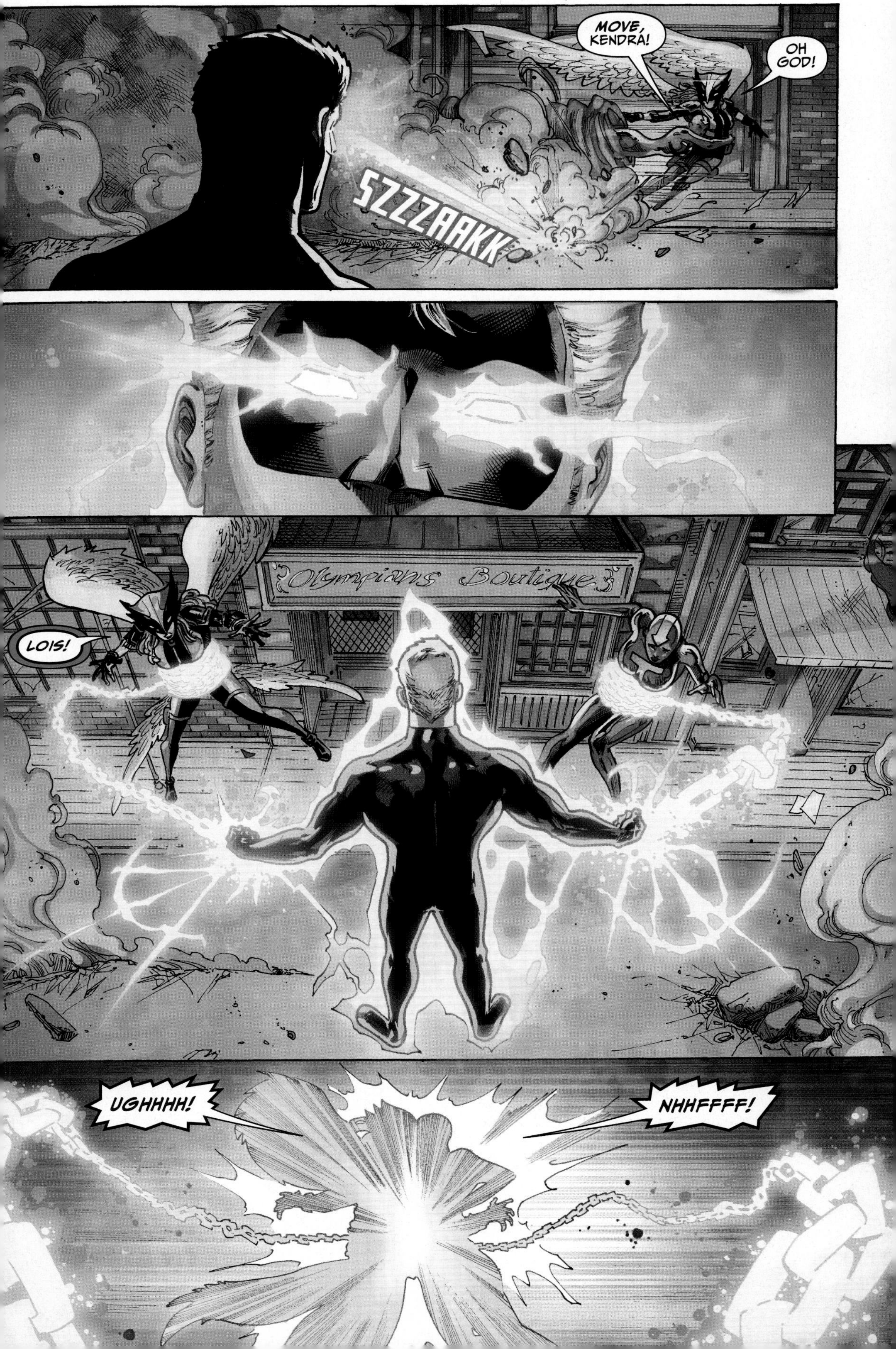
MOVE, KENDRA!
OH GOD!
SZZZAAKK
Olympians Boutique
LOIS!
UGHHHH!
NHHFFFF!

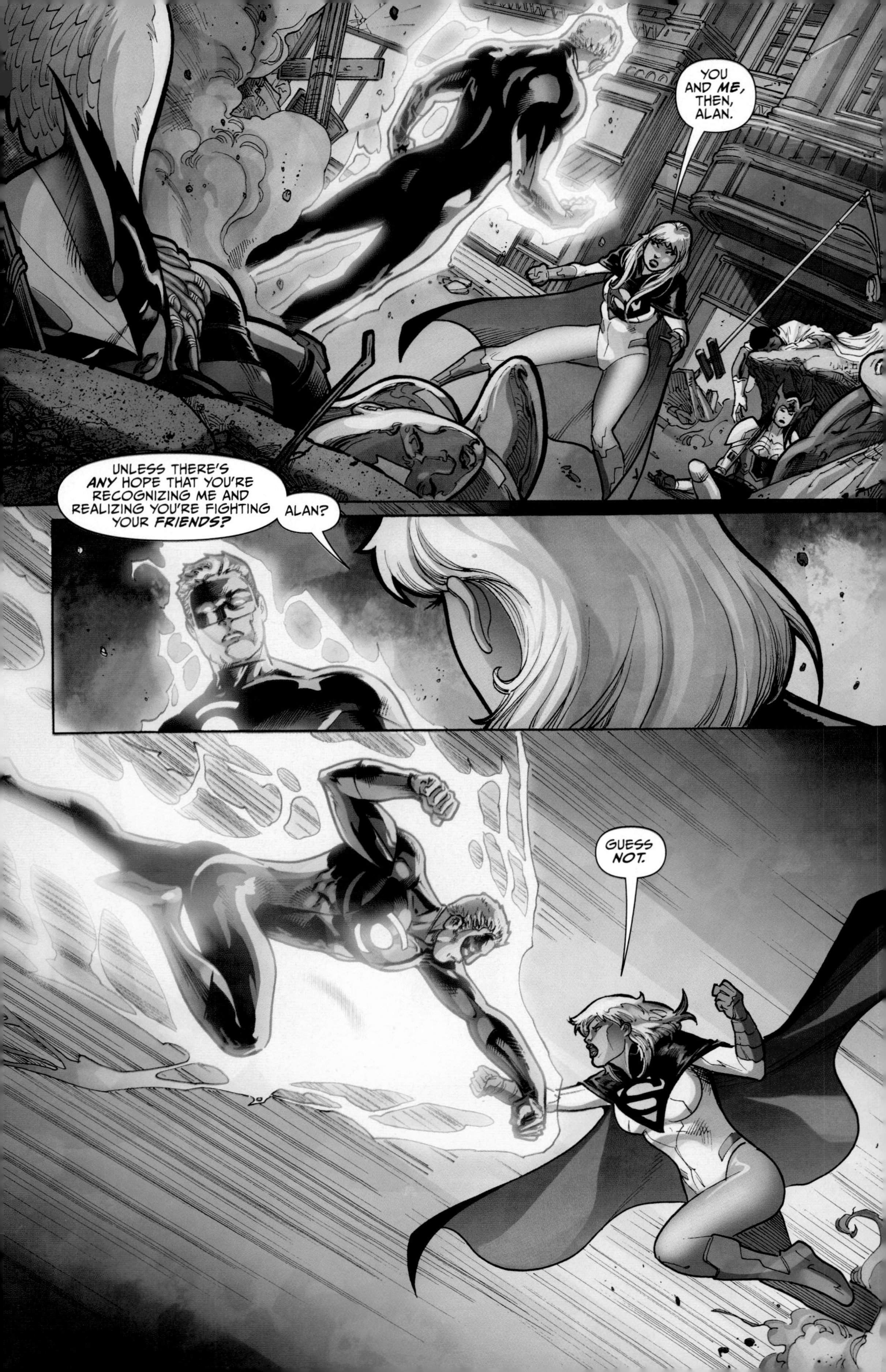
YOU AND ME, THEN, ALAN.
UNLESS THERE'S ANY HOPE THAT YOU'RE RECOGNIZING ME AND REALIZING YOU'RE FIGHTING YOUR FRIENDS?
ALAN?
GUESS NOT.

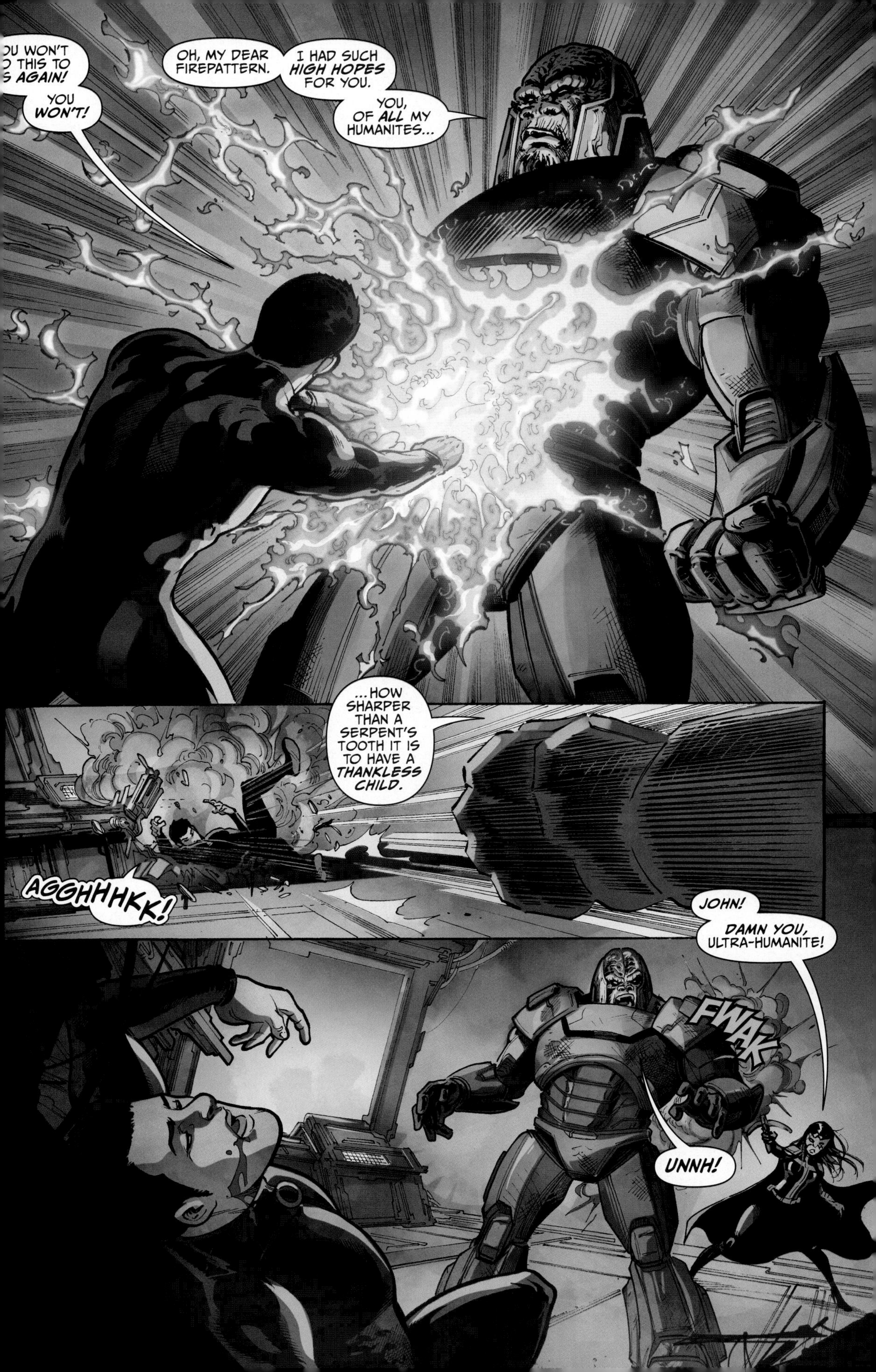

OU WON'T
O THIS TO
S AGAIN!
YOU
WON'T!
OH, MY DEAR FIREPATTERN.
I HAD SUCH HIGH HOPES FOR YOU.
YOU, OF ALL MY HUMANITES...
...HOW SHARPER THAN A SERPENT'S TOOTH IT IS TO HAVE A THANKLESS CHILD.
AGGHHHKK!
JOHN!
DAMN YOU, ULTRA-HUMANITE!
FWAK
UNNH!

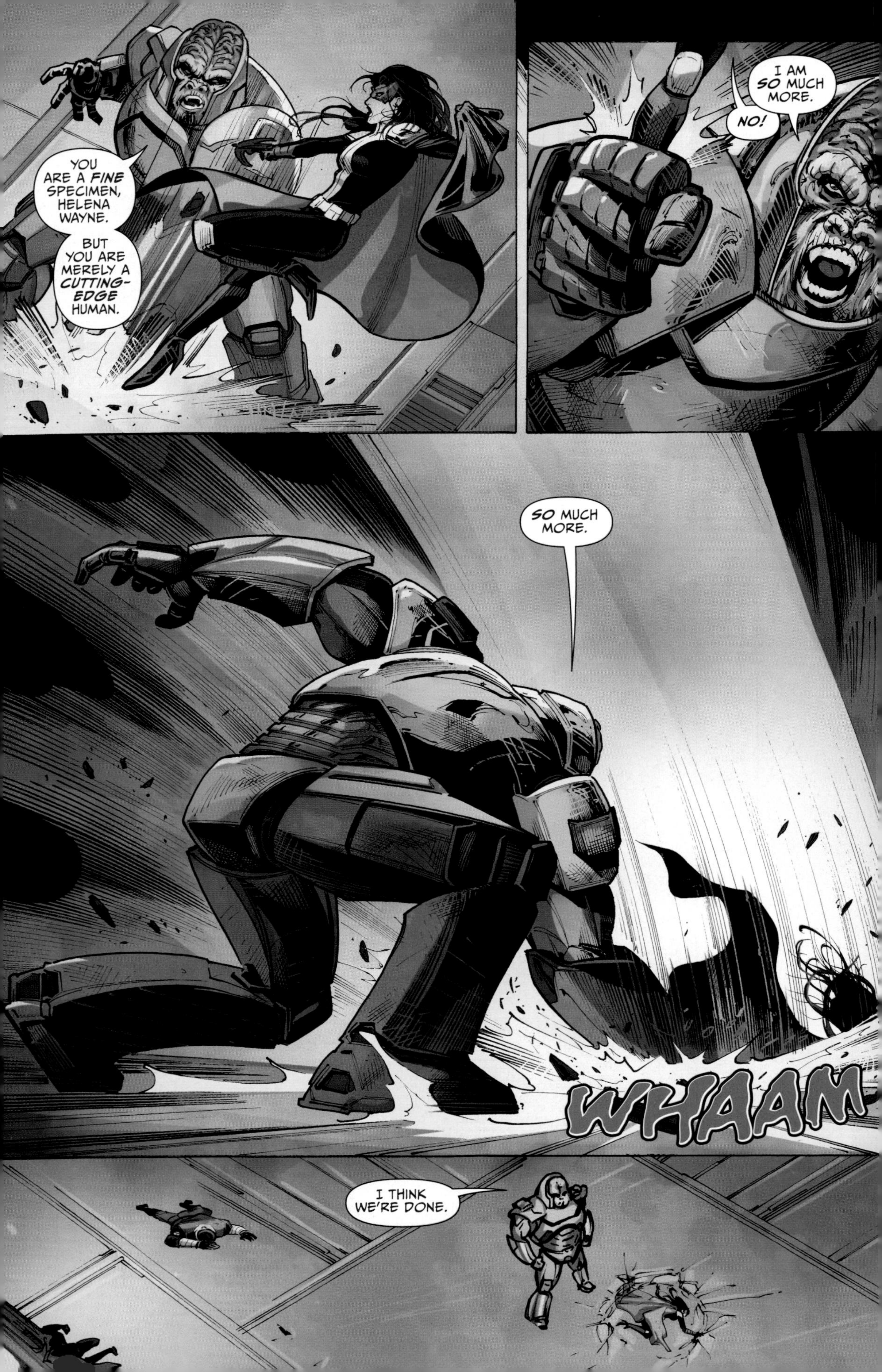
YOU ARE A *FINE* SPECIMEN, HELENA WAYNE.
BUT YOU ARE MERELY A *CUTTING-EDGE* HUMAN.
I AM *SO* MUCH MORE.
NO!
SO MUCH MORE.
WHAAM
I THINK WE'RE DONE.

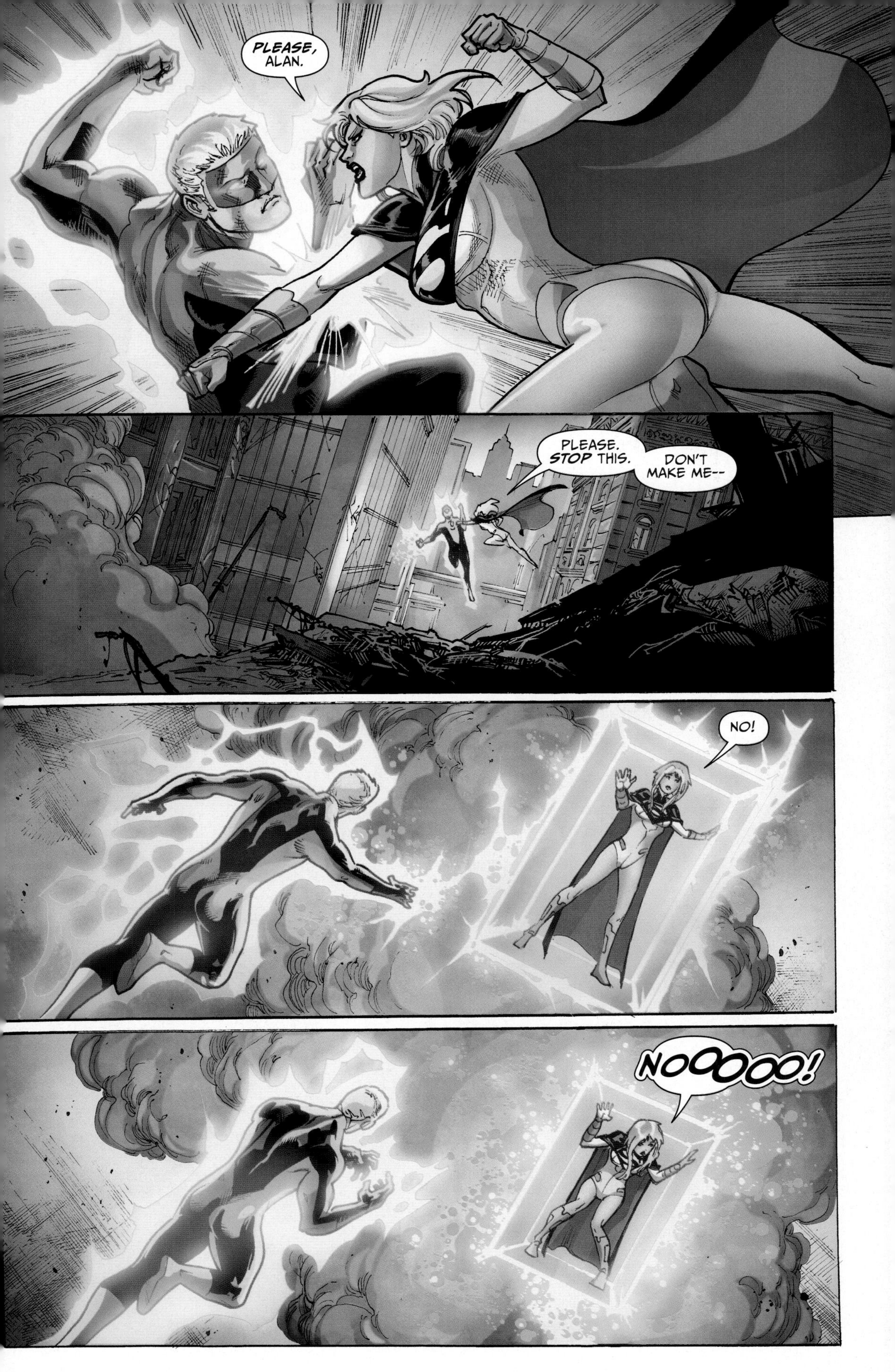
PLEASE, ALAN.
PLEASE. STOP THIS.
DON'T MAKE ME--
NO!
NOOOOO!

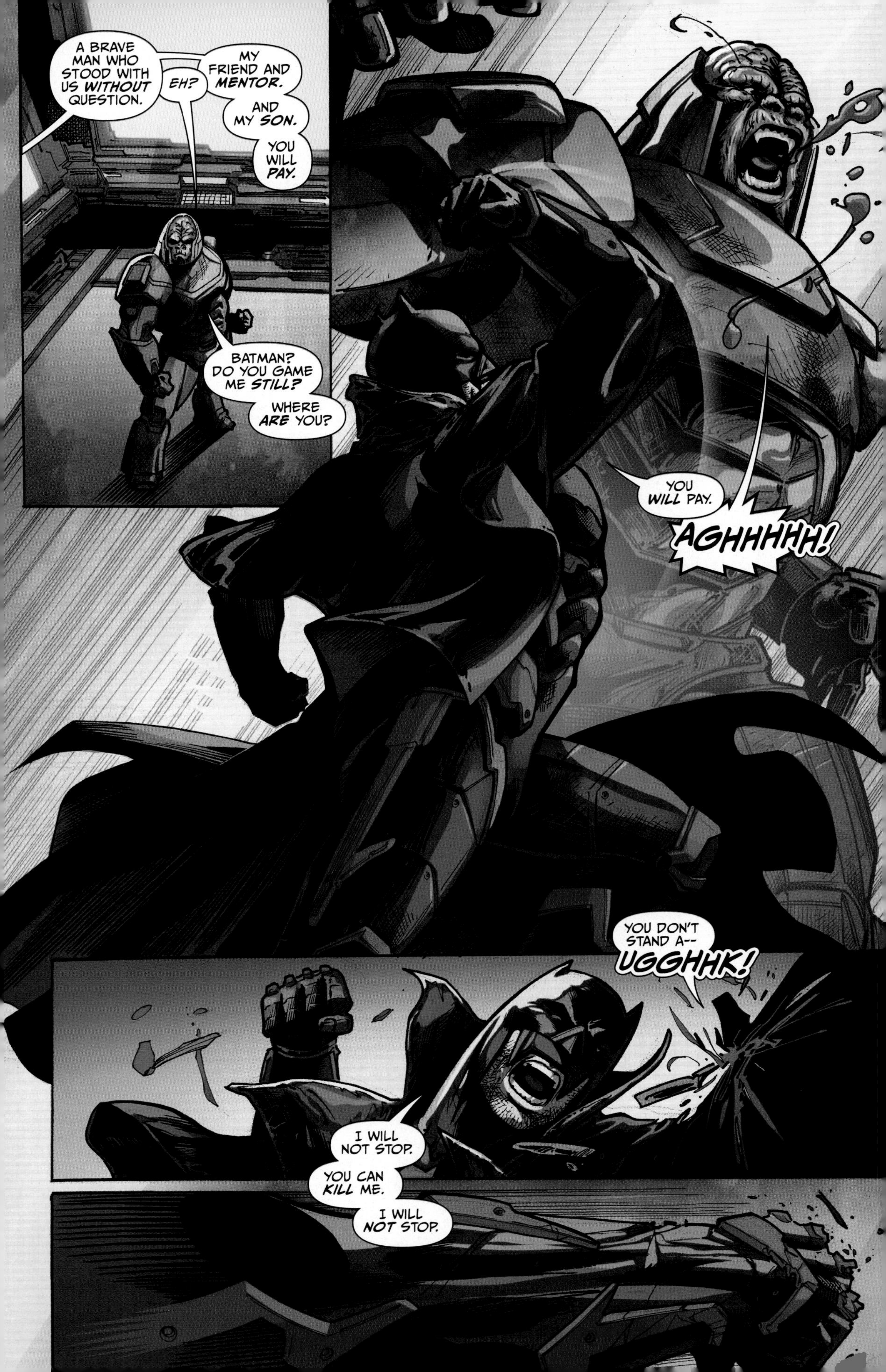
A BRAVE MAN WHO STOOD WITH US WITHOUT QUESTION.
EH?
MY FRIEND AND MENTOR.
AND MY SON.
YOU WILL PAY.
BATMAN? DO YOU GAME ME STILL?
WHERE ARE YOU?
YOU WILL PAY.
AGHHHHH!
YOU DON'T STAND A--
UGGHHK!
I WILL NOT STOP.
YOU CAN KILL ME.
I WILL NOT STOP.

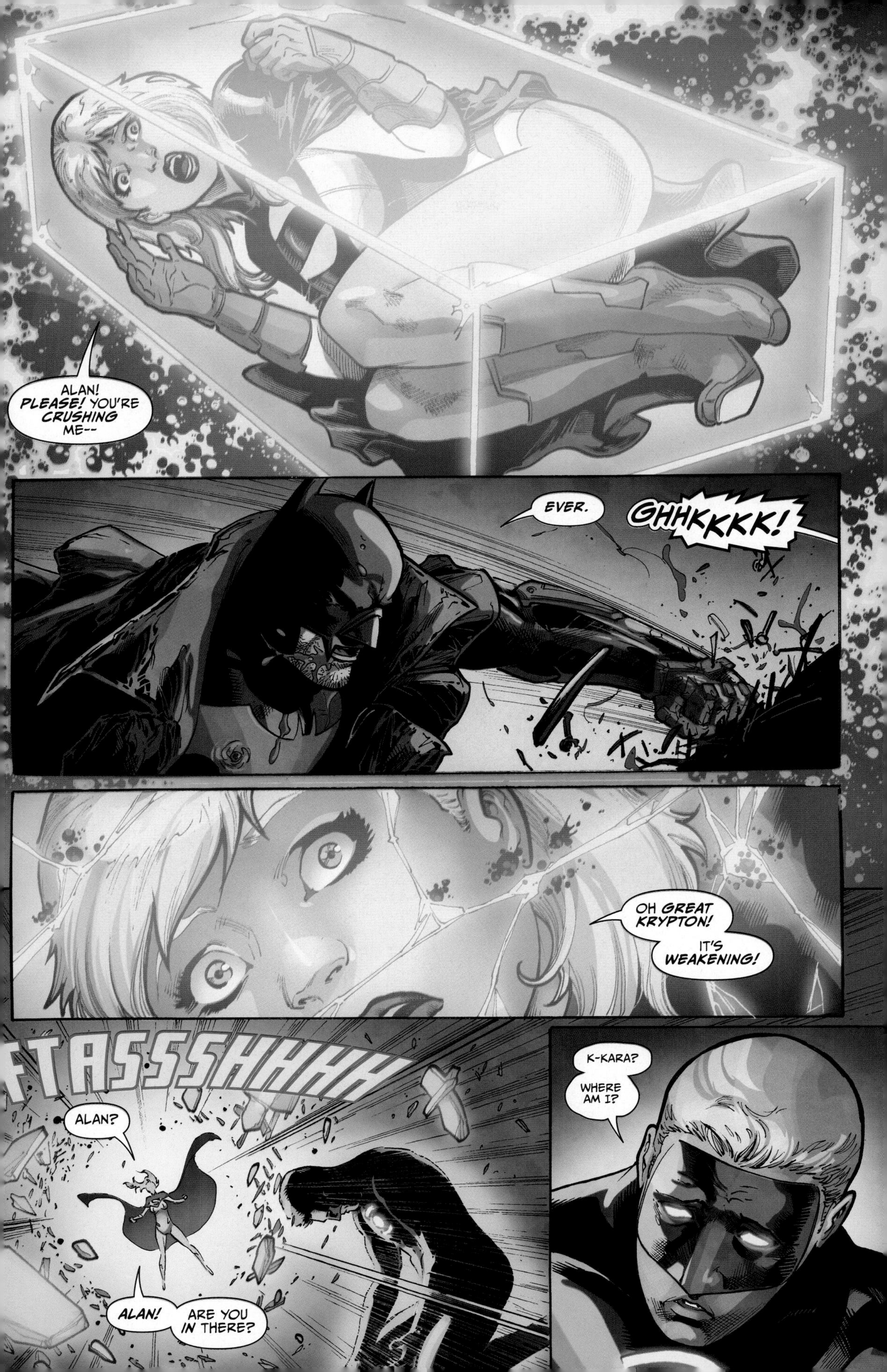
ALAN! PLEASE! YOU'RE CRUSHING ME--
EVER.
GHHKKKK!
OH GREAT KRYPTON!
IT'S WEAKENING!
FTASSSHHHH
ALAN?
ALAN!
ARE YOU IN THERE?
K-KARA?
WHERE AM I?

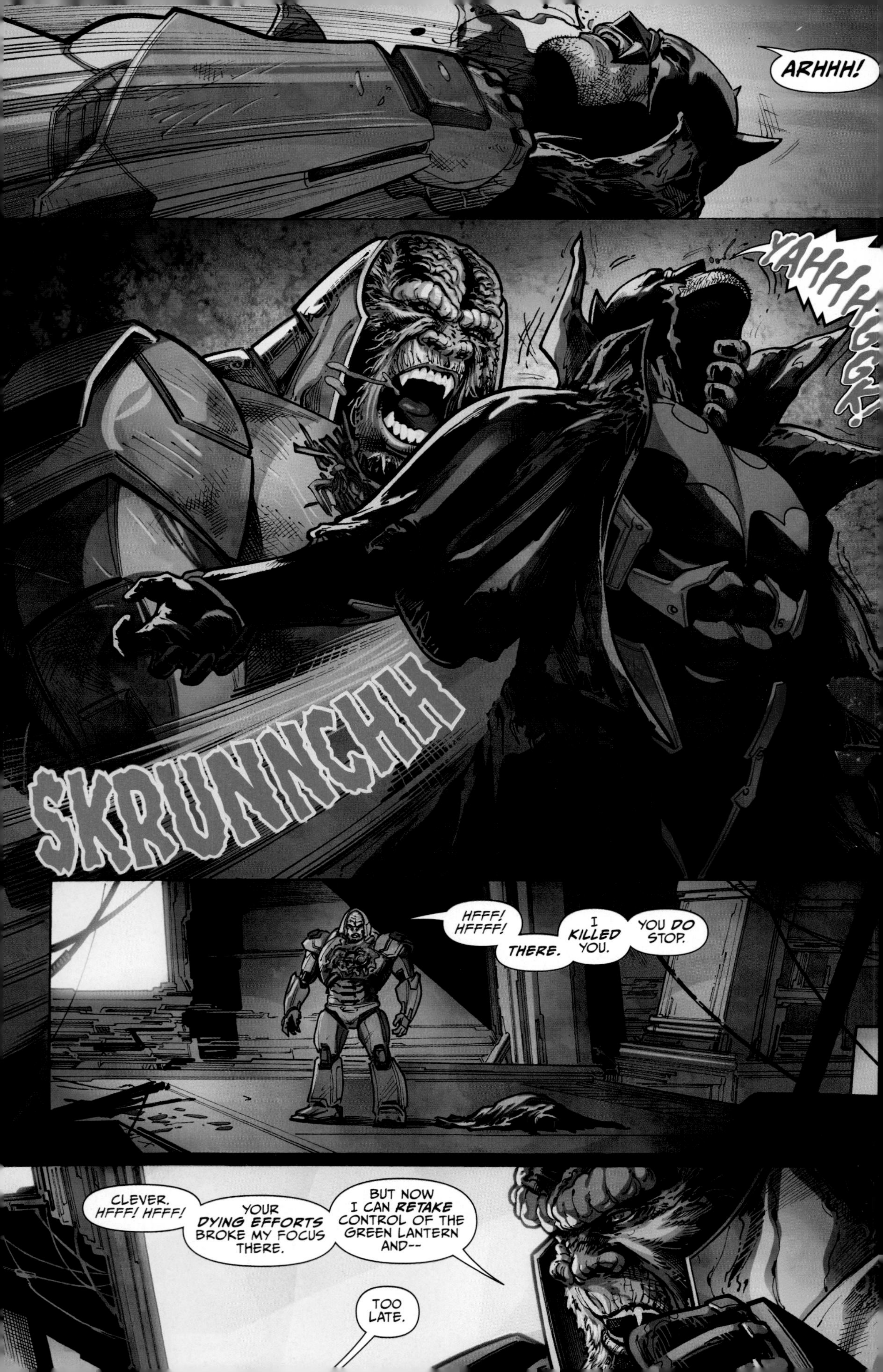
ARHHH!
YAHHHGGK!
SKRUNNCHH
HFFF! HFFFF!
THERE.
I KILLED YOU.
YOU DO STOP.
CLEVER. HFFF! HFFF!
YOUR DYING EFFORTS BROKE MY FOCUS THERE.
BUT NOW I CAN RETAKE CONTROL OF THE GREEN LANTERN AND--
TOO LATE.

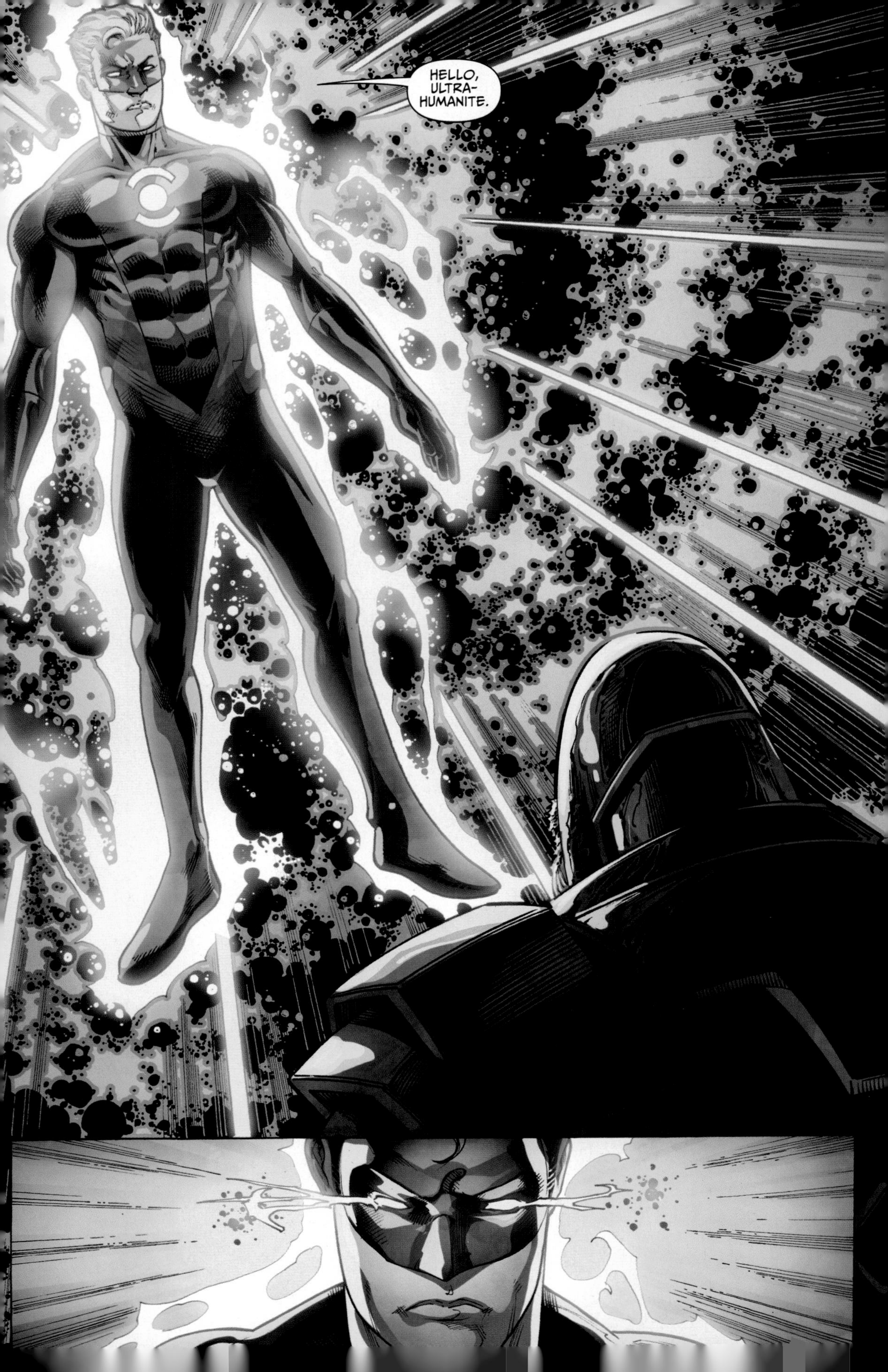
HELLO, ULTRA-HUMANITE.

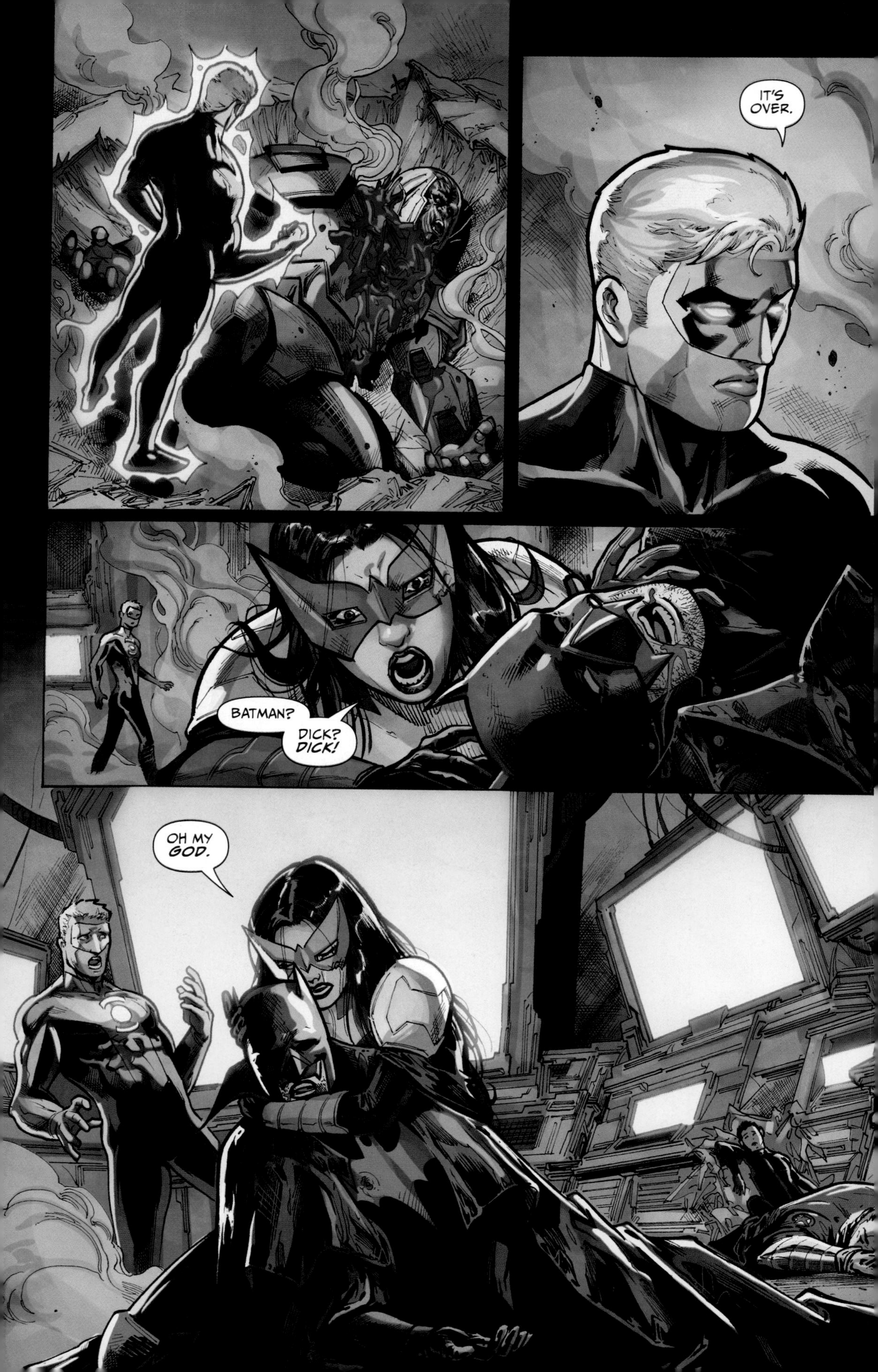
IT'S OVER.
BATMAN?
DICK? DICK!
OH MY GOD.

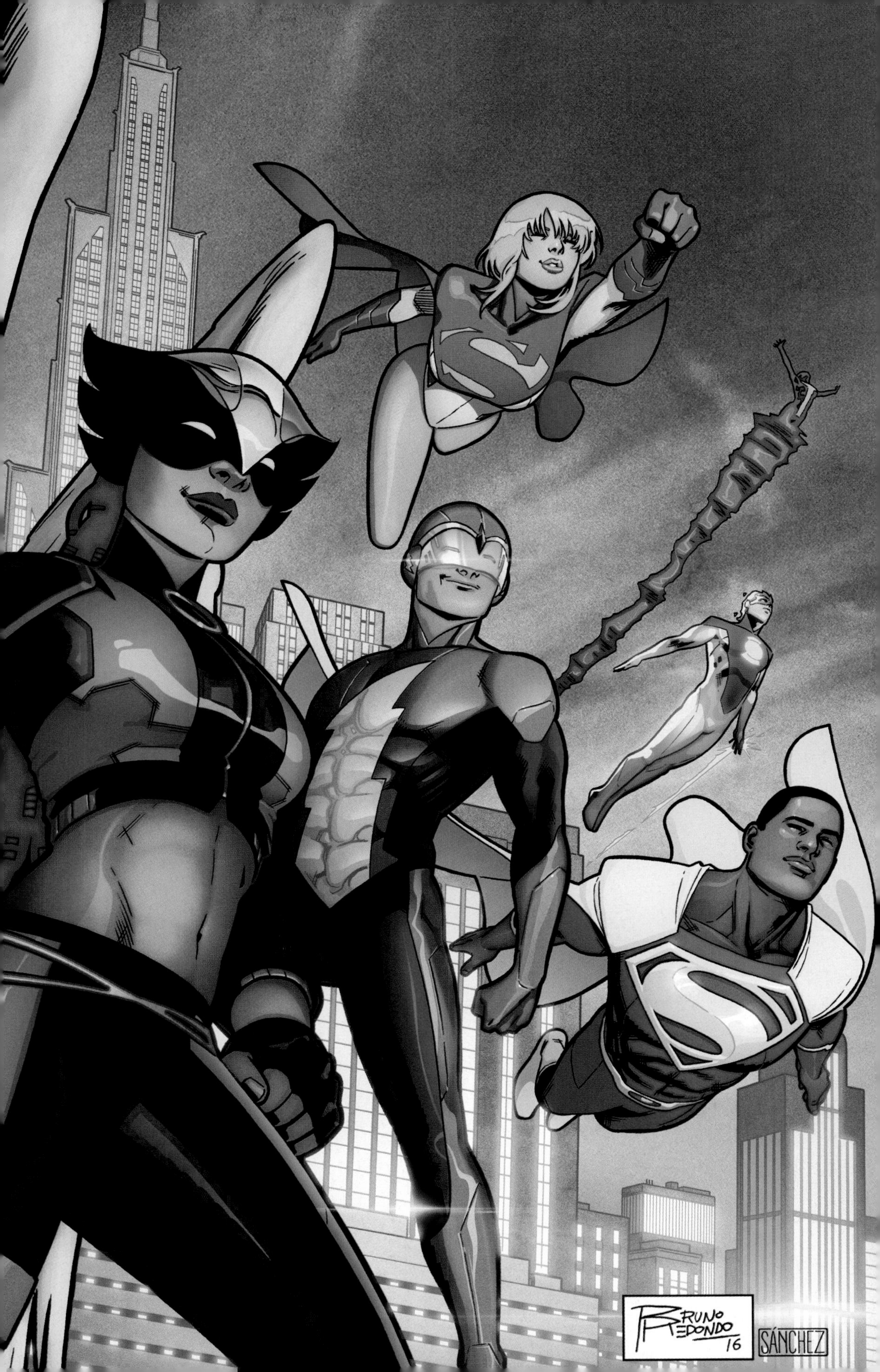
BRUNO REDONDO 16
SÁNCHEZ

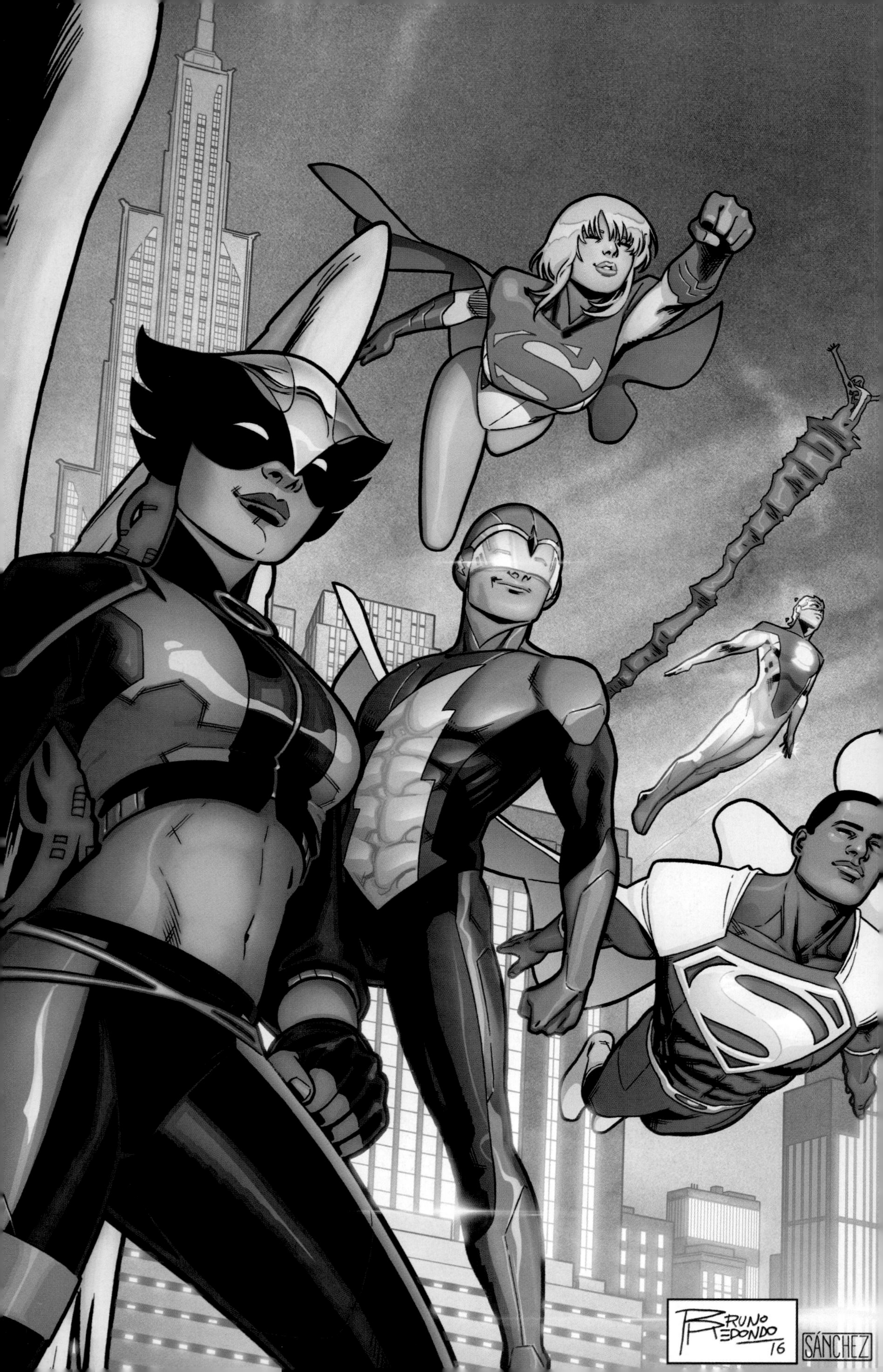
BRUNO REDONDO '16
SÁNCHEZ

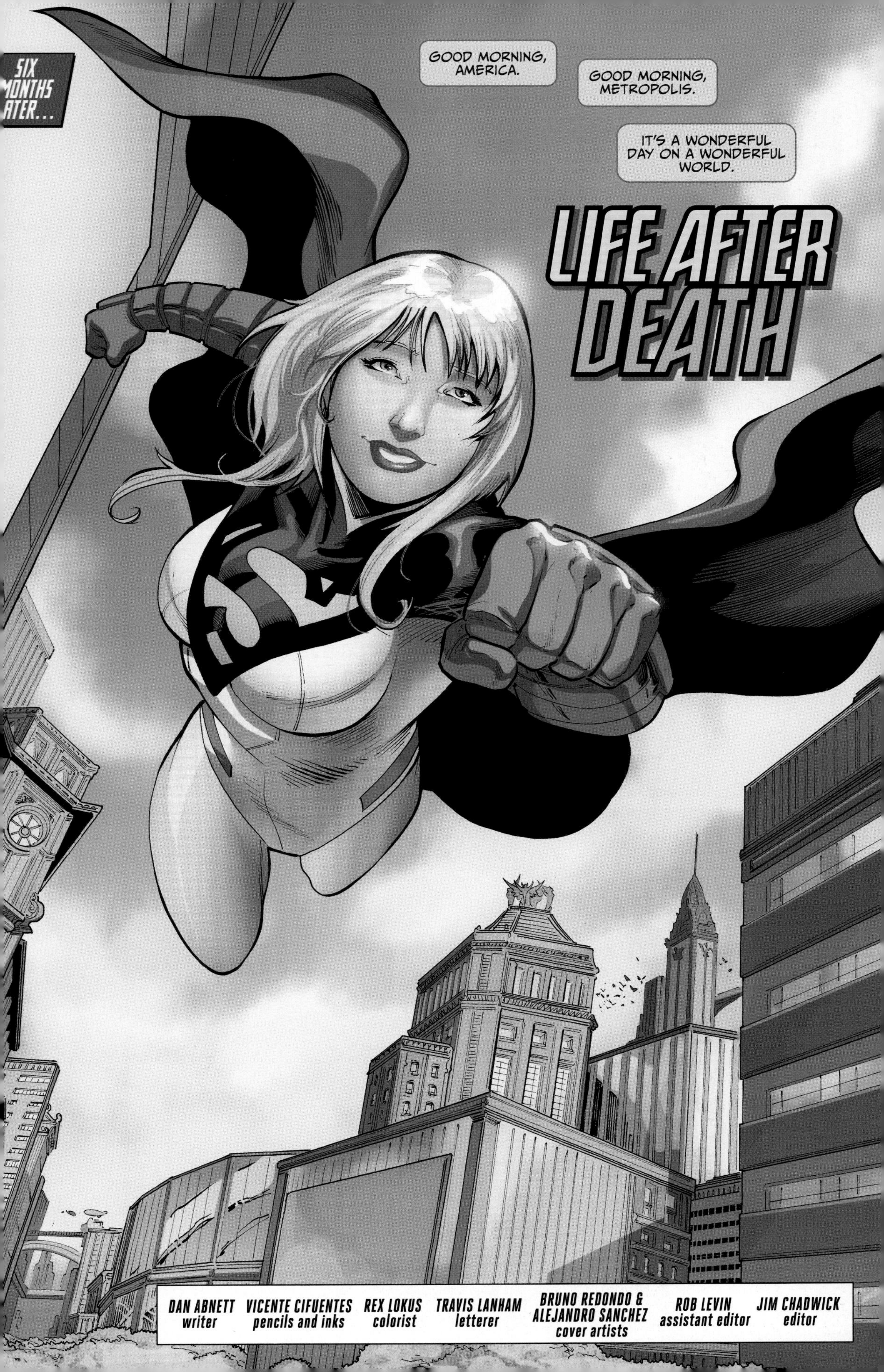
SIX MONTHS LATER...
GOOD MORNING, AMERICA.
GOOD MORNING, METROPOLIS.
IT'S A WONDERFUL DAY ON A WONDERFUL WORLD.
LIFE AFTER DEATH
DAN ABNETT writer
VICENTE CIFUENTES pencils and inks
REX LOKUS colorist
TRAVIS LANHAM letterer
BRUNO REDONDO & ALEJANDRO SANCHEZ cover artists
ROB LEVIN assistant editor
JIM CHADWICK editor

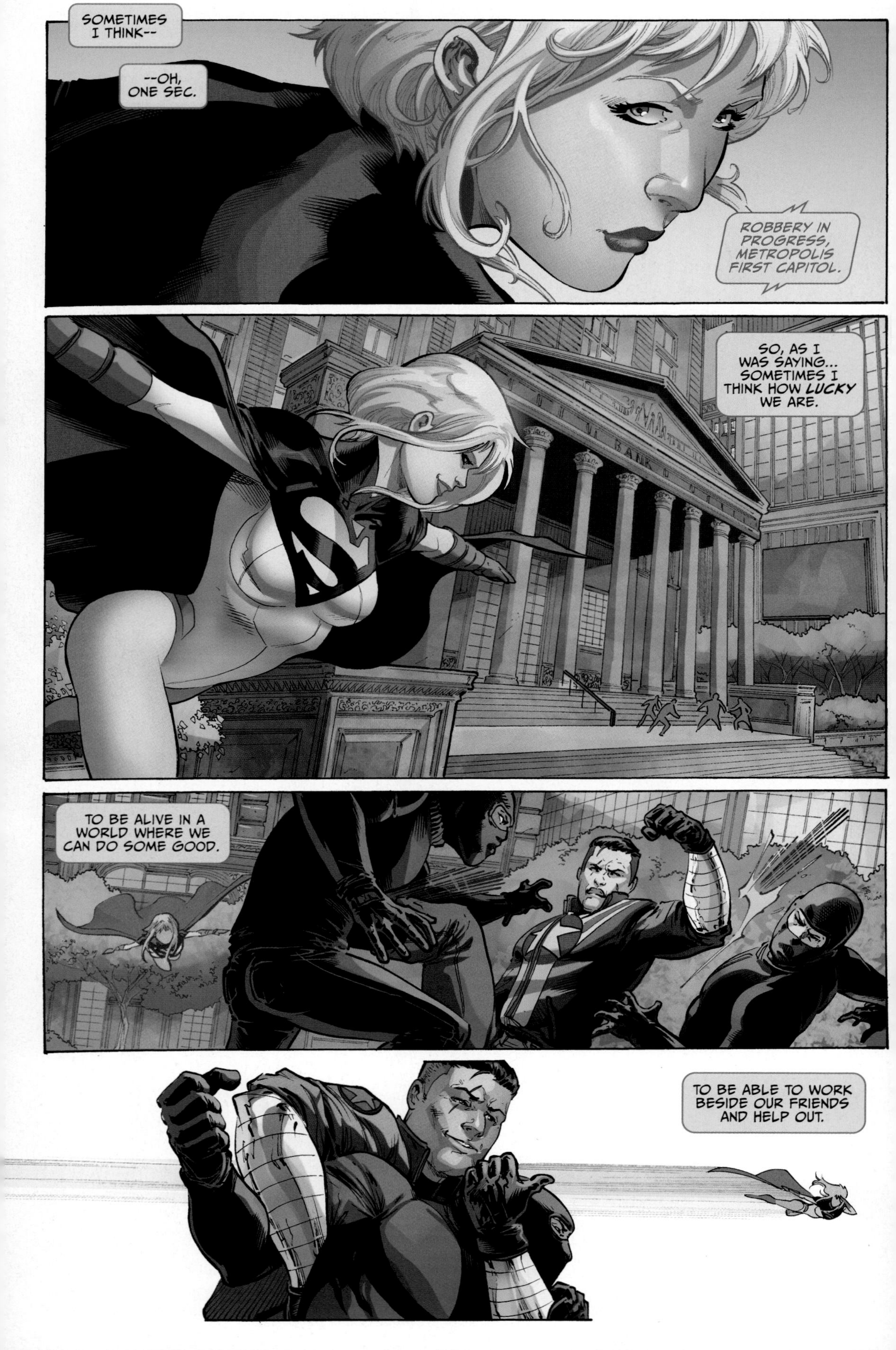
SOMETIMES I THINK--
--OH, ONE SEC.
ROBBERY IN PROGRESS, METROPOLIS FIRST CAPITOL.
SO, AS I WAS SAYING... SOMETIMES I THINK HOW LUCKY WE ARE.
BANK
TO BE ALIVE IN A WORLD WHERE WE CAN DO SOME GOOD.
TO BE ABLE TO WORK BESIDE OUR FRIENDS AND HELP OUT.

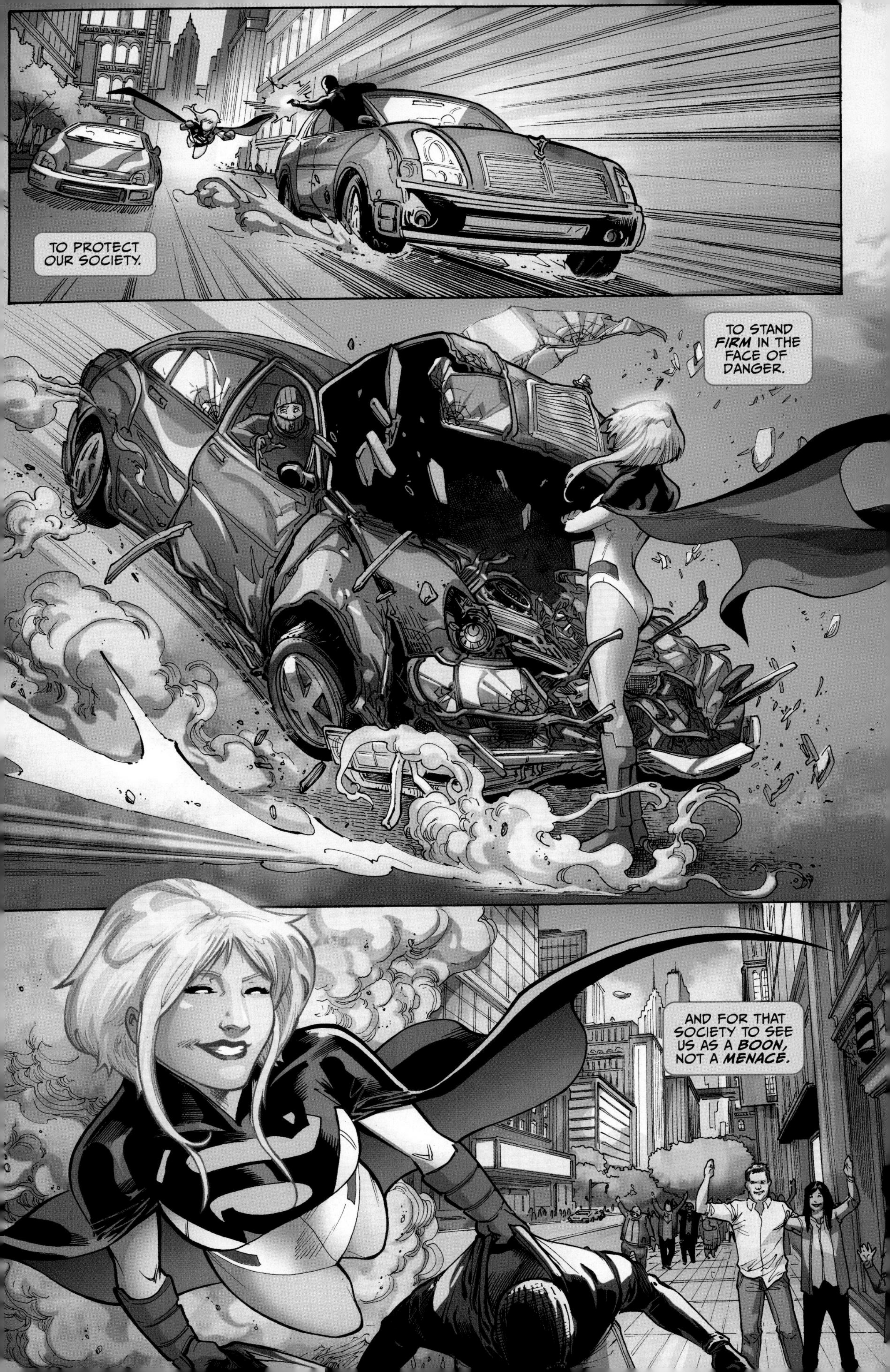
TO PROTECT OUR SOCIETY.
TO STAND FIRM IN THE FACE OF DANGER.
AND FOR THAT SOCIETY TO SEE US AS A BOON, NOT A MENACE.

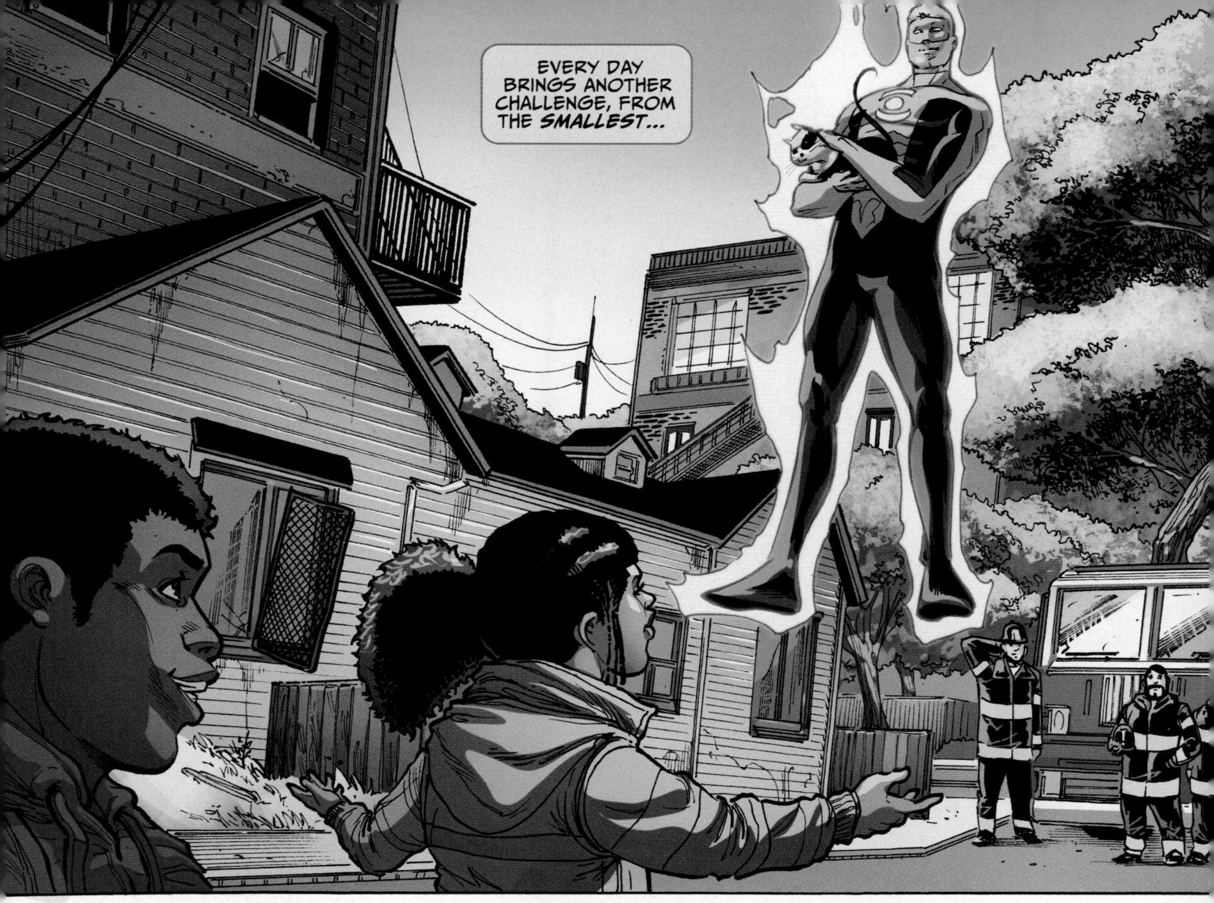
EVERY DAY BRINGS ANOTHER CHALLENGE, FROM THE *SMALLEST*...

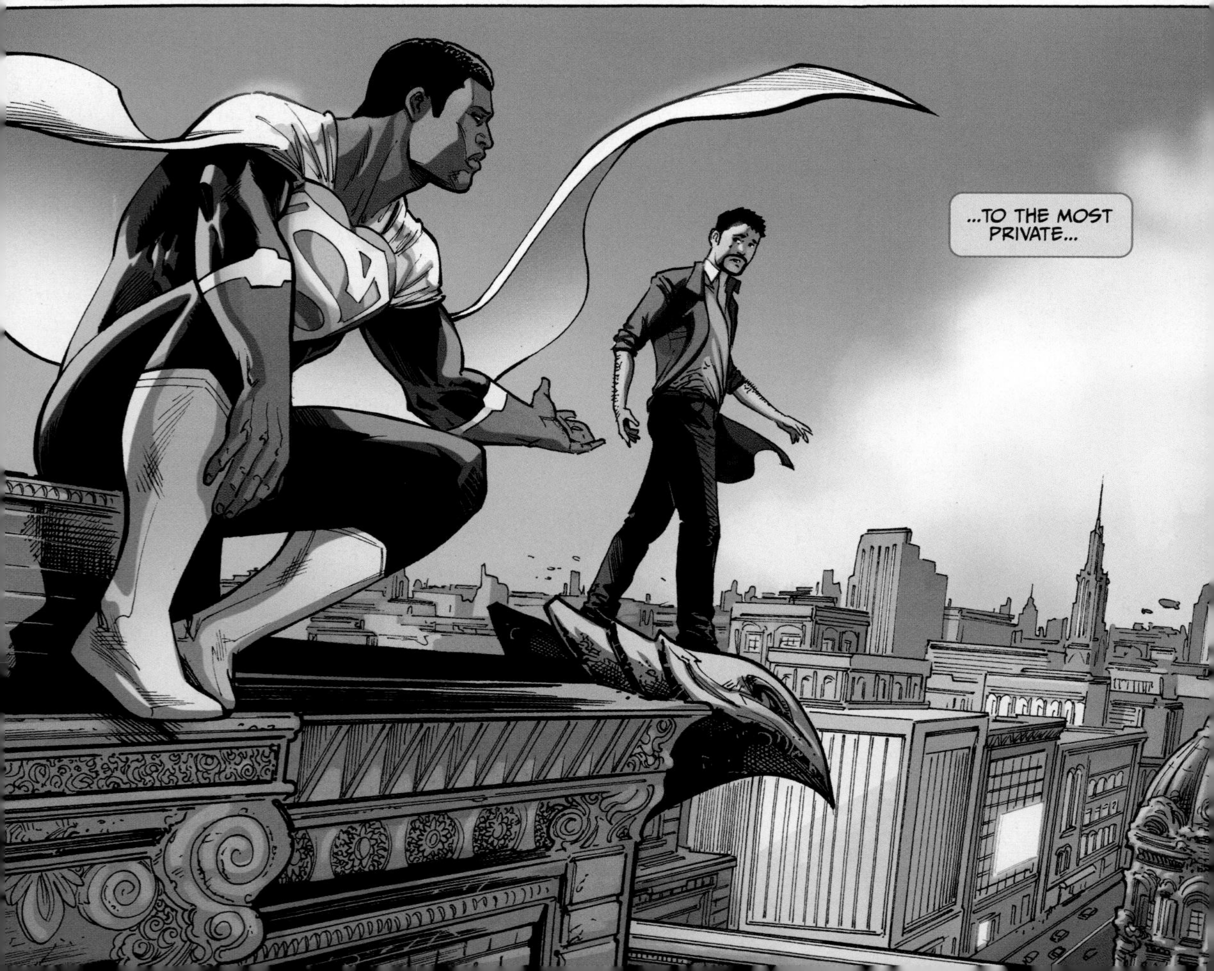
...TO THE MOST PRIVATE...

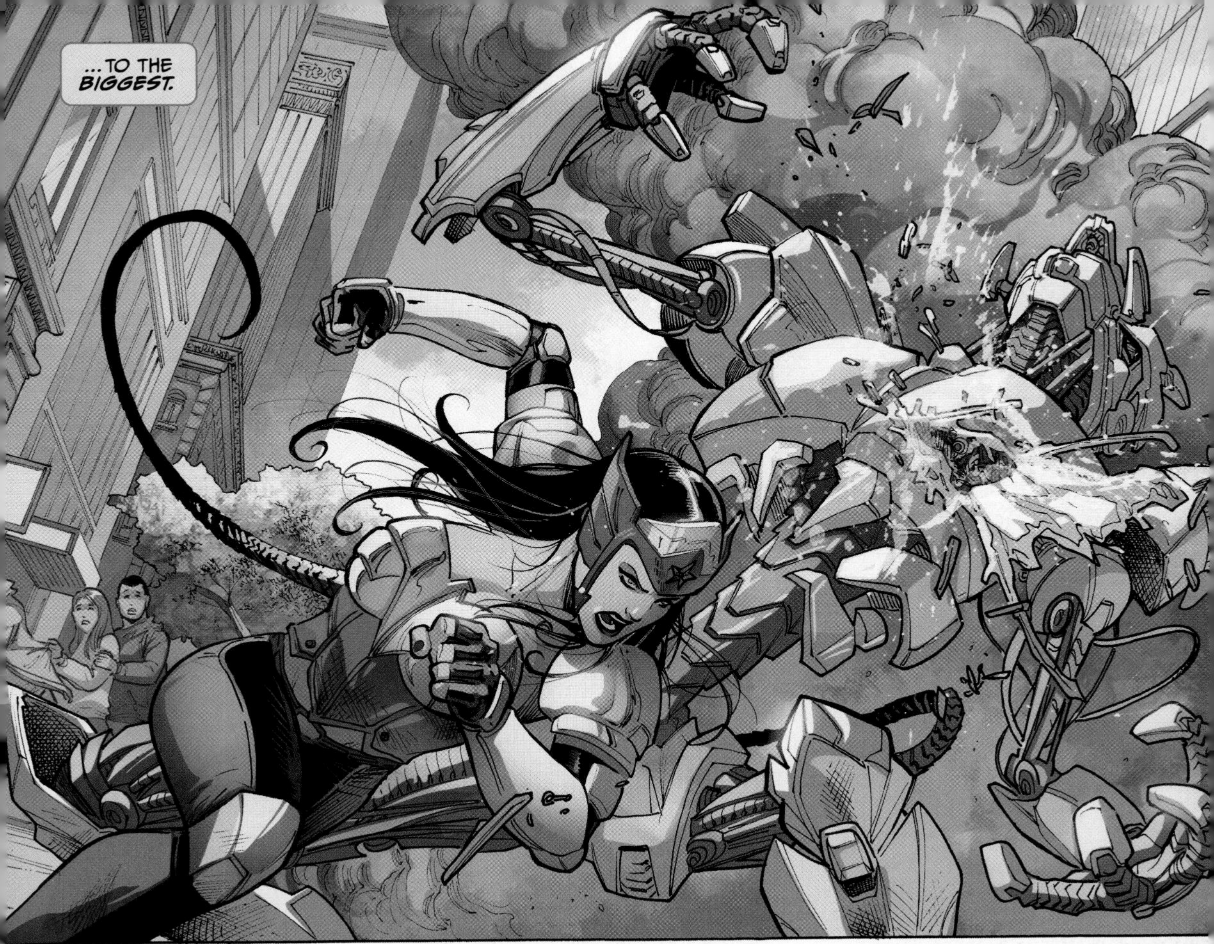
...TO THE BIGGEST.
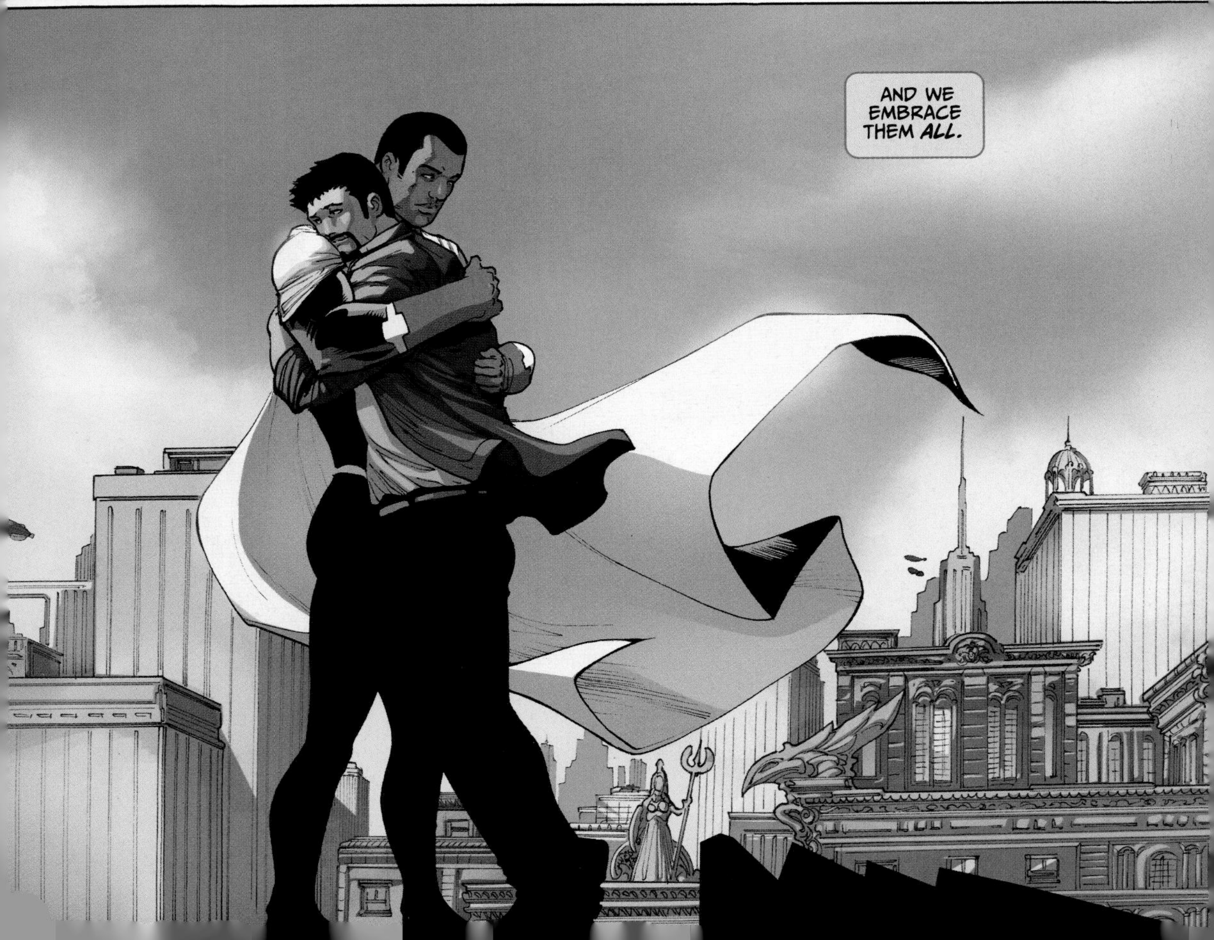
AND WE EMBRACE THEM ALL.

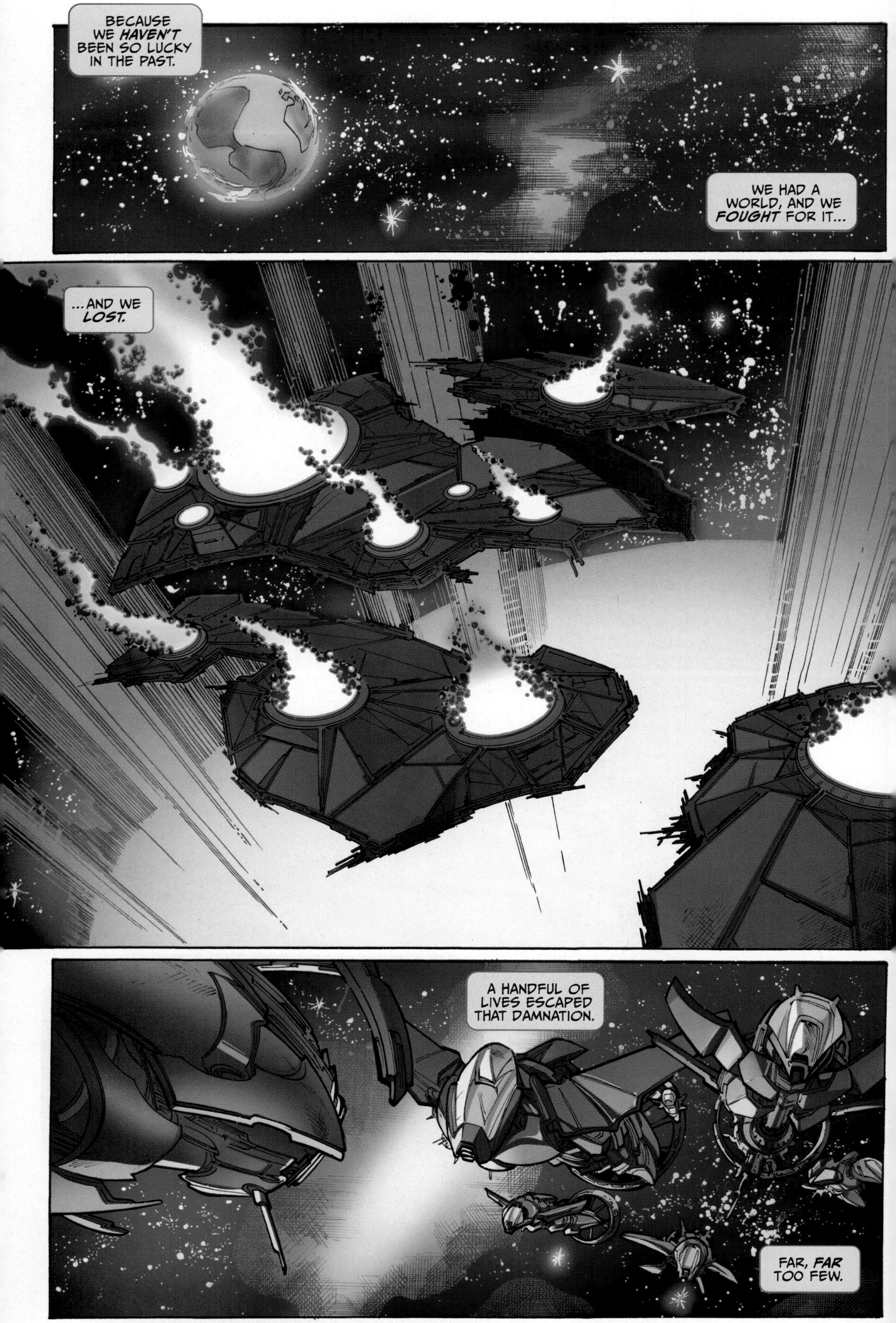
BECAUSE WE HAVEN'T BEEN SO LUCKY IN THE PAST.
WE HAD A WORLD, AND WE FOUGHT FOR IT...
...AND WE LOST.
A HANDFUL OF LIVES ESCAPED THAT DAMNATION.
FAR, FAR TOO FEW.

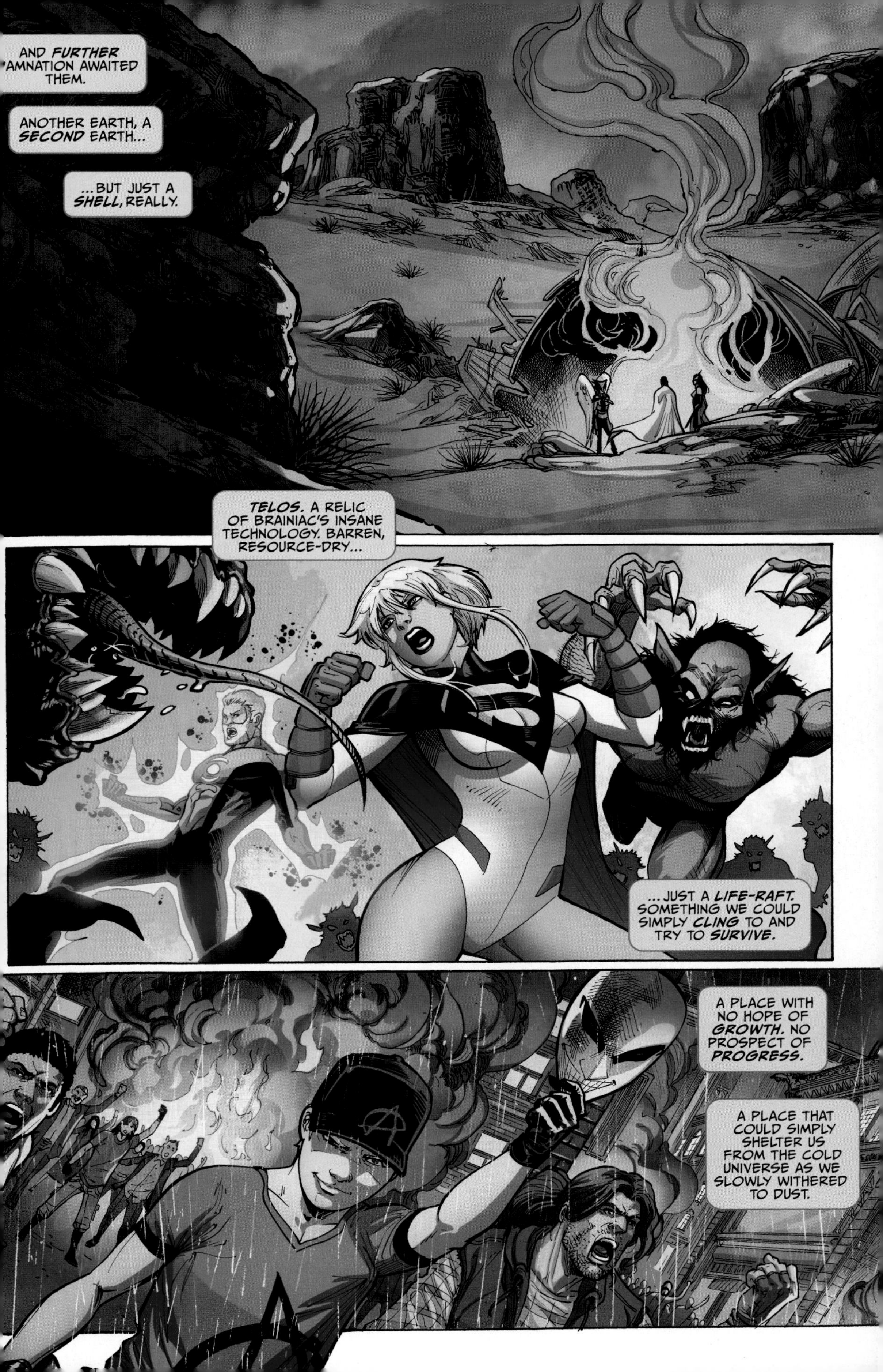
AND FURTHER
AMNATION AWAITED THEM.
ANOTHER EARTH, A SECOND EARTH...
...BUT JUST A SHELL, REALLY.
TELOS. A RELIC OF BRAINIAC'S INSANE TECHNOLOGY. BARREN, RESOURCE-DRY...
...JUST A LIFE-RAFT. SOMETHING WE COULD SIMPLY CLING TO AND TRY TO SURVIVE.
A PLACE WITH NO HOPE OF GROWTH. NO PROSPECT OF PROGRESS.
A PLACE THAT COULD SIMPLY SHELTER US FROM THE COLD UNIVERSE AS WE SLOWLY WITHERED TO DUST.

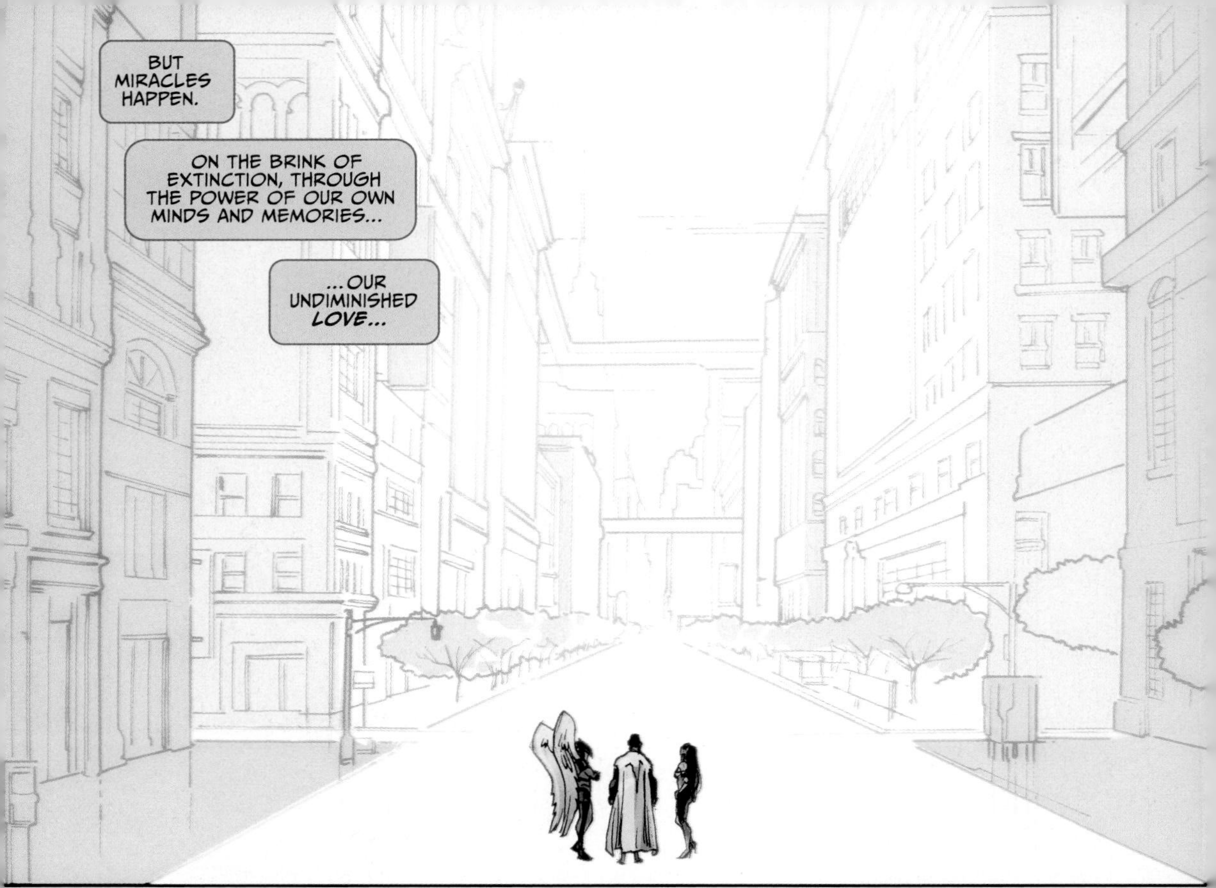
BUT MIRACLES HAPPEN.
ON THE BRINK OF EXTINCTION, THROUGH THE POWER OF OUR OWN MINDS AND MEMORIES...
...OUR UNDIMINISHED LOVE...

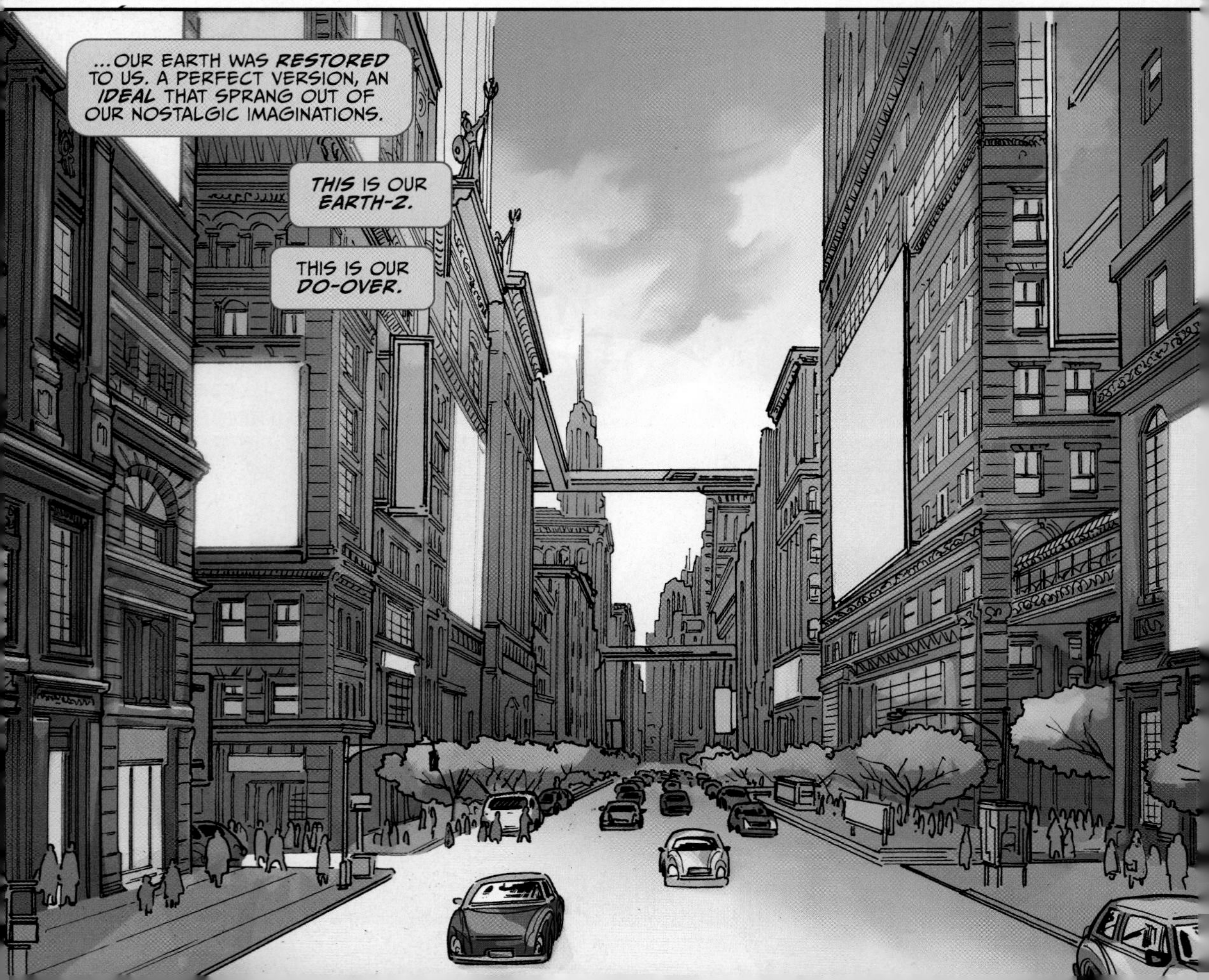
...OUR EARTH WAS RESTORED TO US. A PERFECT VERSION, AN IDEAL THAT SPRANG OUT OF OUR NOSTALGIC IMAGINATIONS.
THIS IS OUR EARTH-2.
THIS IS OUR DO-OVER.

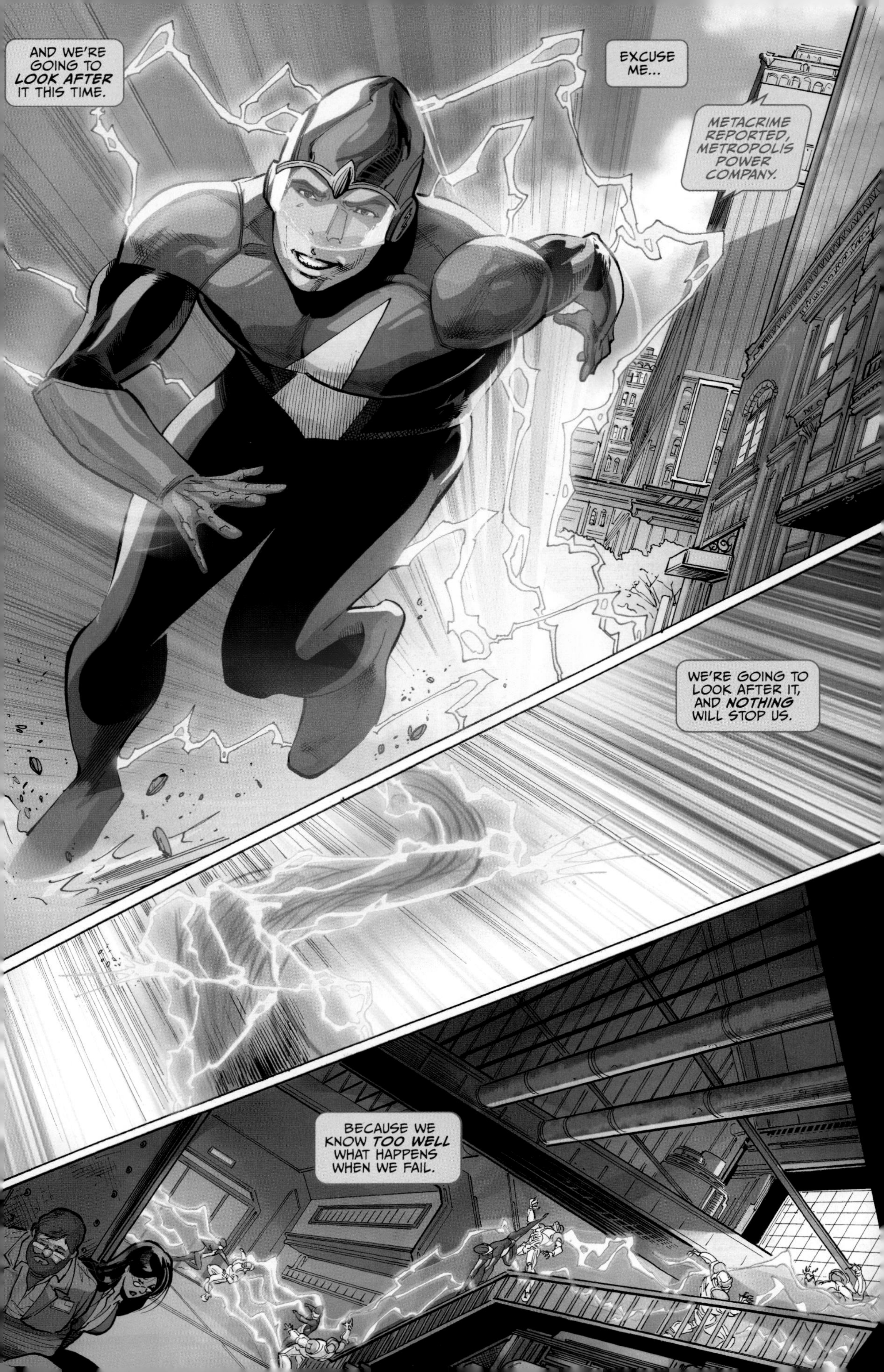
AND WE'RE GOING TO LOOK AFTER IT THIS TIME.
EXCUSE ME...
METACRIME REPORTED, METROPOLIS POWER COMPANY.
WE'RE GOING TO LOOK AFTER IT, AND NOTHING WILL STOP US.
BECAUSE WE KNOW TOO WELL WHAT HAPPENS WHEN WE FAIL.

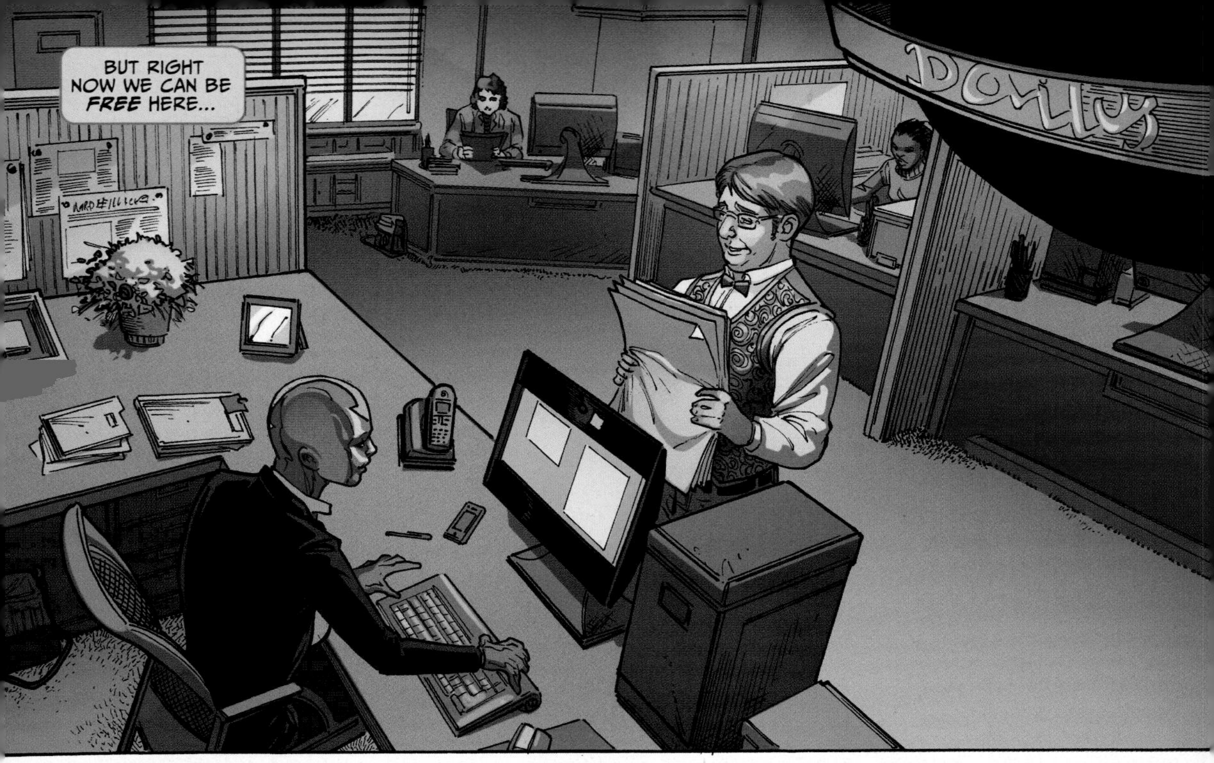
BUT RIGHT NOW WE CAN BE *FREE* HERE...

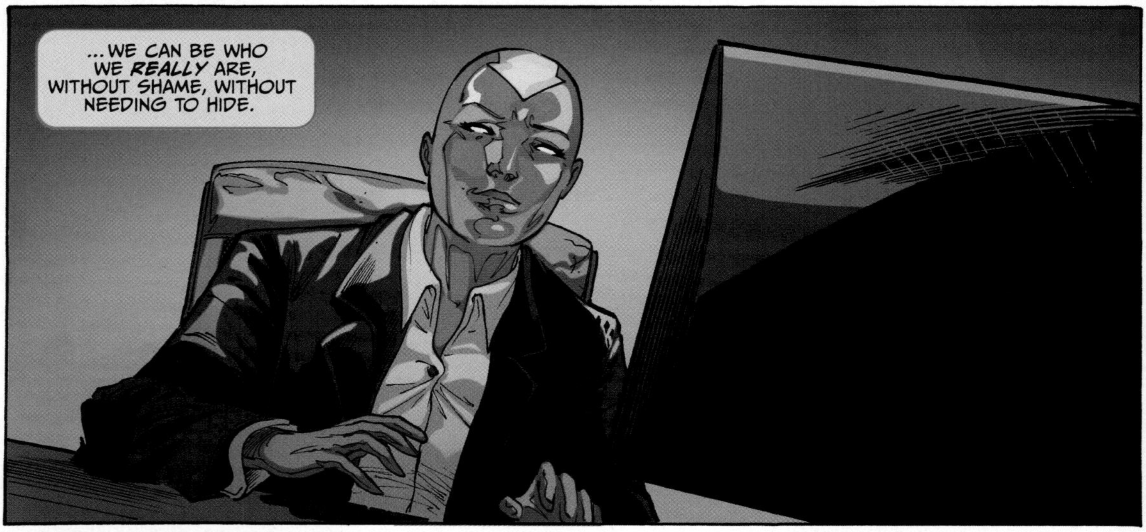
...WE CAN BE WHO WE *REALLY* ARE, WITHOUT SHAME, WITHOUT NEEDING TO HIDE.

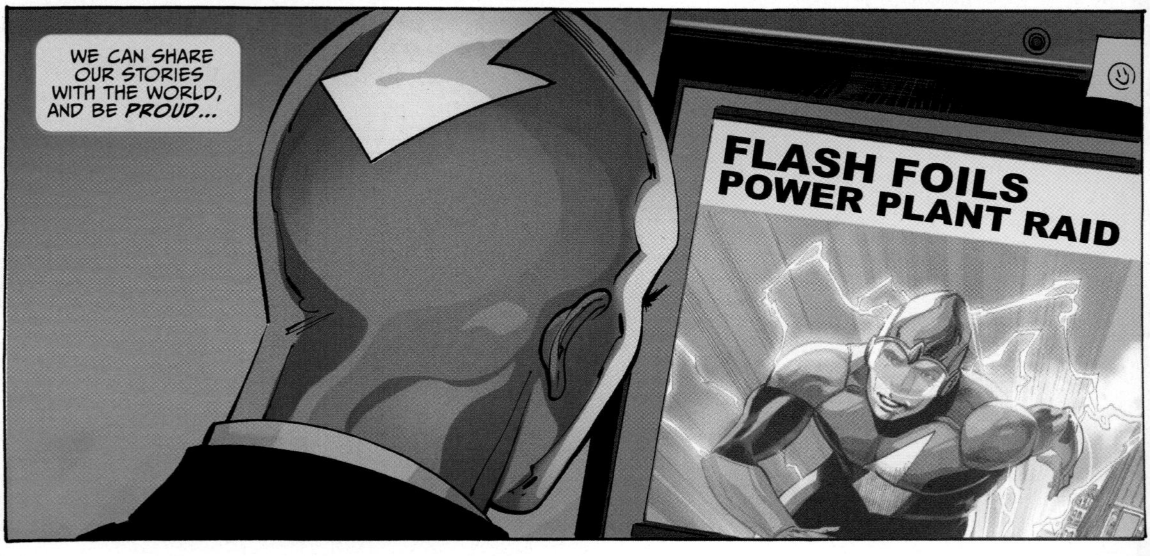
WE CAN SHARE OUR STORIES WITH THE WORLD, AND BE *PROUD*...
FLASH FOILS
POWER PLANT RAID

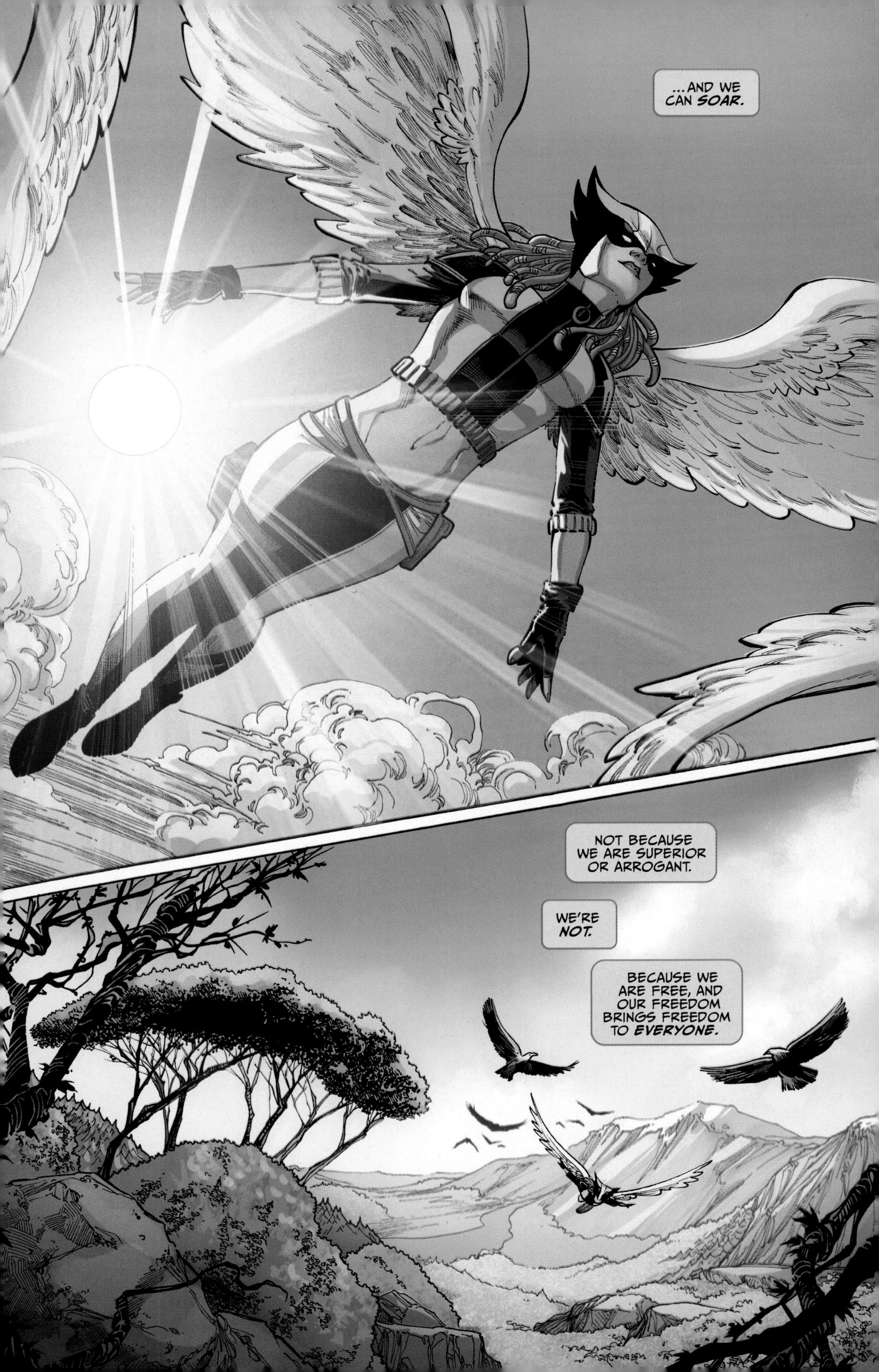
...AND WE CAN SOAR.
NOT BECAUSE WE ARE SUPERIOR OR ARROGANT.
WE'RE NOT.
BECAUSE WE ARE FREE, AND OUR FREEDOM BRINGS FREEDOM TO EVERYONE.

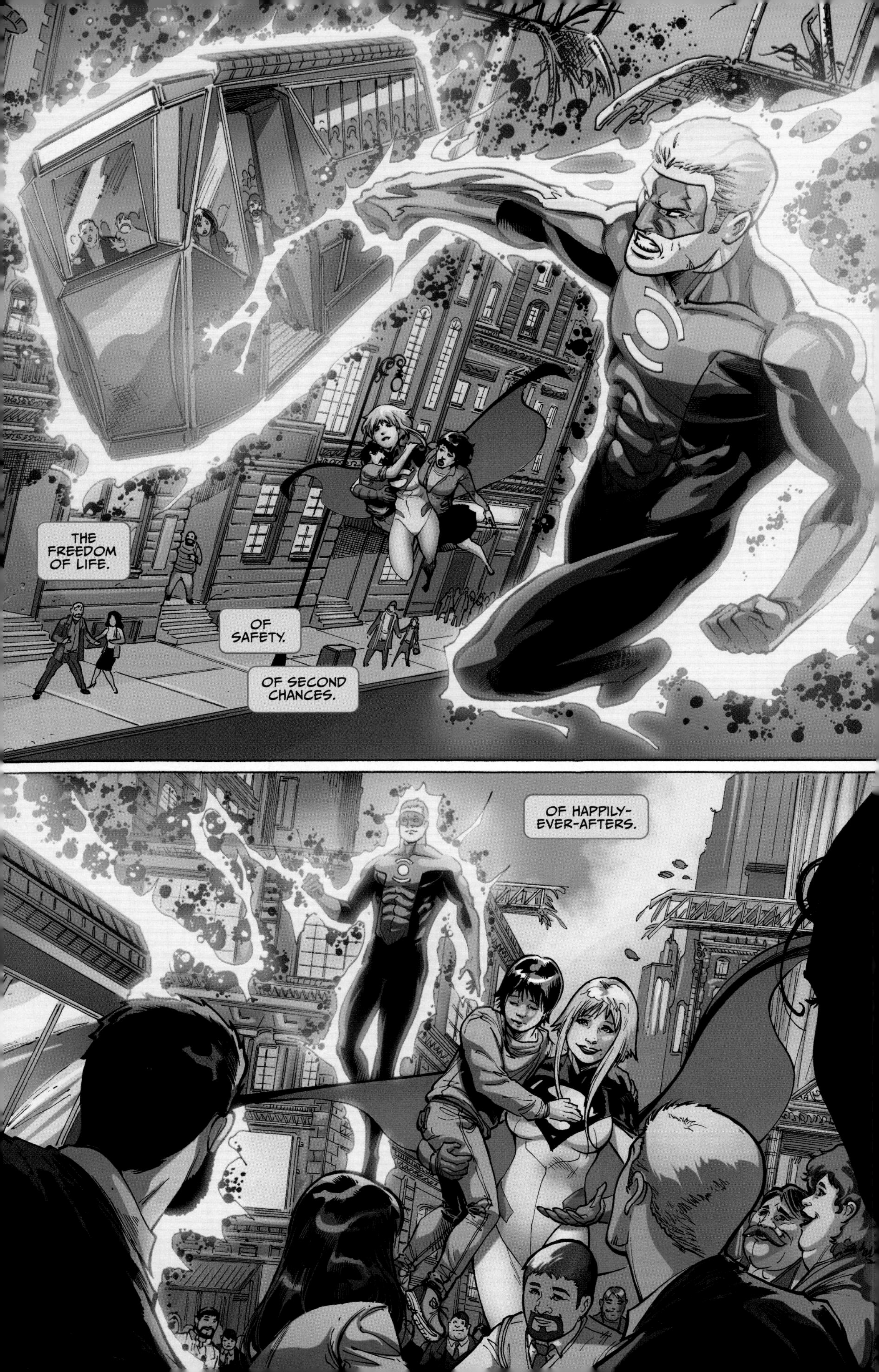
THE FREEDOM OF LIFE.
OF SAFETY.
OF SECOND CHANCES.
OF HAPPILY-EVER-AFTERS.

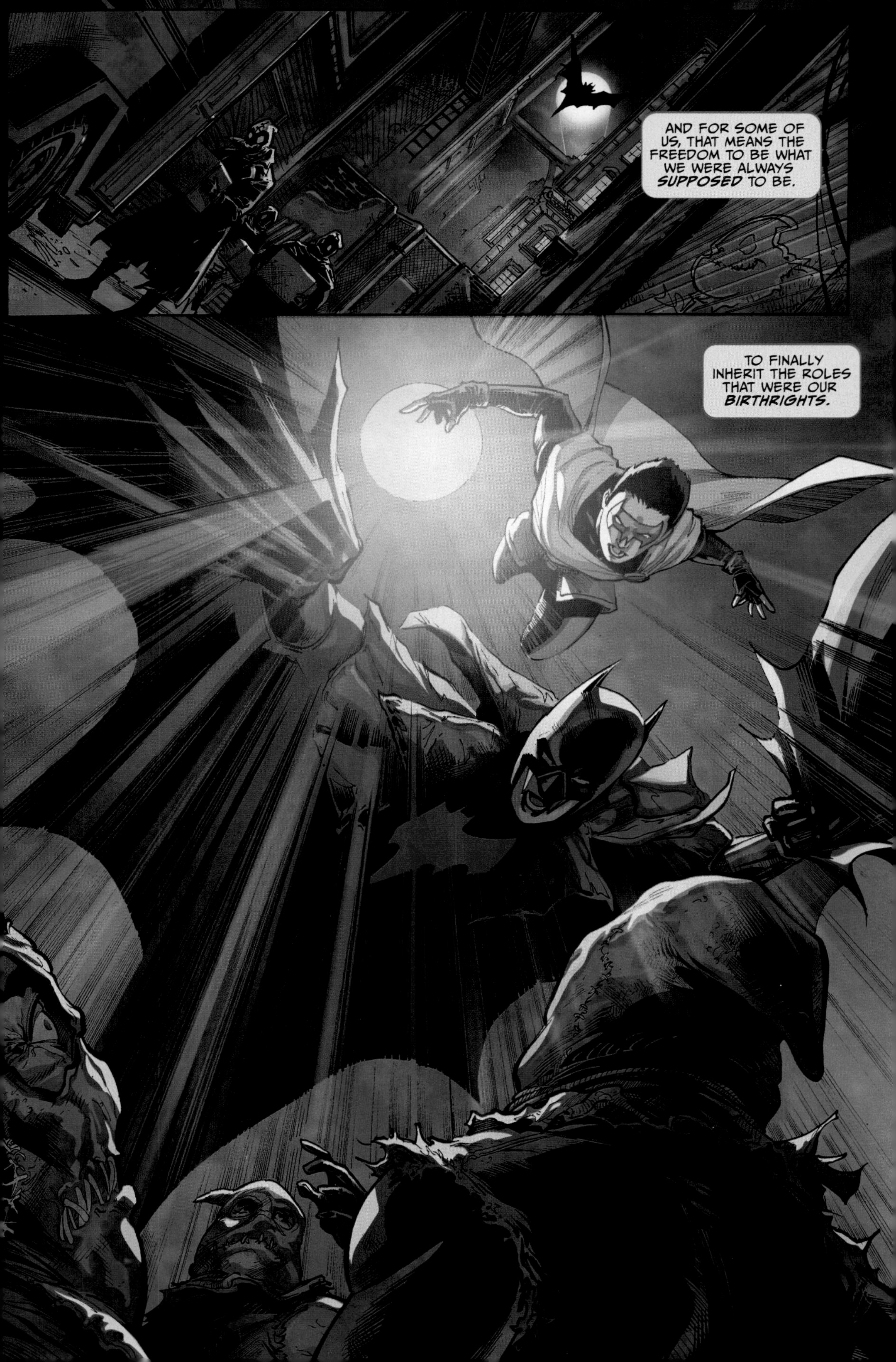
AND FOR SOME OF US, THAT MEANS THE FREEDOM TO BE WHAT WE WERE ALWAYS *SUPPOSED* TO BE.
TO FINALLY INHERIT THE ROLES THAT WERE OUR *BIRTHRIGHTS.*

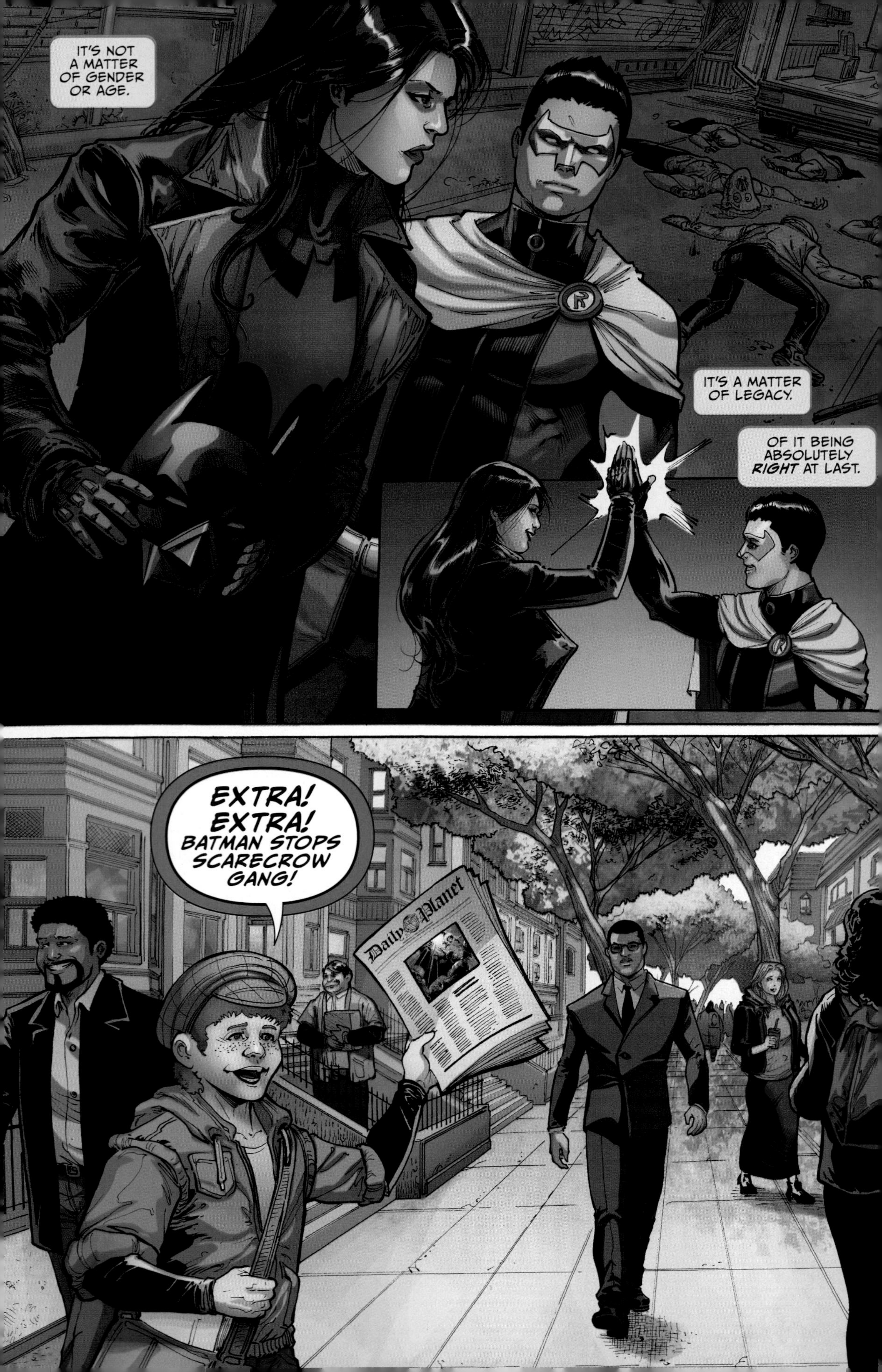
IT'S NOT A MATTER OF GENDER OR AGE.
IT'S A MATTER OF LEGACY.
OF IT BEING ABSOLUTELY RIGHT AT LAST.
EXTRA! EXTRA! BATMAN STOPS SCARECROW GANG!
Daily Planet

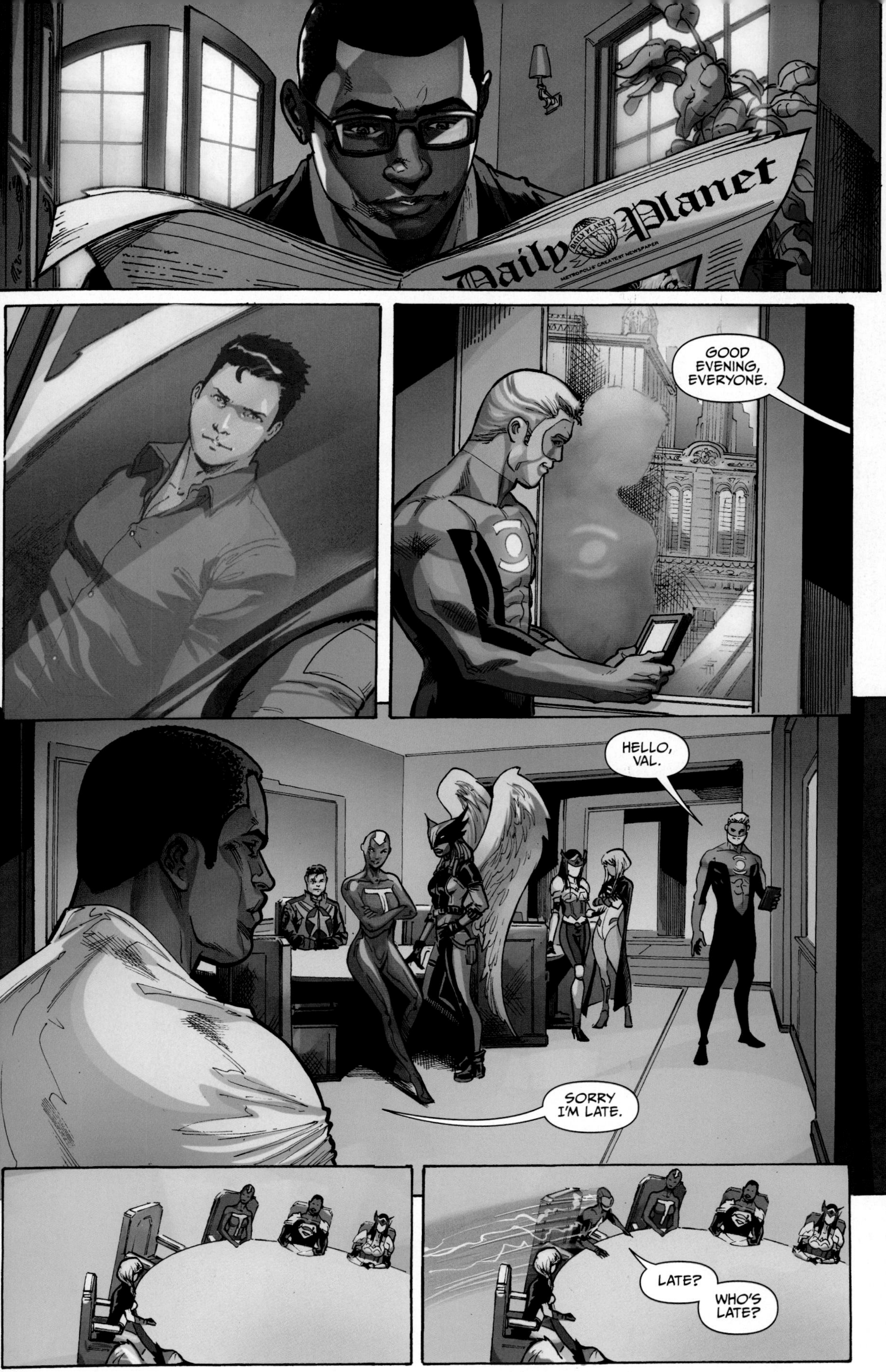
Daily Planet
METROPOLIS' GREATEST NEWSPAPER
GOOD EVENING, EVERYONE.
HELLO, VAL.
SORRY I'M LATE.
LATE?
WHO'S LATE?

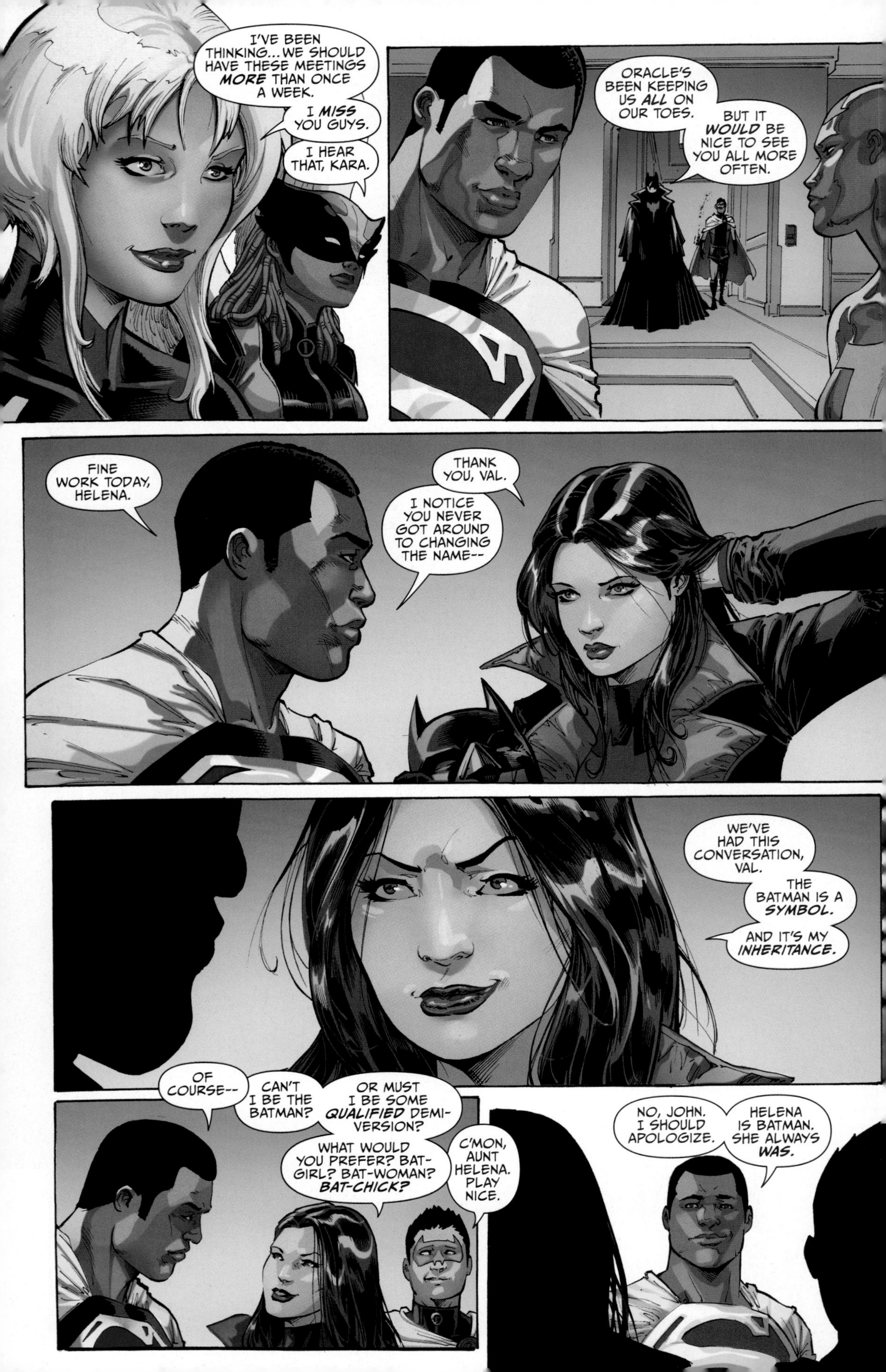
I'VE BEEN THINKING... WE SHOULD HAVE THESE MEETINGS MORE THAN ONCE A WEEK.
I MISS YOU GUYS.
I HEAR THAT, KARA.
ORACLE'S BEEN KEEPING US ALL ON OUR TOES.
BUT IT WOULD BE NICE TO SEE YOU ALL MORE OFTEN.
FINE WORK TODAY, HELENA.
THANK YOU, VAL.
I NOTICE YOU NEVER GOT AROUND TO CHANGING THE NAME--
WE'VE HAD THIS CONVERSATION, VAL.
THE BATMAN IS A SYMBOL.
AND IT'S MY INHERITANCE.
OF COURSE--
CAN'T I BE THE BATMAN?
OR MUST I BE SOME QUALIFIED DEMI-VERSION?
WHAT WOULD YOU PREFER? BAT-GIRL? BAT-WOMAN? BAT-CHICK?
C'MON, AUNT HELENA. PLAY NICE.
NO, JOHN. I SHOULD APOLOGIZE.
HELENA IS BATMAN. SHE ALWAYS WAS.

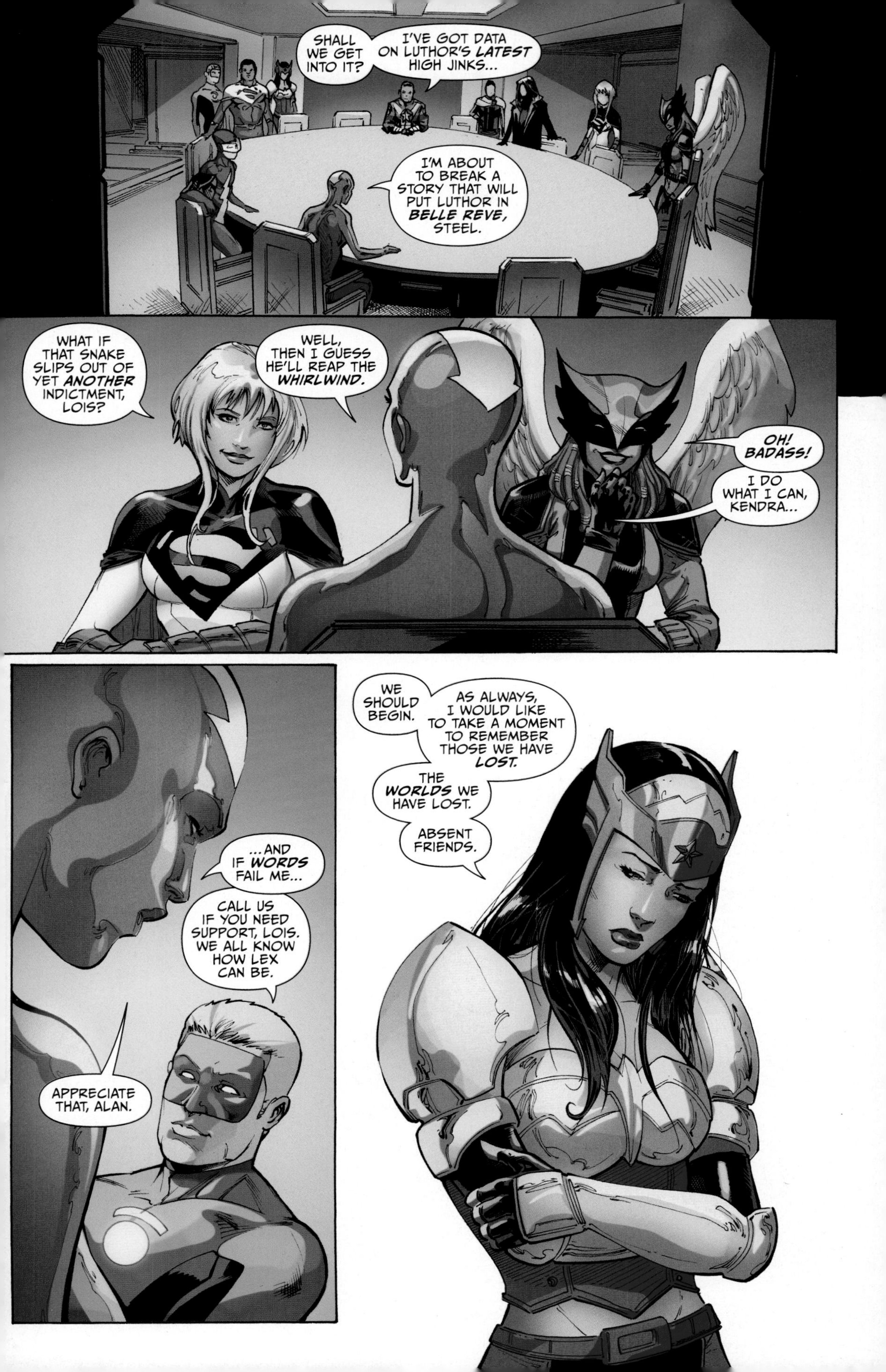
SHALL WE GET INTO IT?
I'VE GOT DATA ON LUTHOR'S *LATEST* HIGH JINKS...
I'M ABOUT TO BREAK A STORY THAT WILL PUT LUTHOR IN *BELLE REVE,* STEEL.
WHAT IF THAT SNAKE SLIPS OUT OF YET *ANOTHER* INDICTMENT, LOIS?
WELL, THEN I GUESS HE'LL REAP THE *WHIRLWIND.*
OH! BADASS!
I DO WHAT I CAN, KENDRA...
...AND IF *WORDS* FAIL ME...
CALL US IF YOU NEED SUPPORT, LOIS. WE ALL KNOW HOW LEX CAN BE.
APPRECIATE THAT, ALAN.
WE SHOULD BEGIN.
AS ALWAYS, I WOULD LIKE TO TAKE A MOMENT TO REMEMBER THOSE WE HAVE *LOST.*
THE *WORLDS* WE HAVE LOST.
ABSENT FRIENDS.

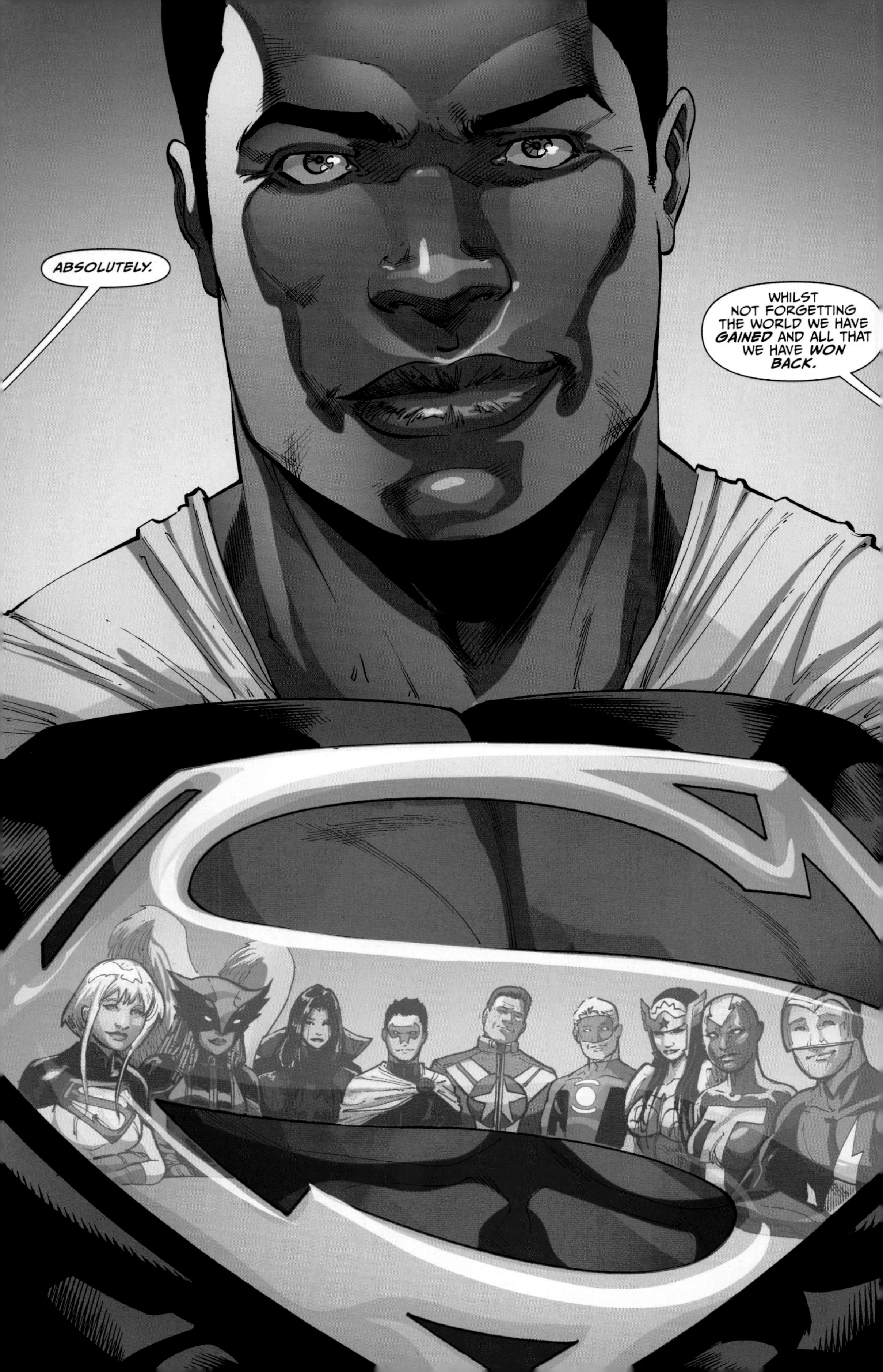
ABSOLUTELY.
WHILST NOT FORGETTING THE WORLD WE HAVE GAINED AND ALL THAT WE HAVE WON BACK.

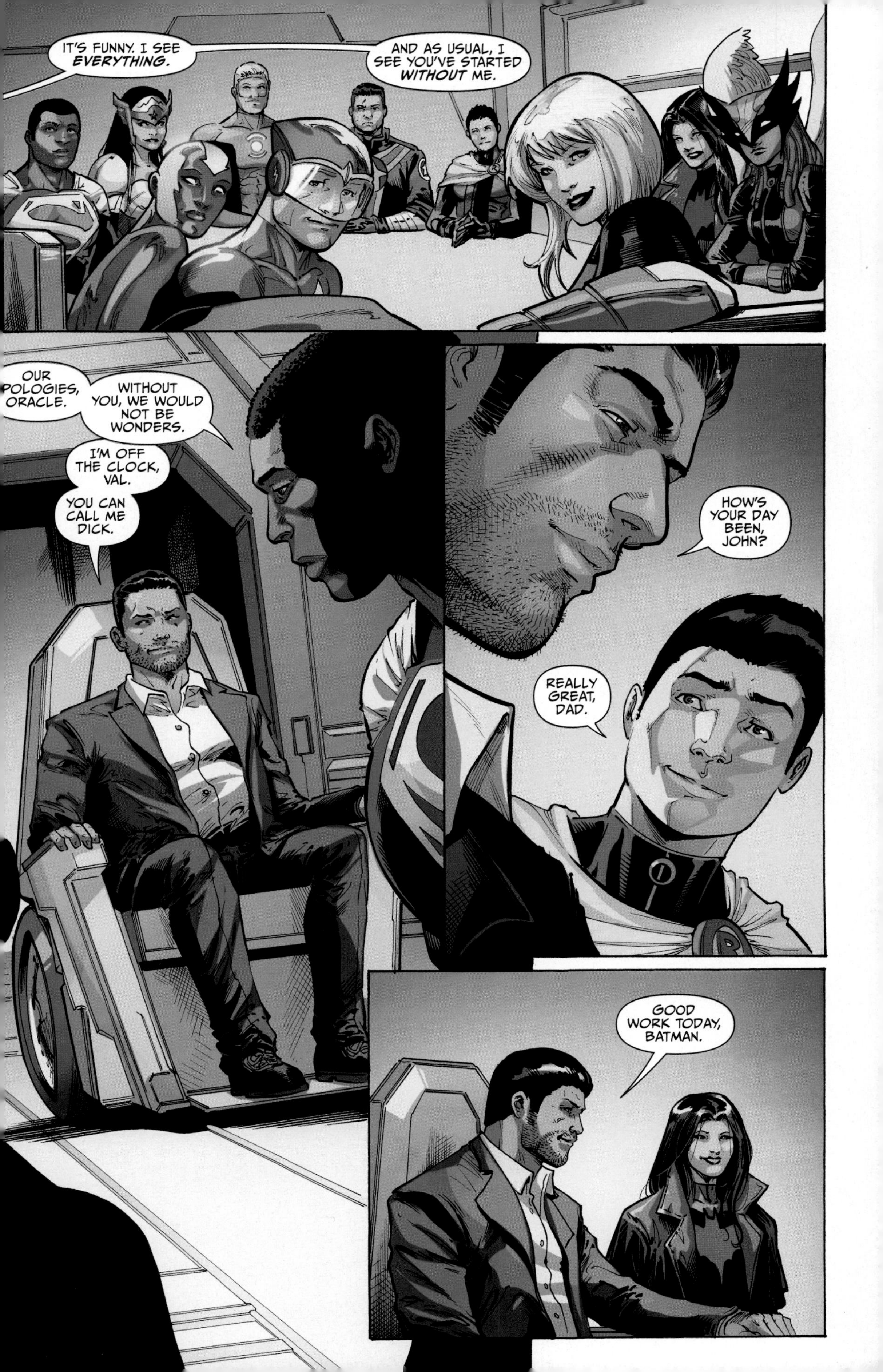
IT'S FUNNY. I SEE EVERYTHING.
AND AS USUAL, I SEE YOU'VE STARTED WITHOUT ME.
OUR POLOGIES, ORACLE.
WITHOUT YOU, WE WOULD NOT BE WONDERS.
I'M OFF THE CLOCK, VAL.
YOU CAN CALL ME DICK.
HOW'S YOUR DAY BEEN, JOHN?
REALLY GREAT, DAD.
GOOD WORK TODAY, BATMAN.

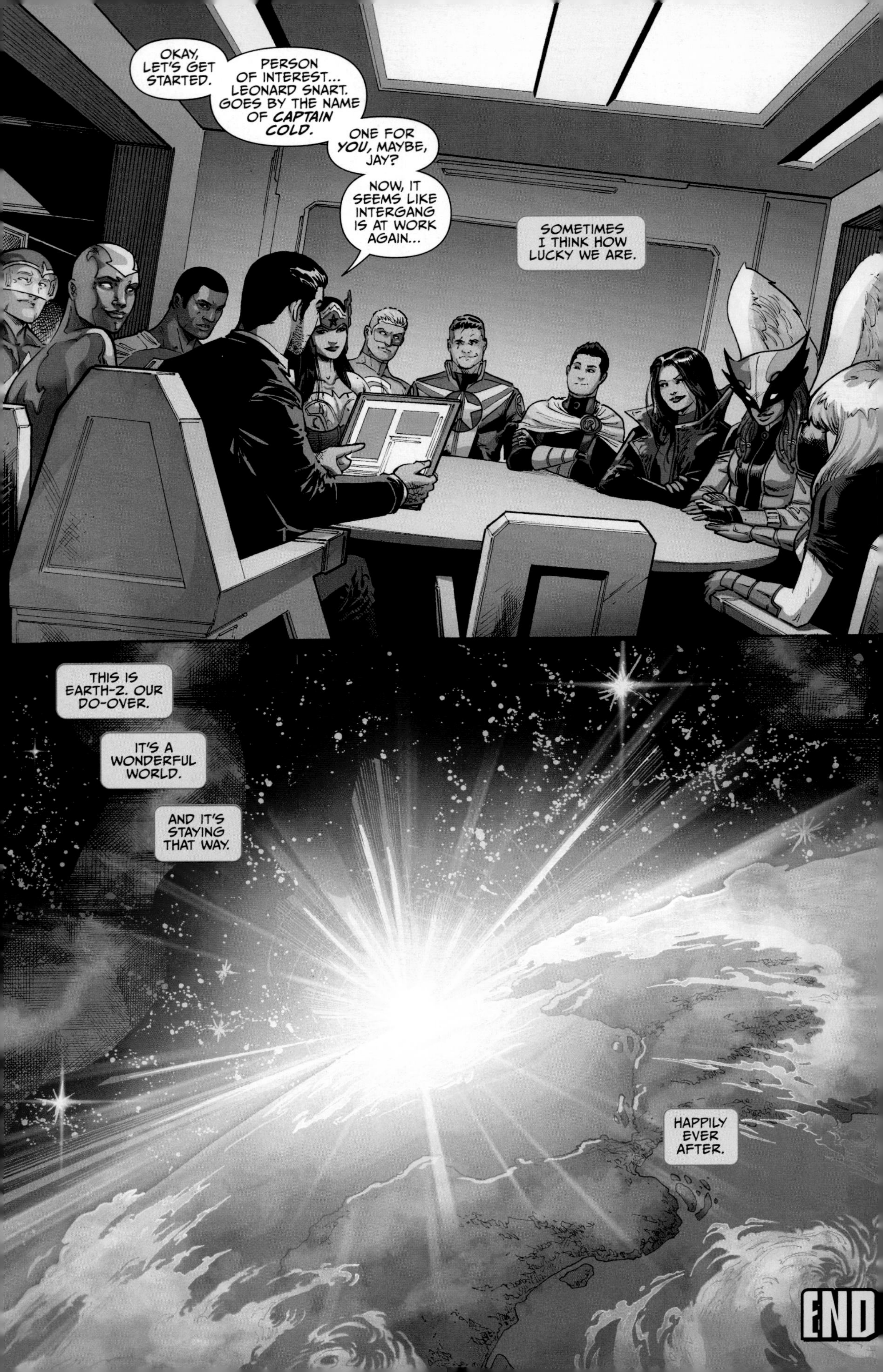
OKAY, LET'S GET STARTED.
PERSON OF INTEREST... LEONARD SNART. GOES BY THE NAME OF CAPTAIN COLD.
ONE FOR YOU, MAYBE, JAY?
NOW, IT SEEMS LIKE INTERGANG IS AT WORK AGAIN...
SOMETIMES I THINK HOW LUCKY WE ARE.
THIS IS EARTH-2. OUR DO-OVER.
IT'S A WONDERFUL WORLD.
AND IT'S STAYING THAT WAY.
HAPPILY EVER AFTER.
END